C453484000

D1760965

Europe's American Revolution

Europe's American Revolution

Edited by

Simon P. Newman

NEWCASTLE LIBRARIES

Bertrams	08/04/2009
973.31	£45.00

Editorial matter, selection, Introduction and chapter 3 © Simon P.
Newman 2006; all remaining chapters © their respective authors 2006

All rights reserved. No reproduction, copy or transmission of this
publication may be made without written permission.

No paragraph of this publication may be reproduced, copied or transmitted
save with written permission or in accordance with the provisions of the
Copyright, Designs and Patents Act 1988, or under the terms of any licence
permitting limited copying issued by the Copyright Licensing Agency, 90
Tottenham Court Road, London W1T 4LP.

Any person who does any unauthorized act in relation to this publication
may be liable to criminal prosecution and civil claims for damages.

The authors have asserted their rights to be identified
as the authors of this work in accordance with the Copyright,
Designs and Patents Act 1988.

First published in 2006 by
PALGRAVE MACMILLAN
Houndmills, Basingstoke, Hampshire RG21 6XS and
175 Fifth Avenue, New York, N.Y. 10010
Companies and representatives throughout the world.

PALGRAVE MACMILLAN is the global academic imprint of the Palgrave
Macmillan division of St. Martin's Press, LLC and of Palgrave Macmillan Ltd.
Macmillan® is a registered trademark in the United States, United Kingdom
and other countries. Palgrave is a registered trademark in the European
Union and other countries.

ISBN-13: 978–1–4039–8997–0 hardback
ISBN-10: 1–4039–8997–4 hardback

This book is printed on paper suitable for recycling and made from fully
managed and sustained forest sources.

A catalogue record for this book is available from the British Library.

Library of Congress Cataloging-in-Publication Data

Europe's American Revolution / edited by Simon P. Newman.
    p. cm.
Includes bibliographical references (p.) and index.
ISBN 1–4039–8997–4
    1. United States – History – Revolution, 1775–1783 – Foreign
public opinion, European. 2. United States – History – Revolution,
1775–1783 – Historiography. 3. Public opinion – Europe. I. Newman,
Simon P. (Simon Peter), 1960–

E249.3.E94 2006
973.3'1—dc22   2006046044

10 9 8 7 6 5 4 3 2 1
15 14 13 12 11 10 09 08 07 06

Printed and bound in Great Britain by
Antony Rowe Ltd, Chippenham and Eastbourne

Contents

Acknowledgements

This book began as a two-session workshop at the biennial conference of the European Association for American Studies in Prague in April 2004. Originally the idea of Michael McDonnell (University of Sidney), the workshop was entitled 'The Relevance of the American Revolution in an Atlantic and Global World.' and it prompted fascinating discussions of the impact of the American Revolution on, and its significance for, Europeans from the late-eighteenth century to the present. All but two of the essays in this volume began as papers at the Prague conference.

I am extremely grateful to Mike McDonnell, to the organizers of the Prague conference and to Michael Strang, our editor at Palgrave Macmillan, for their faith in this exploration of Europe's American Revolution. The two anonymous reviewers provided enormously helpful suggestions for the revision of this volume, which the authors carried out with admirable rapidity. Brad Jones, the author of the first essay, undertook the final copy-editing with all of his usual dedication to detail, and his work and that of the editorial team at Palgrave Macmillan have added considerably to the quality of this volume.

Edinburgh University Press have kindly given permission for the use of portions of Chapter Eight, which appeared in an earlier form in T. McCrisken and A. Pepper's *American History and Contemporary American Film* (Edinburgh, 2005).

Simon Newman
(University of Glasgow)

Notes on Contributors

Thomas Clark (Ph.D., Goethe University, Frankfurt/Main) is Assistant Professor of American History at the University of Kassel, Germany. Focusing on intellectual history, political ideas and transatlantic interactions he has written on the ideology of the American Revolution, Benjamin Rush, Tocqueville, Frederick Remington, *Ecotopia* and Michael Moore. His current project is entitled 'Tocquevillian Moments: Transatlantic Visions of an American Republican Culture'.

Brad A. Jones (Ph.D., University of Glasgow) is an Assistant Professor at California State University, Fresno. His dissertation, entitled, 'The American Revolution and Popular Loyalism in the British Atlantic World', examines the ways in which the Revolution affected the growth and articulation of popular expressions of imperial identity and loyalty throughout the British Empire. He is the author of an essay on the Loyalist lower sort in New York City during the American Revolution, to be published in J.S. Tiedemann and E.R. Fingerhut, eds. *The Other Loyalists: The Common Sort, Royalism and the American Revolution in the Middle Colonies, 1763–1787.*

Csaba Lévai (Ph.D., University of Debrecen) is Associate Professor of History at the University of Debrecen, Hungary. He is the author of *A republikanizmus-vita: Vita az amerikai forradalom eszmetörténeti hátteréröl* (*The Republicanism Debate: Debate about the Intellectual Background of the American Revolution, 2003*), editor of *Új rend egy új világban: Dokumentumok az amerikai politikai gondolkodás korai történetéhez* (*New Order in a New World: Documents for the Study of Early American Political Thought, 1997*), and co-editor of *Tolerance and Intolerance in Historical Perspective (2003)*. He is working on a comparative study of the British and the Habsburg Empires in the eighteenth century.

Anthony McFarlane (Ph.D., University of London) is Professor of History at the University of Warwick. He is the author of *Colombia before Independence: Economy, Society and Politics under Bourbon Rule (1993)* and *The British in the Americas (1994)* and co-editor of *Reform and Insurrection in Bourbon New Granada and Peru (1990)* and *Independence and Revolution: Perspectives and Problems (1999)*. He is currently writing a book on the wars of independence in Spanish America.

Joseph Eugene Mullin (Ph.D., Ohio State University) is Associate Professor of American literature and American society and culture at the University of the Minho, Portugal. He has published extensively on late eighteenth and early nineteenth-century American letters, literary genre and Jack Kerouac.

Simon P. Newman (Ph.D., Princeton University) is Sir Denis Brogan Professor of American Studies at the University of Glasgow. He is the author of *Parades and the Politics of the Street: Festive Culture in the Early American Republic (1997)* and *Embodied History: The Lives of the Poor in Early Philadelphia (2003)* which won the American Studies Network Book Prize in 2004. He is currently working on a study of the transformation of working life and culture in the early modern British Atlantic world.

Andrew Pepper (Ph.D., University of Sussex) lectures in English and American Literature at Queen's University Belfast. He is the author of *The Contemporary American Crime Novel (2000)* and the co-author of *American History and Contemporary Hollywood Film* (2005). His first novel, *The Last Days of Newgate*, will be published in 2006.

Marie-Jeanne Rossignol (Ph.D., University Paris 7–Denis Diderot) is Professor of American Civilization at the University Paris 7–Denis Diderot. She is the author of *The Nationalist Ferment: The Origins of U.S. Foreign Policy, 1789–1812 (2003)*, and is currently working on French and American abolitionism in the revolutionary period.

Introduction

Simon P. Newman

From the firing of the first shots at Lexington, Patriots began the process of constructing the American Revolution as a uniquely American event that would, however, inspire revolutionary transformations all around the world. Building upon the Puritan impulse to create, in John Winthrop's famous phrase, 'a citty upon a hill', and the desire of successive generations of European immigrants to fashion new and better lives for themselves in North America, America's revolutionaries marvelled at their successful war against the mighty British empire and the promise of their new republic.[1] Mercy Otis Warren, one of the Revolution's first historians, concluded her work with the proud proclamation that

> The wisdom and justice of the American governments, and the virtue of the inhabitants, may ... render the United States of America an enviable example to all the world of peace, liberty, righteousness, and truth. The western wilds, which for ages have been little known, may arrive to that stage of improvement and perfection, beyond which the limits of human genius cannot reach; and this last civilized quarter of the globe may exhibit those striking traits of grandeur and magnificence which the Divine Economist may have reserved to crown the closing scene, when the angel of his presence will stand upon the sea and upon the earth, lift up his hand to heaven, and swear by Him that liveth forever and ever, that there shall be time no longer.[2]

Europeans who looked westward across the Atlantic, or who visited the new American republic, picked up on the refrain. As he surveyed the new republic created by the American Revolution, Alexis de Tocqueville believed that something greater and more significant than another nation and polity had emerged, observing that 'in America I saw more than America'. Fascinated by the changes that the French Revolution had triggered in Europe, Tocqueville was confident that other countries would become egalitarian republics, yet he regarded the American Revolution and the republic that it had fashioned as unique.[3]

While Americans celebrated their new republic and the ideals upon which it was founded, it was Tocqueville, a European, who first gave structure and meaning to a theory of American Exceptionalism that lauded the unique role and significance of the United States in world history. Rather than the common histories and ethnicities that defined the nations of the Old World, Tocqueville and those who followed him believed that the United States was founded upon an idea, and that by premising government and nationhood on liberty the American people had created a beacon for others around the world committed to a republican form of government.[4] The principles of this American idea were laid out in the 'Founding' documents of the American Revolution – the Declaration of Independence, the Constitution, and the Bill of Rights – and as the new republic grew rapidly in size, power and wealth, Americans shared a powerful sense of national self-belief and self-confidence, premised upon the distinctive nature and universal significance of their revolution and republic.

Implicitly, and on occasion quite explicitly, historians of the American Revolution in the United States have often echoed Tocqueville and elements of the American Exceptionalist paradigm. The Consensus historiography of the post-World War II period, the ideological debates about the relative significance of classical republicanism and liberalism that followed, and even the new social history have all shared both a relative lack of comparative international frameworks, and the distinct sense that the American Revolution must be understood in its own, unique context.[5] Thus, for all that the American Revolution was fought mainly by men and women of European descent, was founded on European political philosophies, and established institutions of government modeled on European forms, Americans have long defined their Revolution and new republic as a break from the Old World and the creation of a new one.

And yet, inherent in the American Exceptionalist paradigm is the belief that the American Revolution and the creation of the United States were international rather than national events, heralding the dawn of a new age in human society and government. Despite this the work of most historians of the Revolution and early republic at work in the United States implicitly rejects a comparative and international framework of analysis, and only a few of these historians have sought to contextualize the American Revolution in a broad international context. A notable exception was R.R. Palmer, an American citizen but an historian of the French Revolution, which perhaps explains the broader focus of his two-volume epic *The Age of the Democratic Revolution*. Palmer believed that the American Revolution had

> inspired the sense of a new era. It added a new concept to the conception of progress. It gave a whole new dimension to ideas of liberty and equality made familiar by the Enlightenment ... It dethroned England, and set up America as a model for those seeking a better world ... Whether fantasically idealized or seen in a factual way, whether as mirage or reality, America made Europe seem unsatisfactory to many people.[6]

While generally agreeing in a vague and undefined fashion that the American Revolution changed the world, American Revolutionary historiography has remained remarkably insular, a stance that may have been encouraged by the events of the twentieth century and the role that the United States assumed as champion and defender of what Americans and their allies regarded as the free world. However much American support of authoritarian regimes or misguided military interventions such as the war in Vietnam may have undermined the goal, many Americans believed themselves to be engaged in a life-and-death international campaign to defend the very ideals of liberty and self-determination upon which their own nation was founded. Following the Second World War American Studies courses and departments were established all over Western Europe, where intellectuals and academics marvelled at the economic successes of the United States, the affluence of its people, and the use of its overwhelming military strength to defend democratic government and individual rights at home and abroad. The United States, both as an idea and as a material reality, appeared as a beacon illuminating the shadows cast over Europe – and indeed the entire world – by totalitarian fascism and communism.

But if the fascism and communism of mid- to late-twentieth-century Europe defined that continent's understanding of what the United States represented, then the disappearance of those threats to liberty and the emergence of an increasingly integrated western and eastern European society and economy with a firm commitment to individual liberty and human rights mean that in the late-twentieth and early twenty-first centuries European interpretations of the nature and the continued significance of the American Revolution and republic are being reconstructed in entirely new contexts. Inevitably, European perspectives on both the historical significance and the contemporary relevance of the American Revolution are changing. A wide variety of social and cultural factors provide a larger context for these academic reassessments. The power and successes of American corporate capitalism; the failure of the United States to agree to the Kyoto Protocols designed to lessen damaging climate change; the unwillingness of the American government to subject itself to the authority of international bodies such as the United Nations and the World Court; and the disastrous Second Gulf War and the abortive attempts to introduce democratic government as a solution to the problems faced by the people of Iraq have encouraged people all over the world to question the twentieth-century image of the United States as *primus inter pares*.

Contemporary European history has also played a role in the reassessment of the United States. Following the collapse of the Soviet Union, the European Union began a process of expansion, beginning with the reunification of Germany. Already the Czech Republic, Estonia, Hungary, Latvia, Lithuania, Slovakia and Slovenia have joined the Union, and Bulgaria, Croatia, Romania and Turkey are candidates for admission. Europeans who can travel across their continent using a single currency and with minimal border controls no longer look westward across the Atlantic to see a successful federal union of democratic nations. Furthermore, at a time when American policy abroad and an increasingly conservative Supreme Court at home call into question American commitment to the rights enshrined in the Founding documents of the revolutionary era, Europeans look to the European Court of Human Rights (established following the European Convention on Human Rights of 1950) for protection of individual rights and liberties against potentially oppressive national laws and governmental actions.

American historians of the Revolution at work in the United States may know relatively little about the changing political culture of contemporary Europe. But historians of the Revolution who live and work in Europe necessarily operate in a far more comparative framework. Some of the contributors to this volume consider themselves, first and foremost, as historians of early America, yet they have been trained in and teach European history, and they necessarily approach the history of the American Revolution from a comparativist and international perspective. Especially outside of the United Kingdom, difficulties of access to primary and secondary sources, whether in English or in translation, has often encouraged such comparative research and teaching.

As a result, contemporary academics and their students embrace a far more internationalist approach, and of necessity the American Revolution, the Founding documents and the republic that they created can often appear less and less distinctive: the very idea of the revolutionary origins of American Exceptionalism is fading in Europe.

In this volume seven European-based scholars explore the context for and nature of historical and contemporary European reactions to and understandings of the American Revolution. The first two essays explore contemporary reactions to and interpretations of the American Revolution, both shedding new light on such reactions. Brad Jones develops a British case study in order to illustrate that rather than establishing an unparalleled image of republican liberty, the American Revolution solidified patriotic nationalism and a new imperial British identity in the second city of the empire. Focusing on Glasgow, Jones suggests that Scots who had been members of the British Empire for only two generations experienced the 1770s and 1780s as a major step in their creation and articulation of a newly developing loyalty to the British state and empire. The main significance of the American Revolution for Glaswegians and many other Britons, Jones argues, was that it confirmed and deepened loyalty and allegiance to a monarchical and imperial state, premised upon the belief that their political and religious liberties were best protected as British subjects.

Anthony McFarlane paints a rather different picture of Spanish reactions to the American War for Independence. While Spanish rulers were eager to see Britain humbled after its successes at Spanish and French expense in the Seven Years' War, McFarlane explores the very real limitations of this desire for vengeance, given the dangers posed by rebellious colonists and an independent and expanding United States. Although Spain entered the war, it did so with virtually no acknowledgement of the United States, choosing instead to wage a patriotic war with France against Britain. McFarlane concludes that while the ideology of the American Revolution did inspire some Spanish colonists, conditions in Spain did not allow for the positive reception that such ideas enjoyed in France. It was not until Napoleon's invasion that revolutionary change came to the Spanish world.

In Chapters three, four and five, historians of early America based in France, the United Kingdom and Hungary employ case studies to explore the interpretations and uses of the American Revolution in Europe between 1776 and the present day. Marie-Jeanne Rossignol moves beyond R.R. Palmer's comparative international assessment of the American and French revolutions. Ever since the outbreak of the

French Revolution, she argues, the American Revolution has at best been of marginal interest to the public and historians in France. Furthermore, the fact that the French Revolution itself has become less and less germane to contemporary French society and historiography has, Rossignol concludes, rendered the American Revolution all but irrelevant. Simon Newman explores the ways in which nineteenth- and twentieth-century Britons celebrated the ideals enshrined in Founding documents and ideals of the American Revolution, but concludes that while Britons remained fascinated by America they are today far more critical of an American polity that appears to fall short of those ideals. Csaba Lévai explores the sporadic appearances of the American Revolution in Hungarian and Polish society, and the ways in which the distant and quite alien example of the American Revolution and early republic was employed by proponents of constitutional and democratic reform. He argues, however, that although the actions and ideals of the Patriots have occasionally been seized upon by eastern Europeans, these have been employed and interpreted according to local needs and desires.

Modern European constitutional government, both on the national and the European-wide levels, and correlations with the early American republic are the subject of Chapters six and seven. Thomas Clark analyses contemporary German debates about direct and representative democracy, and he established strong parallels between these and the American Revolutionary debates between radical and conservative Patriots. In a similar vein, Joseph Eugene Mullin suggests that the constitutional theories of leading Patriots such as John Taylor continue to have relevance, rehearsing as they do the modern European discussions of the distribution of power and the rights and liberties of the citizen in a federal Europe.

The volume concludes with Andrew Pepper's examination of the Hollywood movies that are the vehicle for most contemporary Europeans' understanding of American history in general, and in this case, the American Revolution. Pepper considers how the formation of the American republic is represented in the only two major films on the subject made in the last quarter-century, *Revolution* (1985) and *The Patriot* (2000). He argues that these very different films – the first largely British-made, the second an American production – illustrate the difficulties facing filmmakers who wish to present the American Revolution to modern audiences in both the United States and abroad, whether in mythical terms as representing liberty, democracy and the American way, or in rather more nuanced and even critical terms.

Almost two centuries have passed since Tocqueville described the exceptional character of the United States for European readers. To successive generations of Americans, and to the Europeans who watched their endeavours, the United States represented what F. Scott Fitzgerald described so memorably as 'the last and greatest of all human dreams'.[7] For millions of nineteenth- and twentieth-century Europeans, the republic established by the American Revolution was best represented by the Statue of Liberty, a gift from a European nation in commemoration of the centenary of the American Revolution, and a powerful symbol that served to welcome millions of immigrants to the United States, the Land of Liberty.

But as the essays in this volume illustrate, the meaning and the significance of the American Revolution for Europeans has never been as fixed and as constant as the Founders and subsequent historians in the United States have assumed. While Europeans from the 1770s to the present have mined America's Founding documents in order to support their own particular arguments for and against political reform, only rarely have Europeans wholeheartedly embraced the American precedent. While nineteenth- and twentieth-century Europeans from Britain to Hungary regarded the Declaration of Independence, the Constitution and the Bill of Rights as the founding documents of a nation based upon higher ideals, from the very beginning many other Europeans in Glasgow, Paris and elsewhere rejected this special American role. Moreover, the idealism of the 'American Century' has eroded significantly over the past quarter-century, and pan-European institutions have fashioned viable alternatives to American constitutional models. While the American republican experience can inform contemporary European debate, many European scholars and politicians find that current American policies betray the ideals enshrined in the Founding documents of the Revolution. All around contemporary Europe, more and more people are committed to human rights and democratic government, yet seldom have the examples of the Founders appeared less directly and uniquely relevant. In the early twenty-first century, Europeans seldom look westward across the Atlantic for inspiration as they discuss democracy, individual rights and representative government.

Notes

1. J. Winthrop, 'A Modell of Christian Charity'; (1630), in S. Mitchell, ed., *Winthrop Papers, 1498–1649* (Boston, MA: Massachusetts Historical Society, 1931), II, p.295.

2. M.O. Warren, *'History of the Rise, Progress and Termination of the American Revolution. Interspersed with Biographical, Political, and Moral Observations'* (Boston, MA: Manning and Loring, 1805), III, pp.435–6.
3. A. de Tocqueville, *'Democracy in America'*, transl. H. Reeve (New York: George Dearborn & Co., 1838), p.xxiii.
4. There is a huge secondary literature in American Exceptionalism. Recent works include S.M. Lipset, *'American Exceptionalism': A Double-Edged Sword* (New York: W.W. Norton, 1996); D.T. Rodgers, 'Exceptionalism', in A. Molho and G.S. Wood, eds, *'Imagined Histories: American Historians Interpret Their Past* (Princeton, NJ: Princeton University Press, 1998)', pp.21–40; M. Kammen, 'The Problem of American Exceptionalism' *American Quarterly*, XLV (1993) 1–43.
5. For a discussion of this historiography, see S.P. Newman, 'Writing the History of the American Revolution,' in M. Stokes, ed., *The State of U.S. History* (Oxford: Berg, 2002), pp.23–44.
6. R.R. Palmer, *'The Age of the Democratic Revolution': A Political History of Europe and America, 1760–1800* (Princeton, NJ: Princeton University Press, 1959), I, p.282. A more recent example is P.L.R. Higgonet, *Sister Republics: The Origins of French and American Republicanism* (Cambridge, MA: Harvard University Press, 1988). Like Palmer, Higonnet is a French historian, and few American historians of the revolutionary era have seldom ventured into this comparative terrain.
7. F.S. Fizgerald, *'The Great Gatsby (1926)'* (Harmondsworth, Middlesex: Penguin, 1978), p.187.

1

The American Revolution, Glasgow, and the Making of the Second City of the Empire

Brad A. Jones

For years historians have argued that the American Revolution informed and influenced revolutionaries throughout the world. R.R. Palmer, in his pivotal work on the subject, argued that it

> inspired the sense of a new era. It added a new content to the conceptions of progress. It gave a whole new dimension to ideas of liberty and equality made familiar by the Enlightenment ... It dethroned England, and set up America, as a model for those seeking a better world ... Whether fantastically idealized or seen in a factual way, whether as mirage or as reality, America made Europe seem unsatisfactory to many people of the middle and lower classes, and to those of the upper classes who wished them well.[1]

To Palmer and many subsequent historians, the American Revolution's contagion of liberty infected communities and countries throughout the western world and on occasion helped trigger other revolutionary movements.

However, historians have all but ignored the nature and effects of European opposition to the American Revolution. This chapter will explore how members of the key provincial British Atlantic community of Glasgow, Scotland, interpreted and reacted to the political ideology of the American Patriots in an effort to articulate their own loyalty to Great Britain. The American Revolution served as a catalyst for Glasgow's late eighteenth-century and nineteenth-century emergence as the 'Second City of the Empire', and the city's public response to revolutionary ideas and the events of the war enabled Glaswegians to demonstrate and articulate their loyalty to a new British union that was barely two generations old. In effect, the American War for Independence awakened a

1

new, uniquely British political consciousness in Glasgow. The events of the war provided Glaswegians with the opportunity to patriotically affirm their rights and liberties as established members of the British Empire, and they did so by rejecting the ideas of American revolutionaries in favour of a patriotic imperial nationalism.

Enormous economic growth over the course of the eighteenth-century provided the context for Glasgow's patriotic loyalism during the American Revolution. The eighteenth century was a period of intense and unprecedented expansion in the British Empire, which was accompanied by both an elite and popular elaboration of a British imperial identity. Military success against the French and Spanish, the emergence and expansion of a powerful Atlantic trade economy, and the growth of an accessible and influential print culture allowed subjects from all corners of the rapidly expanding Empire to participate in these public processes of identity formation. In Glasgow, the initial unpopularity of the 1707 Act of Union with England gradually subsided as the economic benefits of membership in the Empire became ever more apparent. As early as the 1720s, the English traveller and pro-Unionist Daniel Defoe had remarked that 'Glasgow is a *City of Business* and has the face of Foreign as well as Domestic Trade; nay, I may say, 'tis the only City in Scotland, at this time, that apparently increases in both. The *Union* has, indeed, answered its end to them, more than to any other Part of the Kingdom, their Trade being new formed by it.'[2] However biased Defoe's unionism may have been, the city's landscape had begun to illustrate Glasgow's economic rise through trade as an imperial British city.

In fact, access to English trading routes had been one of the principal motives for Scots, particularly in Atlantic trading communities such as Glasgow, to become Britons.[3] Scotland had struggled throughout the seventeenth century to compete with its English neighbours in the colonial trade, and the Scottish Parliament regularly petitioned Westminster for wider access to the English colonial markets. In the late-seventeenth century the Company of Scotland, a group of wealthy merchants who had united to cultivate the country's foreign market economy, attempted to establish a Scottish colony at Darien, located in present-day Panama. Enormous sums of money were invested and the public was inundated with promises from the government that it would resurrect the nation's fading economy. In Glasgow, which was to serve as the Company's trading headquarters, the Council subscribed a considerable sum of £3,450 to the venture, and the local public contributed nearly four times as much.[4] Yet, amid poor planning, lack of military protection and widespread disease, the venture ultimately collapsed.

In retrospect, the failure of the Darien venture was more than just a disastrous attempt by the Scots to expand their markets across the Atlantic. Rather, it illustrated Scottish determination to participate in and benefit from the Atlantic world trade, and the Scots' aspirations alone to mount such an expedition showed that at least the beginnings of an Atlantic market economy had already begun to take root in Scotland years before union with England.[5] Yet, it was not until nearly the middle of the eighteenth-century that Scotland in general, and Glasgow in particular, began to develop a truly expansive trans-Atlantic trade network with the prosperous American colonial markets.[6]

Thereafter, the staggering growth of the Atlantic economy, based as it was on the profitable tobacco and sugar trade with the American and Caribbean colonies, positioned the city as one of the major commercial centres in the Empire, competing with the likes of Liverpool, Bristol, and even London. Their success, as Tom Devine has convincingly shown, was to a large degree a result of the faster, less dangerous, and more direct shipping routes across the Atlantic, as well as improved methods of business with the colonial tobacco and sugar planters.[7] By 1741, for example, tobacco imports from the thirteen American Colonies had risen to roughly 8 million pounds, more than 40 times the yearly rate imported in the 1680s. Three decades of remarkable growth ensued: by 1745, imports had jumped to 13 million pounds, increasing to 15 million pounds in 1755, and peaking at 47 million pounds on the eve of the American War for Independence.[8] By the late 1750s, tobacco imports in Glasgow had surpassed those of London and all other English ports combined, and by 1765 it had already accounted for nearly 40 per cent of all of Britain's Atlantic trade.[9] The success of the trade also spurred the growth of other industries in the city to supply goods and provisions to their colonial planters, so that by the 1750s and 1760s Glasgow had a complex urban economy with established connections all across the Atlantic world.[10] Visitors to Glasgow took note of the diverse urban economy, and the direction of trade: one recorded seeing,

> a vast nailery, a stone-ware manufactory, and a great porter brewery: besides these are manufactures of linnens, cambricks, lawns, fustians, tapes, and striped linnens; sugar-houses and glass-houses; great roperies; vast manufactures of shoes, boots and saddles, and all sorts of horse furniture; also vast tanneries … chiefly for the use of the colonists. The magazine of saddles, and other works respecting that business, is an amazing sight: all these are destined for *America*, no port equaling this for the conveniency of situation, and speedily supplying that market.[11]

The wealth generated through the tobacco trade had important political ramifications as well. During the 1760s, at the height of the Glasgow's Atlantic supremacy, nearly every Lord Provost and town councillor had direct ties to the American trade, and thus an increasingly heightened interest in the emerging imperial crises.[12]

The successful incorporation of Scots into the newly emerging British political and economic system required more than just access to English trade routes. To many Glaswegians, a transformation of identity was required to consolidate their position within the British polity and Empire. To reinvent themselves as British required Scots, and Glaswegians in particular, to relocate themselves within the traditional rhetoric of English rights and liberties. To be sure, by the middle of the eighteenth-century the financial rewards of the Atlantic trade had convinced many of the benefits of membership in the British Empire, but just as important were the failures of the previous century. 'From the 1690's', Colin Kidd has argued, 'there had been a large element of self-doubt in Scottish political culture about the nation's collective institutional failures, and this cast of mind, which was to predate Union, was to ease the capitulation of eighteenth-century North Britons to an English political identity'.[13] The Act of Union brought Scotland from the peripheries of political and economic modernization into the progressively advanced ideas and practices of the developing British Empire. Despite the vital significance of Scottish political and economic thinkers, ideas such as representative government, individual rights and liberties and taxation by elected representatives were all re-cast as British. To British enthusiasts, Scotland was trapped in a feudal, agrarian-based communal society and it had quickly fallen behind the political, social and economic growth of mainland Europe. At the same time, England, which had been, at best, a marginal power throughout much of the sixteenth- and seventeenth-centuries, had modernized and was emerging as a major international military, political and economic power.[14] Consequently, by the middle of the eighteenth-century many enlightened Scottish writers, both in popular and elite print culture, had 'rendered their native country' in a sense a 'historyless nation'.[15] In their essays, correspondence, sermons and speeches, Scotland's past was reimagined within a new Anglo-British history that allowed Scots to successfully adopt the English Protestant whig heritage as their own.

The 'salutary neglect' of successive early-eighteenth century British governments also helped to ease tension between Scotland and England.[16] By and large, Parliament avoided interfering in the political or economic lives of the Scots, while the Act of the Union guaranteed that many Scottish traditions, institutions and privileges, such as the legal, education and religious institutions remained virtually independent.[17] Devout Presbyterians in Glasgow had initially feared that the union would undermine the Church of Scotland, but those fears subsided as the century progressed. Eventually, the freedom to remain Presbyterian actually served to strengthen loyalty to Britain in Glasgow, and became a means by which Scots could express their loyalty and patriotism to Britain in a way that still preserved their own sense of a uniquely Scottish heritage. When Scots were denied the formation of a militia in the 1750s, largely due to the fears of a Jacobite revival that still persisted after the rebellion of 1745, they reacted bitterly toward the British government. This was not because they resented being a part of Britain, but rather the absence of a militia deprived them of the means by which they could physically express their loyalty to the Crown and Empire. Furthermore, as Britons they resented being denied the right to bear arms enjoyed by Englishmen.[18]

The success of the British government's salutary neglect toward Scotland was reflected in the steady development of popular expressions of loyalty. Scots faithfully supported the Empire and fought in battles in Europe, North America and the Caribbean, and as merchants, shippers, factors and workers they played a vital role in the expansion of the Empire's powerful Atlantic trade economy. By the 1750s, public expressions of loyalty and patriotism surrounding important events on the British calendar, such as the birthdays of the King and Queen, and coronation and accession anniversaries, were widely celebrated and reported in local newspapers. These events provided Glaswegians, along with Britons throughout the Atlantic world, with regular, public opportunities to express themselves as loyal British subjects. Local Glasgow newspapers also began reprinting reports of celebrations going on elsewhere in Scotland, England and across Britain's Atlantic Empire, in order to place the loyalty of Glaswegians within the broader context of a shared Empire-wide British identity.

The ideological importance of the popular print culture of the newspapers, magazines, pamphlets and broadsides that was so vital to these processes has been acknowledged by historians of England and early America, but has been somewhat neglected by Scottish historians.[19] These printed materials constituted an easily accessible and consumable source of information for all of the public and played a crucial role in encouraging readers to confront issues of identity and Britishness. They not only reported on patriotic activities and news in local communities, but also reprinted editorials and accounts of patriotic events occurring further afield. Describing the origins of an American nationalist ideology, David Waldstreicher notes that 'Celebrations and printed accounts of them embodied and mobilized a nationalist ideology, an ideology that made consensus the basis of patriotism.'[20] The resulting flow of information around the British Atlantic helped foster an imagined community of British subjects who were able to find commonality in this shared sense of identity.[21]

Throughout much of the eighteenth-century, Glaswegians relied heavily on the periodical press in Edinburgh for their news. Successive stamp tax increases, as a result of Britain's mounting war debt, in addition to a lack of competent printers and financial backers, inhibited the growth of a successful popular print culture in Glasgow.[22] Moreover, the relatively close geographical proximity of Edinburgh appeared to negate the need for a local newspaper in Glasgow. As an intellectual centre of the Enlightenment and the political capital of Scotland, Edinburgh had nurtured a vibrant periodical press, and until 1788, despite earlier petitions from the Glasgow magistrates, all news from London first went through the capital.[23]

Glasgow's first newspaper, the *Glasgow Courant*, appeared in 1715, but it was another 25 years later before the city's second paper, *The Glasgow Journal*, joined the competition. The *Courant's* run ended shortly after the British victory at Quebec in 1759, while *The Glasgow Journal* continued to supply its readers with a weekly issue throughout the American Revolution. *The Glasgow Chronicle or, Weekly Intelligencer*, which may have begun its life as *The Glasgow Weekly Chronicle* in 1766, continued until at least 1778, when the last known issue appeared. In the same year, *The Glasgow Mercury* first appeared as a new competitor.[24] Various weekly and monthly magazines, containing articles on moral and spiritual guidance, histories of cities or countries, poems and songs about various subjects and selections of foreign and domestic news taken directly from the newspapers, also appeared in Glasgow during the Revolutionary War, but none lasted longer than a year and only a few issues survive today.

The sheer volume of Edinburgh newspapers and magazines demonstrated the Scottish capital's domination of the Glasgow press. Eight newspapers and 12 magazines were published during the Revolutionary War, including such internationally recognized titles as the *Caledonian Mercury, Edinburgh Advertiser, Edinburgh Evening Courant* and *Ruddiman's Weekly Journal*. The *Scots Magazine*, modelled on the popular London periodical, *The Gentlemen's Magazine*, was unquestionably the most widely read monthly publication in Edinburgh, Glasgow, and throughout all of Scotland.[25]

Since Edinburgh publications were readily available in Glasgow, residents of the latter city were able to read a good deal about colonial affairs.[26] Nearly a dozen newspapers, even more magazines, plus pamphlets, broadsheets and letters from friends, family and business acquaintances from across the Empire meant that Glaswegians were relatively well informed. News about Britain, the Empire and the American Revolutionary War all required Glaswegians to consider issues relating to their government, political ideology and patriotism. There is evidence to suggest that interest in the news was widespread across social classes, and that many Glaswegians devoured the latest news at home or in taverns, coffeehouses and their places of work. Even those that could not read, or were too poor to afford a periodical, often had access to the news of the day through a process known as 'bridging', by which the popular prints in a community were routinely read aloud at a certain spot in town.[27] An early historian of the city recalled how 'Old Citizens, still living, remember the "Lazy Corner" in the Bridgegate being an important one. In the days before every man was pestered to Subscribe to, or Buy, a Newspaper, the Citizens used to assemble at this Spot in great numbers, and learn the News of the day – the progress of the Rebels in 1715 and 1745; and the Events of the American War some time later, in which Glasgow was deeply interested, from the extent of her Virginian Trade'.[28] There, and in the local taverns and coffeehouses, Glaswegians would deliberate over the latest military news from abroad and contemplate the latest decisions in Parliament, all the while considering their own opinions on the state of the Empire and their place within it.

Together, the economic benefits of the Union, the lax political control of successive eighteenth-century British governments and the emergence of an accessible popular print culture helped to enhance the loyalty of Scots to the Crown and Empire. By the outbreak of the Seven Years' War in the mid-eighteenth century, Glaswegians demonstrated and articulated their opposition to France – Scotland's traditional ally – as loyal British subjects who had adopted the English's long-established Francophobia. Scottish newspapers drew upon a profound anti-Catholic sentiment in order to illustrate the superiority of the British Protestant identity.[29] In a 1755 issue of the *Glasgow Courant* a writer calling himself Decius more precisely highlighted these differences:

Our Contention is not with Protestants, but professed ROMAN CATHOLICS. – A People (however loyal, and pacific, many noble, and ancient Families in this Kingdom have on all occasions behaved themselves toward the present happy Establishment) yet our Enemies on the Continent are a People whose Religion is principally Maintained by forgery, and Falsehood: repugnant to the Laws of Nature, and Nations; composed of Human Devices, in no sort to be deduc'd, or proved out of Holy Scripture; keeping its deluded Votaries in Blindness, and ignorance of God! and real Goodness.[30]

A few weeks later, Decius used Britain's Protestant identity to unite the Scots, the English and their North American colonists against their common enemy:

> I therefore take the Freedom in this Manner, to join every Friend, Briton, and Protestant in their Joy on the [recent] Accounts arrived from the Coast of Virginia ... There is no Distinction, I hope, of Party, of Principle, or, of Northern, or Southern Country amongst us. No such Distinction, I say, can, or ought, to prevail; We are all Britains; inhabiting one island; acknowledging one God! one King, one Faith. – Let us convince our Gallic Enemies of the Unity amongst us; and every Scheme they meditate to the Prejudice of Great Britain, will certainly prove abortive.[31]

Another letter, this time from a resident of New York City, expressed fear at rumours of a savage attack by the French on the city. The writer pictured 'the sacking of a city, by a cruel and merciless enemy!' He continued with an apocalyptic description of 'our streets streaming of blood! our houses in a blaze! our aged trampled under foot! our wives a prey to lust! our virgins ravished! our infants torn from their fond mother's breast, and inhumanely dashed against the walls! these are the heartbreaking calamities which we may suffer from a French fleet and army'.[32]

This kind of imagery of the French as barbaric, inhumane, cruel and without morals, was nothing new to mid-eighteenth century Britons. Historians of eighteenth-century Britain have argued that these representations of France were of vital importance in the origins and growth of a British national identity.[33] Through imperial conquest, a rapidly expanding network of trade, and a rich, vibrant and widely accessible popular print culture, the eighteenth-century British Empire had fostered the development of a new, popular conception of what it meant to be British. At the heart of this identity lay a determined opposition to Britain's long-standing enemy, France. French absolutism and the Catholic religion that supported it, invoked a powerful, unifying and accessible language of identity that Protestant Britons living in Glasgow, and throughout the Empire for that matter, could readily adopt and share in common.[34] More simply put, France allowed a newly emerging nation of 'diverse inhabitants to focus on what they had in common, rather than on what divided them'.[35]

Furthermore, by linking French absolutism with the Catholic religion British subjects were able to celebrate the superiority of the British Church and state over those of their traditional enemy. The emerging popular print culture employed rhetoric and symbols in which Catholic political rule was made synonymous with the perceived absolutism, tyranny and brutality of the religion. In turn, such rule produced a population of backward, barbaric, subordinate subjects, who lacked the ability to think, reason and mature, both as individuals, and then more broadly as a nation. The pervasiveness of this rhetoric in elite and popular culture enabled Britons to identify with themselves and against their enemies in broad socio-political terms that helped define patriotic and nationalist political culture.[36]

Despite an increasingly diverse population, Britons throughout the Empire were able to find commonality in the rights and liberties secured in their constitution and defended in wars against Catholic France.[37] 'Anti-catholicism', as Colin Haydon has argued, 'was an ideology which promoted national cohesion, countering, though not submerging, the kingdom's political divisions and social tensions'.[38] However, in no small way the pervasiveness of this rhetoric depended upon the presence of Britain's eternal enemy. British rights and liberties came into focus when framed in opposition to the Catholic empires of mainland Europe. This grand narrative, accessible and influential to so many, was, at the same time, dependent upon the presence of the French 'other'.[39] The comprehensive British victory in the Seven Years' War provided the ultimate justification for Protestant British supremacy and firmly implanted in the minds of its subjects the idea that they were a part of the most advanced and successful empire in the world. As a young Charles Fox declared to his fellow members of Parliament, 'Observe the magnificence of our metropolis – the extent of our empire – the immensity of our commerce and the opulence of our people.'[40]

Few cities in the Empire better fit Fox's description than Glasgow. By the 1760s, the city and its 30,000 residents had emerged as a vitally important and loyal British Atlantic community.[41] During his tour through Scotland in the early 1770s, the Welsh traveller Thomas Pennant declared, 'GLASGOW: the best built of any second-rate city I ever saw', the view from the Cross, 'has an air of vast magnificence'.[42]

The wealth and influence generated by their successful Atlantic trade created more opportunities for Scots to infiltrate the predominately-English social and political structure. Additionally, while the backlash of anti-Scottish sentiment generated by John Wilkes during this period highlighted the still tenuous nature of their relationship, it also proved, quite blatantly, that Scots were acquiring power and influence within Great Britain to an unprecedented degree.[43] In the poetic words of the Wilkite Charles Churchill, 'Into our places, states, and beds they creep, They've a sense to get that we want sense to keep.'[44] Proudly, defiantly and successfully British, Glaswegians depended for much of their economic success and political influence on trade with Britain's American colonies. Thus, while the wars against France had consolidated British identity in Scotland, the imperial crises and ensuing American War for Independence challenged the loyalty and identity of Glaswegians.

To make matters more difficult, the emerging conflict with the American colonists was notably different from previous wars of the eighteenth-century. This time the enemy was not France, but rather fellow British subjects, who adhered to the Protestant heritage that Britons throughout the Empire had come to define themselves by. Assisted by an equally influential and accessible print culture, the Revolutionary ideology of the American Patriots thus challenged the very nature of eighteenth-century conceptions of Britishness, and thereby drew into question the perceived superiority of the newly emerging Empire. Just as Americans began to create a new, American national identity, Britons were forced to redefine, rearticulate and defend their own identity. This was a difficult process, made more complicated by the fact that both sides were arguing very similar cases. And access to both British and American popular print culture throughout the Atlantic world allowed Britons everywhere to see and read both sides of the conflict, making it increasingly difficult for them to comprehend and define an enemy once considered to be a friend.[45]

In the early years of the imperial crisis, the popular print culture in Glasgow relied upon a rhetoric that challenged the legitimacy of the Revolutionary cause. News of extra-legal associations, committees of correspondence, and the influence of the Sons of Liberty, particularly in New England, raised concern over the legality of the protest and increased speculation that it was orchestrated by a few corrupt and self-interested gentlemen.[46] In 1768, *The Glasgow Journal* printed a letter from a Bostonian that reported on the arrival of General Gage and his British troops to restore order to the city. The author reported that

The poor unthinkable multitudes have been wretchedly misled by a few factious popular men, who, disguising their own self-interested designs, under the specious pretext of liberty, have worked them up to such a pitch, that the men of sense and good principle were afraid of declaring their sentiments.[47]

In another letter, addressed to the printer of *The Edinburgh Advertiser*, the writer confessed his earlier sympathy for the colonists, 'but some of their late proceedings have convinced me, that their opposition is not dictated by true patriotism, but by a spirit of tyranny and despotism'. He complained that the colonial leaders had destroyed the liberty of speech and press, forced peaceful citizens to subscribe to associations contrary to their principles and opinions, and deprived them of the right to trial by jury, before concluding, 'Shall the sacred name of liberty be made the instrument to glut the avarice, the tyranny of such enemies to civil society?'[48] The pervasiveness of this rhetoric even extended beyond discussions of the political crises occurring in the American colonies. When a group of sailors at Port Glasgow rioted for higher wages early in 1773, their leader wrote a letter to the editor of *The Glasgow Journal* explaining that 'we did not intend a Mob, Riot, or what d'ye call it? we only mistook our plan, and by having some Chips off the old Block from Boston, as well as some Irish Runners among us, they soon convinced us, that the best way of doing Work was "to do none." '[49]

At times, the tactics used by the rebellious colonists to oppose imperial policy overshadowed the imagery of corrupt and self-interested Patriot leaders that were employed to discount the American revolutionary cause. Colonial non-importation, first in 1768, and then more widely in 1774, was greeted with indignation by the merchant community in Glasgow. One writer asserted that it 'is alarming as well as a very unexpected height of insolence, and ought to remind us of the duty we all owe, in our respective stations, to our country, her trade, and manufactures, which must suffer very considerably if this [non-importation] spirit is allowed to go on without being properly checked in the bud'.[50] He went on to state that mercantilist colonial taxation was necessary because it kept the colonists from selling and buying outside of Britain's Atlantic trade network. He then concluded, 'Thus we should at once secure our trade, our manufactures, and our existence; and encrease [sic] our revenues by these very means, which American selfishness had contrived for subverting them.'[51] The writer framed a problem suffered by Glaswegians in imperial terms, placing it within the context of a broader British Atlantic community. He presented the selfishness of American colonists as directly affecting the general wellbeing of communities across the Empire, and for many Glaswegians that was the real issue at stake.

Similarly, in a letter printed in an August 1774 issue of *The Glasgow Journal*, a loyalist New York City resident divided those colonists who were in support of the non-importation agreement into three categories so that the reader 'may guess of our present stock of Patriotism'. The first, he says,

> really think that life, estate, and every thing else is concerned in the debate about who shall have the laying on of a paltry three penny tax ... There are other men who trade to Spain, Portugal, &c. in wheat and flour, who never deal in English goods, these are very zealous about non-importation, for then trade will run entirely though their own hands ... There is a third set more numerous than both of these put together, they are men who intend to make fortunes by breaking agreements, which they hope others will be such fools to keep.[52]

Besides disrupting Glasgow's prosperous colonial trade, the American revolutionaries were challenging the authority and legitimacy of the King and Parliament, and the enlightened polity over which they presided. 'The great art of government', according to Britannus, writing in *The Glasgow Journal*, 'consists in keeping a due medium between well-bounded Liberty and unbounded Licentiousness, and devising such checks and dependencies between subject and sovereign, that we may be either slaves or libertines', and Britain should only 'let the Americans enjoy all the sweets of legal freedom, and extend their commerce as far as they can, under proper restriction.' With that in mind, he warned that 'if they assume a power to themselves of undermining the very basis of our constitution, by erecting twenty distinct parliaments, and each of them with supreme authority ... 'tis high time to make them sensible, that so daring an attempt will not escape with impunity'.[53] The colonists' formation of extra-legal, self-interested groups constituted an illegal challenge to the authority of the British constitution. The constitution had become a bulwark of British society, responsible for ensuring that the rights and liberties of all subjects would be protected in times of need. To challenge it, was to challenge the very essence of Britishness.[54]

The portrayal of the American Patriots as tyrannical, despotic, and self-interested – essentially as un-British – was especially evident in the coverage of the British siege of New York City. An account from London boasted that because 'of the shameful retreat of the rebels at New York, many people are of opinion that they will make the best of their way at Kingsbridge also'. It continues, 'Even some of the warmest advocates for the Americans begin now to give them up; they say, if they will not fight for their liberties, they deserve to lose them.'[55] The subsequent fire in New York City, reported to have been caused by the retreating Patriots, provided further evidence of their bad character. A letter printed in *The Glasgow Chronicle* reported that the residents 'all behave themselves as yet become good subjects; I mean the New Yorkers, not the New England people, some of who I find stayed behind for the villanous purpose of setting fire to the city which, 'tis verily believed, was concerted by some great ones among the Rebels, and that the poor wretches who did the business were only their tools'. In an effort to inflame the loyal readers, the writer reported that the fire was set 'in a part of town where the labouring people lived, as also where the English Protestant churches were, as well as the college'. Attacks on the moral, religious and educational foundations of British society, as well as the long-suffering working class 'lower sorts' would have resonated with nearly the entire Glaswegian public. The arrival of the British in New York City was reported as bringing a return to stability, morality and prosperity as Glaswegians learned that 'the distressed inhabitants begin again to return, and the place seems already [half] alive, goods are plenty, provisions of all kinds moderate, and the people healthy. While the town was in the hands of the rebels, it was almost quite deserted.'[56]

During the early years of the American Revolution Scottish newspapers repeatedly printed reports such as these to challenge the legitimacy of the revolutionary cause and to remind loyal British readers of the benefits of membership in the Empire. However, this line of rhetoric was fragile. It relied upon an interpretation of the events going on in the American colonies that was open to questioning, which is exactly what happened. Just as the British popular political culture challenged the American revolutionary ideology, the emerging and influential American print culture turned the language of British liberty on its head. Patriots defended the actions of American crowds and popular politics as the actions of Britons who were denied the very rights and liberties the Constitution was designed to protect.

But the Franco-American alliance of 1778 changed the ways in which the British public perceived the war by renewing the traditional and persuasive rhetoric of loyalty, or what Stephen Conway has colourfully labelled the 'old-style gallophobia' that Britain had come to define itself by.[57] On the surface, the alliance allowed the broader public, not just in Glasgow, but throughout the Empire, to identify an enemy that defied simple definition. Britons rejoiced in what they saw as the hypocrisy of a rebellion supposedly based on a greater appreciation of individual rights and liberties, which was now associated with an oppressive and arbitrary empire. French participation in the conflict enabled Glaswegians to reconstruct the meaning of the war and their place within it. They were able to redefine the American Patriots as political and religious enemies, while simultaneously celebrating Glaswegian loyalty and identity within a broader Empire-wide conception of Britishness.[58]

Early in 1778, shortly after news of Burgoyne's humiliating defeat at Saratoga, and amid rumours of the impending alliance, Glasgow's town councillors and many of the trade incorporations subscribed funds to raise new regiments needed to fight an unexpectedly troublesome enemy. The raising of these regiments quickly became a means by which Glaswegians of all levels in society could publicly profess their loyalty to the British cause. *The Glasgow Mercury* reported that 'the inhabitants, animated by that zeal for their excellent constitution, and for the prosperity of their country, (which has in all times of public danger characterized the city of Glasgow,) subscribed most liberally.'[59] Despite their own suffering occasioned by the interruption in trade, the 'Journeyman Weavers in Glasgow' displayed 'the ardent loyalty of this place, among all the lovers of liberty, of their country and of our happy constitution' in a letter to the Lord Provost printed in *The Glasgow Mercury*.[60] British newspapers throughout the Empire reported on the determined efforts of Glaswegians to raise troops in support of the war effort. *The Royal Gazette* in New York City reported that the 'sum subscribed for raising the Glasgow battalions, already exceeds £9000' and provided a detailed account of the different amounts given by the city council and each of the trade incorporations.[61] *The London Chronicle* reprinted a letter from a Glaswegian that spoke of the continued and absolute loyalty of that city's residents. 'The Citizens of Glasgow', the writer acknowledged, 'have ever been distinguished for their loyalty and patriotism; but upon no occasion have they exerted themselves more than in the present case; all ranks of men seem determined to contribute liberally to support the constitutional rights of Great Britain over her misled and refractory Colonies.'[62] British newspapers reported on similar efforts in communities such Edinburgh, Liverpool, Manchester and Bristol, in order to highlight the unity and solidarity of British subjects in the face of their Franco-American enemies.[63]

However, amid the public outpouring of support for the new war against the French and Americans, the British government made a decidedly unpopular and eventually costly decision. The presence of France had expanded the geographical reach of the war. Britons were no longer fighting just a small, disorganized colonial militia on a distant continent, for they now also faced a formidable, well-trained enemy in a war that stretched throughout the Empire. In Glasgow, rumours of a French invasion surfaced regularly in the periodical press from 1778 onward, exacerbated by reports of the infamous American privateer, John Paul Jones, who threatened his own attacks on the coasts of Scotland and England.[64] Such threats made it glaringly obvious that the current size of the British military was insufficient to deal with this new enemy, and the North ministry decided to repeal certain penal laws against Catholics living in England so that they would be eligible for military service.[65]

The decision had little immediate impact in England, but provoked a strong reaction in Scotland. By October, newspapers began to report that the government was planning to do the same for Scottish Catholics, and Scots immediately began mobilizing in opposition. Associations and committees of correspondence, modelled on those created by the American revolutionaries during the 1760s, were formed to coordinate and express the public's outrage. In Glasgow and the city's hinterland, members of trade incorporations, elite merchants and politicians, prominent clergymen and citizens from all levels of society organized together as 'the Eighty-five Private Societies in and about Glasgow'.[66] Within a matter of months, they drew up petitions against the proposed legislation and utilized the local press in Glasgow and Edinburgh to list their grievances and print their proclamations.[67]

The speed, extent and vehemence of the Scottish response was remarkable. From October 1778 to January 1779, over three hundred and fifty petitions from churches, towns and societies throughout Scotland were published, and in the Glasgow area alone, organizers were said to have collected over eighty-eight thousand signatures.[68] For many, fears of the proposed legislation centred less on the religious consequences of enabling Catholics to fight for Britain, and more on the broader socio-political threat of Catholic relief. *The Scots Magazine* reported that a meeting in Glasgow of 'many hundreds of the friends of the *Protestant Interest* ... declared it as their unanimous opinion, that such a measure would be highly prejudicial to the interest of the Protestant religion in Scotland, dangerous to our constitution civil and religious, a direct violation of the treaty of Union, inconsistent with the King's honour, and destructive of the peace and security of his best subjects'.[69] The 'Paisley Ayr Shire Society' warned that such relief would 'give the death's stab to our civil and religious liberties', while the 'Society of Weavers in Pollockshaws' reminded readers that nearly five years earlier the government had made similar allowances for Catholics living in Canada, which had set off a chain of events that ultimately led to the revolted American colonists allying themselves with those 'under-handed, double-dealing, perfidious Papists, our natural enemies, THE FRENCH.'[70] The actions of the government threatened to undermine the loyalty of British subjects and challenged the very definition of Britishness that they were so strongly asserting. France's involvement in the war had brought about a renewed spirit of loyalty amongst the broader population, encouraging many to profess their patriotic support for the British cause and vow to defend their Protestant nation against a Catholic enemy.

However, by legislating in favour of Catholics, the King and Parliament risked betraying this identity. Their policies harkened back to monarchs who had threatened national security through pro-Catholic conces-sions, and their actions even led some to wonder if Lord North's government was embracing a Catholic, absolute form of rule in order to continue the war in America. The petition from the heritors and heads of family in the parish of Carluke, printed in *The Glasgow Mercury*, drew upon a familiar rhetoric of loyalty in order to express their anger at the actions of the government.

> Great Britain hath long been considered as the bulwark of the Protestant cause. The power of her arm, and the terror of her right arm, kept the Popish nations in awe. To annihilate, therefore, or diminish her power, is giving a mortal blow to Protestantism. – It fills our breasts with indignation, to behold a set of men entrusted by their King and country, effectuate in a few years by ****** (we are at a loss to give it a name,) what the united force of the Popish powers have attempted so often in vain. – They have lost America. – The West Indies in danger. – Trade and manufactures in a ruinous state. – Protestant alliances neglected or despised, while the Popish powers are closely united, and our internal safety thereby rendered very precarious.[71]

It was the threat of Catholic toleration that persuaded lower sort Glaswegians to take to the streets. Violence ensued in early February 1779, ironically just days after Parliament had withdrawn the bill from consideration. A mob burnt and destroyed the home of an English Catholic named Robert Bagnal,[72] which was believed to be the site where Catholics met to worship, and continued to wreak havoc in the city until a regiment of the Western Fencibles disbanded the angry citizens.[73] A similar, if not more violent riot occurred at the same time in nearby Edinburgh, where a newly built Catholic church was demolished and local Catholics roughly treated. The situation could have turned much worse had it not been for the efforts of local newspaper printers to assure the public that the government had concluded not to bring the proposed legislation to a vote.

While this may have averted more violent opposition in Scotland, the failure of the government to do the same in England allowed debates over identity, loyalty and the war with the French and Americans to continue to dominate the popular political prints. Lord George Gordon and his newly formed Protestant Association played upon the united response of the Scots in opposing Catholic relief to initiate a similar campaign in England. In a speech before the Parliament in November 1779, Gordon defended his anti-Catholic sentiments by claiming that the 'government will find 120,000 men at my back who will avow and support them!'[74] And in doing so, Gordon achieved a level of celebrity north of the border that illustrated the Scots continuing commitment to the Protestant cause. When he made a tour of Glasgow in early September 1779 bonfires blazed, firework displays lit up the night sky, and windows throughout the town were illuminated in honour of the peer. In the neighbouring town of Paisley, Gordon was treated to a parade featuring members of the local trade incorporations who turned out in great numbers to honour the man 'who had so lately distinguished himself in protecting their religion, liberties, and trade'.[75]

Even after the disastrous consequences of five days of rioting in London in early June 1780, Gordon and the cause he championed continued to be held in high regard by many Scots.[76] In early February 1782, 'The PRAESES of the 85 SOCIETIES in GLASGOW, and its Neighbourhood, and a Numerous and Respectable Company of the Friends of LORD GEORGE, and zealous Well-wishers to the *Protestant Cause*' assembled at the Saracen's Head Inn in Glasgow to celebrate the anniversary of Gordon's acquittal from charges of treason. Toasts given throughout the evening not only honoured 'The Protestant Interest' and 'LORD GEORGE GORDON', but also 'The Protestant Association at London, Edinburgh, and Glasgow, and all the Friends and Well-wishers to the Protestant Interest', thereby linking the loyalty of Glaswegians with British subjects living in the two most important political centres on the British mainland.[77]

Months later, during an annual celebration of the King's birthday, *The Glasgow Journal* reported that 'a number of gentlemen well affected to government, and zealous wishers to the Protestant interest, assembled at the house of Mr. JOHN PATERSON, Praeses of the different Societies, in order to celebrate the anniversary of the birth of our most Gracious

Sovereign.' Besides the usual toasts to the King and Queen, those present also gave honour to 'Lord George Gordon, [and] the Praeses of the 85 Societies'. Additionally, recent news of Admiral Rodney's improbable victory over the Comte De Grasse in the British West Indies, which secured Britain's position in the Caribbean and restored their naval dominance of the Atlantic, led to a series of toasts to 'Lord Rodney, Lord Hood ... the whole gallant Captains and Officers under Lord Rodney, [and] the Brave Tars who gained the late glorious victory over De Grasse.'[78] Together, the toasts given on the day – loyalty to the King and Royal family, support of and identification with Britain's Protestant heritage, and a joyous celebration in honour of Britain's resounding victory over the Catholic French navy – spoke volumes about the British loyalty and self-identification of those present.

Popular opposition to Catholicism and widespread support for Britain's Protestant heritage remained a vital means by which Glaswegians were able to articulate their loyalty to Great Britain in the latter stages of the war. This was abetted, in part, by the presence of the Catholic empires of France, and then Spain, in the conflict. From 1778 onward their presence enabled the British public to revert to a traditionally conservative language and rhetoric of loyalty that centred upon the authority of the King and Parliament as the protectors and guarantors of the cherished rights and liberties of British subjects.

The Glasgow press continued to challenge the legitimacy of the American revolutionary ideology even as it became clear that Britain could not win the war. In an air of apparent resentment towards the colonies' stance on British taxation, they mistakenly reported various claims that the new and unstable American government had resorted to excessive taxation to pay for their massive war debt. One such report stated that 'The government of America have imposed such taxes on the people, as will enable Congress ... to keep the whole country in the most perfect subordination and quietness.'[79] A story reprinted from the *Virginia Gazette* carried the alleged tax crisis a step further, reporting that 'wherein several estates are held forth for public sale, for the payment of taxes levied upon them, and among which, however singular it may appear, is one of George Washington's, containing 3087 acres, which had been seized for eight pounds five shillings and threepence.'[80]

Taxation was not the only example of American oppression reported by Glasgow newspapers. Accounts of Loyalists being stripped of their rights and liberties continued to surface throughout the summer and autumn of 1783, raising questions about the ability of the American government to ensure the protection of their citizens' rights and liberties. *The Glasgow Journal* testified that 'three or four loyalists who had returned to their habitations in the United States on the proclamation of peace, had been treated with so much severity, that they thought themselves happy in getting back to New York with their families, and the loss of the greatest part of their property.'[81] A report from a frightened and dejected gentleman in New York City recognized that all hope for reconciliation was lost.

> This city swarms with those we lately called rebels; and daily accounts are brought in of the most violent resolves entered into by different associations to murder all those who shall be found here upon the evacuation by the King's troops, under a hope of being permitted to return to their families. When the dreadful day arrives, I hope we shall not find our fears realized ... Under this impression, great numbers of people ... are going to the deserts of Nova Scotia. What will be their fate, where they will find places to cover their heads, or how they will subsist, it is impossible even to conjecture. In my own opinion, I have already consigned two-thirds of them to the grave.[82]

Such reports, truthful or otherwise, were meant to illustrate the lawlessness and chaos of the new American government and its inability to live up to the lofty, if not naive ideals of the revolutionary cause. These failures were as much attributed to the misguided intentions of the revolutionary leaders as they were to the influence of their French allies. Heavy taxes and instances of violent and oppressive rule, both commonly associated with Catholic France, offered glaring proof of the baleful influence of the French on their American allies. A letter from a loyal Briton, printed in *The Glasgow Journal* shortly after news of the Peace Treaty in 1783, played upon these popular perceptions in order to reassure the British public of the superiority of their Protestant whig heritage.

> The Americans, desirous of consecrating their gratitude to our Monarch, propose to erect in the principal square of Philadelphia, facing the palace of the Congress, a statue of brass, with this inscription in French, 'A Louis XVI. Liberateur des Americains.'[83]

Linda Colley has argued that following the end of the American War for Independence British popular politics adopted a more conservative, geographically limited interpretation of Britishness, honing an identity that excluded non-white, non-Protestant, and non-British mainland peoples against the backdrop of an increasingly diverse Empire.[84] Eliga Gould has agreed that the American war produced a 'counter-revolutionary turn,' forcing Britons to recognize the limits of their own Britishness.[85] Stephen Conway has suggested that the unfulfilled claims of the American colonists to the rights and liberties of British subjects made 'an inclusive, Greater-Britain type of Britishness untenable.'[86] In many ways their assertions are correct, but none of these historians have truly appreciated the impact of the American Revolution on popular conceptions of identity amongst the Scottish population. They have all but forgotten that at the outset of colonial opposition to imperial rule, the Scots themselves were still struggling to find their own place within the newly emerging Empire.

For those Scots living in the important British Atlantic community of Glasgow, the American war presented a series of crises and opportunities. The loss of the Atlantic tobacco trade, while having an immediate and devastating impact, provoking great anger during the critical years of colonial non-importation and impending war, proved in the long term to pave the way for the city's extensive economic growth.[87] As Tom Devine as argued, the 'social and economic dominance [of the elite tobacco merchants] had depended to a considerable degree on the absence of competing groups in Glasgow business society'. However, the weakening of the trade with America, coupled with the expanding cotton and sugar trade with the British West Indies, allowed Glasgow's influential merchant and manufacturing community to expand and new fortunes to be made. Within a matter of decades, the city's population had doubled to nearly eighty thousand inhabitants, and its diverse trades and manufacturers had made Glasgow one of the most important centres of trade and industry in the British Empire.[88]

However, to focus wholly on the economic consequences of the American Revolution in the development of Glasgow as the 'Second City' of the British Empire is to ignore the equally important political and ideological factors involved. Debates over identity and loyalty stirred up by the American colonists and covered in great detail in the emerging Empire-wide popular print culture forced Glaswegians to develop and articulate their own assumptions about their rights and liberties as British subjects, and the superiority of their Protestant British heritage. Critically important to this debate was the alliance between France and America, which weakened the legitimacy of the revolutionary cause, enabling the broader British public – Glasgow included – to regard

Americans who shared in the political and religious heritage of true Britons as having become alien, 'other' and un-British. At the same time, the alliance also created an opportunity for members of the broader public to reassert their own rights and liberties as members of the British Empire. From 1778 onwards, the public loudly and on occasion violently proposed a conservative rearticulation of Britishness that emphasized the sovereignty of Parliament and the authority of the Monarch as defenders of Britain's Protestant heritage. In Glasgow, this reaffirmation of Britishness served to not only deepen the roots of loyalty in the community, but also to strengthen the city's political ties to the rest of the Empire. In doing so, Glasgow emerged from the American Revolution with a deepened sense of loyalty and patriotism to Great Britain that had important consequences on the city's emergence as the Second City of the Empire.

Notes

1. R.R. Palmer, *The Age of the Democratic Revolution: A Political History of Europe and America, 1760–1800* (Princeton: Princeton University Press, 1959), p.282.
2. J. McUre, *Glasghu Facies: A View of the City of Glasgow* (Glasgow: John Tweed, 1872), I, p.16.
3. N.C. Landsman, 'Nation, Migration, and the Province in the First British Empire: Scotland and the Americas, 1600–1800', *The American Historical Review*, CIV (1999) 464.
4. G. Jackson, 'Glasgow in transition, c. 1660–c. 1740', in T.M. Devine and G. Jackson, eds, *Glasgow: Volume 1: Beginnings to 1830* (Manchester: Manchester University Press, 1995), pp.73–4.
5. D. Armitage, 'Making the Empire British: Scotland in the Atlantic World, 1542–1707', *Past and Present*, CLV (May 1997) 57–9; T.M. Devine, *Scotland's Empire, 1600–1815* (London: Penguin Books Ltd., 2004), pp.40–9; G. Pratt Insh, *The Company of Scotland Trading to Africa and the Indies* (London: Scribner, 1932); J. Prebble, *The Darien Disaster* (London: Secker & Warburg, 1968); M. Lynch, *Scotland: A New History* (London: Pimlico, 1992), pp.307–9.
6. One historian has estimated that smuggling was so excessive in the 1720s that Glasgow merchants paid duties on only one-half to two-thirds of all their imports. R.C. Nash, 'The English and Scottish Tobacco Trades in the Seventeenth and Eighteenth Centuries: Legal and Illegal Trade', *Economic History Review*, XXXV (1982) 354–72.
7. T.M. Devine, *The Tobacco Lords: A Study of the Tobacco Merchants of Glasgow and their Trading Activities c. 1740–1790* (Edinburgh: Donald, 1975), pp.55–71; Devine, *Scotland's Empire*, pp.74–88.
8. Devine, *The Tobacco Lords*, pp.73, 108; Lynch, *Scotland*, p.380.
9. T.M. Devine, 'The Golden Age of Tobacco', in Devine and Jackson, eds, *Glasgow*, pp.76, 140–3.

22   *Brad A. Jones*

10. I. Maver, *Glasgow* (Edinburgh: Edinburgh University Press, 2000), pp.18–20; R. H. Campbell, 'The Making of the Industrial City', in Devine and Jackson, eds, *Glasgow*, pp.188–90.
11. T. Pennant, *A Tour in Scotland, and Voyage to the Hebrides* (Chester: Printed by John Monk, 1774), I, p.131.
12. Devine, *The Golden Age of Tobacco*, 164–5; D. I. Fagerstrom 'Scottish Opinion and the American Revolution', *William and Mary Quarterly*, 3rd ser, XI (1954) 274; I. Maver, 'The Guardianship of the Community: Civic Authority Prior to 1833', in Devine and Jackson, eds, *Glasgow*, pp.239–77.
13. C. Kidd, 'North Britishness and the Nature of Eighteenth-Century British Patriotisms', *The Historical Journal*, XXXIX (1996) 363.
14. J. Brewer, *The Sinews of Power* (London: Unwin Hyman Inc., 1989), pg. xiii.
15. C. Kidd, *Subverting Scotland's Past: Scottish Whig Historians and the Creation of Anglo-British Identity, 1689–c.1830* (Cambridge: Cambridge University Press, 1993), p.209.
16. J. Henretta, *Salutary Neglect: Colonial Administration Under the Duke of Newcastle* (Princeton: Princeton University Press, 1972), pp.3–60.
17. F. O'Gorman, *The Long Eighteenth Century: British Political and Social History, 1688–1832* (London: Arnold, 1997), pp.97–9.
18. Kidd, 'North Britishness', 381.
19. The one exception being, Fagerstrom, 'Scottish Opinion'.
20. D. Waldstreicher, 'Rites of Rebellion, Rites of Assent: Celebrations, Print Culture, and the Origins of American Nationalism', *The Journal of American History*, LXXXII (1995) 38.
21. B. Anderson, *Imagined Communities: Reflections on the Origins and Spread of Nationalism* (London: Verso, 1983), pp.44–5, 61, 62; S.P. Newman, *Parades and the Politics of the Street: Festive Culture in the Early American Republic* (Philadelphia: University of Pennsylvania Press, 1997), pp.186–7.
22. The first Stamp Act was introduced in 1712, followed by a tax on advertisements. It increased from 1 1/2d to 2d in 1725, to 2 1/2d in 1757, 3d. in 1776 and by 1780, up to 4d. H. Barker, *Newspapers, Politics and English Society: 1695–1855* (Singapore: Addison Wesley Longman Ltd., 2000), p.40.
23. M.E. Craig, *The Scottish Periodical Press, 1750–1789* (Edinburgh: Oliver and Boyd, 1931), p.20.
24. *Ibid.*, pp.41–4.
25. *Ibid.*, pp.23–5.
26. R. Harris, *Politics and the Rise of the Press: Britain and France, 1620–1800* (London: Routledge, 1996), pp.21–2.
27. J. Brewer, *Party Ideology and Popular Politics at the Accession of George the Third* (Cambridge: Cambridge University Press, 1976), pp.155–8; R.S. Schofield, 'The Measurement of Literacy in Pre-Industrial England', in J. Goody, ed., *Literacy in Traditional Societies* (London: Cambridge University Press, 1968), pp.312–13.
28. McUre, *Glasghu Facies*, I, p.462.
29. L. Colley, *Britons: Forging the Nation 1707–1837* (New Haven, CT: Yale University Press, 1992), pp.11–54
30. 'A letter from Decius, July 5, 1755', *Glasgow Courant*, 14 July 1755.
31. 'A letter from Decius, July 23, 1755', *Glasgow Courant*, 4 August 1755.
32. *The Glasgow Journal*, 13 January 1755, printed in the *New York Gazette and Weekly Mercury*, 23 September 1754.

33. Colley, *Britons*; L. Colley, 'Britishness and Otherness: An Argument', *The Journal of British Studies*, XXXI (1992) 309–29. Colley's work has generated a wealth of research on this subject. See J.P. Greene, 'Empire and Identity from the Glorious Revolution to the American Revolution', in P.J. Marshall, ed., *The Eighteenth Century* (Oxford: Oxford University Press, 1998), II, pp.208–30; E.H. Gould, *The Persistence of Empire: British Political Culture in the Age of the American Revolution* (Chapel Hill, NC: University of North Carolina Press, 2000); T. Claydon and I. McBride, eds, *Protestantism and National Identity: Britain and Ireland, c. 1650–c. 1850* (Cambridge: Cambridge University Press, 1998); C. Kidd, *British Identities before Nationalism: Ethnicity and Nationhood in the Atlantic World, 1600–1800* (Cambridge: Cambridge University Press, 1999); Kidd, 'North Britishness', 361–82; S. Conway, 'A Joy Unknown for Years Past': The American War, Britishness, and the Celebration of Rodney's Victory at the Saints', *History*, LXXXVI (2001) 180–99; S. Conway, 'From Fellow-Nationals to Foreigners: British Perceptions of the Americans, circa 1739–1783', *The William and Mary Quarterly*, LIX (2002), 65–100.

34. H.T. Dickinson, *The Politics of the People in Eighteenth-Century Britain* (New York: St. Martin's Press, 1995) pp.266–7.

35. Colley, 'Britishness and Otherness', 316.

36. Harris, *Politics and the Rise of the Press*, pp.82–96.

37. Colin Kidd has done the most to advance ideas about the ways in which different regional identities operated within a broader British national identity. See Kidd, 'North Britishness', 361–82.

38. C. Haydon, ' "I love my King and my Country, but a Roman Catholic I hate": Anti-Catholicism, Xenophobia and National Identity in Eighteenth-Century England', in Claydon and McBride, eds, *Protestantism and National Identity*, p.49.

39. Colley, 'Britishness and Otherness', 309–29; more specifically, 316.

40. Quoted in Colley, *Britons*, p.101.

41. J. Bell and J. Paton, *Glasgow: Its Municipal Organization and Administration* (Glasgow: James MacLehose & Sons, 1896), p.3.

42. Pennant, *A Tour in Scotland*, I, p.127.

43. Much of the popular resentment directed toward the Scots at this time was in reaction to the political influence of Charles Stuart, Lord Bute. J. Brewer, 'The Misfortunes of Lord Bute: A Case-Study in Eighteenth-Century Political Argument and Public Opinion', *The Historical Journal*, XVI (1973), 19–23.

44. Quoted in Colley, *Britons*, pp.120–1.

45. D. Wahrman, 'The English Problem of Identity in the American Revolution', *The American Historical Review*, CVI (2001) 1–23.

46. J. Flavell, 'British Perceptions of New England and the Decision for a Coercive Policy, 1774–1775', in J. Flavell and S. Conway, eds, *Britain and America Go to War: The Impact of War and Warfare in Anglo-America, 1754–1815* (Gainesville, FL: The University of Florida Press, 2004), pp.95–115.

47. *The Glasgow Journal*, 17 November 1768.

48. 'Appius- To the Printer', *The Edinburgh Advertiser*, 27 September 1776.

49. *The Glasgow Journal*, 18 March 1773.

50. *The Glasgow Journal*, 31 December 1767.

51. *Ibid.*

52. *The Glasgow Journal*, 25 August 1774.

53. *The Glasgow Journal*, 8 April 1766.
54. E.H. Gould, 'American Independence and Britain's Counter-Revolution', *Past and Present*, CLIV (1997) 113–17.
55. *The Glasgow Chronicle or, Weekly Intelligencer*, 14 November 1776.
56. *Ibid.*
57. Conway, 'A Joy Unknown for Years Past', 194.
58. Fagerstrom 'Scottish Opinion', 271
59. *The Glasgow Mercury*, 8 January 1778.
60. *Ibid.*
61. *The Royal Gazette* (New York City), 21 March 1778.
62. *The London Chronicle*, 15 January 1778.
63. S. Conway, *The British Isles and the War of American Independence* (New York: Oxford University Press, 2000), pp.196–99; S. Conway, 'British Mobilization in the War of American Independence', *Historical Research* LXXII (1999), 66–71; Conway, '"Like the Irish"? Volunteer Corps and Volunteering in Britain during the American War', in J. Flavell and S. Conway, *Britain and America Go to War*, pp.143–69.
64. The situation was especially tense in Scotland, where there was very little military protection and no local militias. J. Oughton to Lord Suffolk, Edinburgh, 19 May 1778, The National Archives (TNA): Public Record Office (PRO): SP 54/47/135; J. Oughton to George the Third, Edinburgh, 7 September 1778, TNA: PRO: 54/47/187; W. Hamilton to Lord Viscount Weymouth, Edinburgh, 29 October 1779, TNA: PRO: 54/47/346–7.
65. R.K. Donovan, 'The Military Origins of the Roman Catholic Relief Programme of 1778', *The Historical Journal*, XXVIII (1985) 79–102.
66. R.K. Donovan, *No Popery and Radicalism: Opposition to Roman Catholic Relief in Scotland, 1778–1782* (New York: Garland, 1987), p.58; *Transactions of the eighty-five societies, in and about Glasgow: United ... to oppose a repeal of the penal statues against Papists in Scotland* (Glasgow, 1779).
67. Many of the public declarations made in opposition to the Catholic Relief Act mentioned France's alliance with the Americans. See *The Glasgow Mercury*, 7 January 1779, 14 January 1779, and 21 January 1779; *The Scots Magazine*, February 1779. Also see 'Supplement to the Glasgow Journal, No. 1957', TNA: PRO: SP 54/47/210–11.
68. Donovan, *No Popery and Radicalism*, p.67.
69. *The Scots Magazine*, February 1779.
70. *The Glasgow Mercury*, 28 January 1779; *The Glasgow Mercury*, 4 February 1779.
71. *The Glasgow Mercury*, 28 January 1779.
72. His surname also appears as Baynal, Bagnall, and Baynall in various publications. See J.D. Marwick and R. Renwick, ed., *Extracts from the Records of the Burgh of Glasgow with Charters and other Documents*, (Glasgow: Scottish Burgh Records Society, 1912), VIII, pp.547–53.
73. J. Oughton to Lord Suffolk, Edinburgh, 12 February 1779, TNA: PRO: SP 54/47/228.
74. Gordon quoted in J. P. de Castro, *The Gordon Riots* (London: Oxford University Press, 1926), pp.17–18.
75. 'A Short ACCOUNT of the kindly Reception the Right Honourable Lord GEORGE GORDON met within the City of GLASGOW, and other Places in

the West', in *Transactions of the eighty-five societies*, pp.26–7; Donovan, *No Popery and Radicalism*, pp.36–7.

76. For more on the Gordon Riots see, G. Rudé, 'The Gordon Riots: A Study of the Rioters and their Victims', *Transactions of the Royal Historical Society*, 5th Series, VI (1956) 93–114; C. Hibbert, *King Mob: The Story of Lord George Gordon and the Riots of 1780* (London: Longmans, Green & Co., 1958); Castro, *The Gordon Riots*.

77. *The Glasgow Journal*, 6 February 1782.

78. *The Glasgow Journal*, 6 June 1782; Conway provides a fascinating account of the political and ideological consequences of Rodney's victory in England, and to a lesser extent Ireland, but curiously says little about the response in Scotland. Conway, 'A Joy Unknown for Years Past', 180–99.

79. *The Glasgow Magazine and Review; Or Universal Miscellany*, October 1783.

80. *Ibid.*

81. *The Glasgow Journal*, 10 July 1783.

82. *The Glasgow Journal*, 19 June 1783.

83. *The Glasgow Journal*, 6 March 1783.

84. Colley, *Britons*, pp.144–5.

85. Gould, 'American Independence', 108–12.

86. Conway, 'A Joy Unknown for Years Past', 194.

87. M.L. Robertson, 'Scottish Commerce and the American War of Independence', *The Economic History Review*, IX (1956) 123–4.

88. Devine, *The Tobacco Lords*, p. 166; Robertson, 'Scottish Commerce', 130–1.

2
The American Revolution and the Spanish Monarchy

Anthony McFarlane

The contribution which France made to the success of the American Revolution by providing financial and military support to the American rebels in their war of independence against Britain is well understood. So, too, are the consequences for the French monarchy of involvement with the American Revolution in the war, since its victory was so promptly followed by the fiscal and political crisis which triggered the French Revolution. Spain's role and its consequences are less well known. This is no doubt partly because Spain took a less prominent role in the war and partly because the Spanish Bourbon state did not suffer the catastrophic after-effects that the war brought to its French counterpart. The American Revolution was, nonetheless, an important moment in the history of Spain and its empire, not only because the defeat of Britain altered the balance of colonial power in the Americas, but also because Spain's engagement in the war interacted with political reforms and cultural changes within Spain and its American colonies.

To explore these issues, this essay will focus on three major facets of Spain's engagement with British America and the American Revolution. These are, first, Spanish perceptions of colonial British America and their influence on Spanish responses to the revolution; second, Spain's engagement with the revolutionary crisis and war of independence in America; and, finally, the repercussions of the American Revolution in the political life of the Spanish monarchy, both in Spain itself and in the wider world of Spanish governance and politics in Spain's American colonies.

Spain and the British North American colonies

In 1772, Colonel Francisco Douché wrote a memorandum for the Conde de Ricla, then Spain's Minister for War, in which he warned that the

British colonies in North America represented an imminent threat to Spanish sovereignty in Mexico.[1] The report commands attention because Douché had held high rank in the Viceroyalty of New Spain from 1767 and, after a shipwreck on the return voyage from Mexico to Spain, had spent nine months in Britain's North American colonies. It was this latter experience which he placed at the forefront of his letter; indeed, his observations about the British North American colonies, when contrasted with his experience in Mexico, were the keystone of a rhetorical strategy designed to show why Spanish sovereignty in Mexico faced a dangerous threat from the colonies of Britain which lay to its north.

At one level, Douché's report was conventional enough. Concern with British aggression and expansion ranked high among the preoccupations of Spanish civil and military officials amidst the aftershock of the Seven Years' War. Such was Spain's alarm about future British intentions that, scarcely was peace restored in 1763 than the Spanish crown embarked on a programme for structural reform of colonial defences at key points in America. Colonel Douché's term of service in Mexico was in fact itself an expression of that process of reform, as he was one of the first of several senior officers despatched from Spain with a post-war mission to revitalise the colony's defences. However, while Douché's identification of Britain as a serious danger may seem banal, his analysis of Spain's capacity to respond to this threat had several special features, all designed to show the British colonies in a new light.

In the first place, he offered an unconventional appraisal of the form that the British menace would take. Whereas Spanish military men were traditionally obsessed with defending New Spain against external attack by amphibious assault on Veracruz, Douché warned that the real threat now lay in an overland attack from the British colonies in North America. To support this claim, he supplied the minister with a factual assessment of British military strength in North America that demonstrated the enemy's ability to launch an invasion by land. There were, he stated, twenty battalions from Britain and two raised in the colonies on North American soil, together with numerous well-armed militias, busy shipyards, foundries for cannon and cannonballs, and gunpowder mills in plenty. These forces were ready to move together, since they were united under a single commander, General Gage, and, having seen them parade and manoeuvre, Douché was convinced that they equalled the best in Europe. And, he added, the object of all this military might was perfectly plain. At dinner-table conversations, where he was frequently an honoured guest afforded all the niceties owing to his rank, English officers in their cups boasted that Britain would seize Louisiana and invade New Spain. To Douché, such boasts were deeply alarming because they were backed by powerful forces. Britain, he said, had twenty-two regular regiments in its colonies, and talked of adding another twenty; New Spain had only five. British American militiamen all had personal arms; New Spain's militias relied on people who had mostly never seen arms, let alone used them. British America abounded in men suitable for soldiering and did not allow evasion of militia service; New Spain had few men of military quality and allowed many to escape militia duty. British America had plenty of arms and replacements; he had found not a single firearm or sword of respectable manufacture among all fifty-three mounted companies of the Legions of San Carlos and the Príncipe.

If Douché gave a novel turn to military analysis by suggesting that British aggression against Spain's empire would come by land rather than sea, his commentary was also unusual for the mode of analysis he adopted. Rather than focusing simply on the organisational details of Spanish military deficiencies, as Spanish army officers routinely did, Douché offered an analysis of New Spain's defence which directly related military weakness to the colony's social structure.[2] He did not question the orthodoxy then prevailing in Bourbon governing circles, that defence of the colonies had to rest primarily on colonial subjects; indeed, his analysis rested on the implicit premise that successful states must be able to mobilise their societies for war. However, he raised fundamental questions about the ability of the Spanish state to manage such mobilization in New Spain, and identified ethnic variety and racial mixture as a key source of weakness. Spain could not rely on its colonial subjects to defend Spanish sovereignty, he argued, not just because New Spain was a colony but because it was a colony of a particular kind. The ethnic composition of New Spain's people, the backwardness of New Spain's economy and the outmoded character of its government were all markers of weakness and inadequacy. And this, Douché argued, was made obvious by comparing social and political conditions in New Spain with those in the British North American colonies, the neighbouring territories where he perceived a very different colonial world.

In Britain's colonies, he observed a model society. Its provinces, he proclaimed, were well-governed, had a highly-productive agriculture, made ample use of cultivable land, and enjoyed a flourishing commerce; its cities were equal to the most beautiful in Europe, and its 'numerous people' were 'all white, all robust, all clean', without poverty or an 'indiada' (Indian peasantry). This linkage of poverty, weakness and impurity set the tone for the racist tenor that pervaded his analysis. For Douché, the success of the British colonies and their military strength derived from the European character of the population, without the 'Indians, mulattos, mestizos and other castas that taint our America'. Indeed, Douché not only admired Britain's policy of allowing European immigrants into its colonies and integrating them into an English-speaking culture; he also applauded the colonists' destruction of native American cultures by what he called the 'ingenious method' of addicting Indians to rum and gin. This pushed the Indians back into the interior, where they died 'happy to be drunk', leaving their lands free to be appropriated by European settlers.

British America was, then, presented as a prosperous neo-European society, and, by the same token, a much stronger base for imperial defence and expansion than anything that New Spain, for all its wealth, could provide for the Bourbon monarchy. The great strength of British America was 'a free people who breathe contentment', in sharp contrast to New Spain, 'a land of taxes and a land oppressed' whose people were of doubtful loyalty. If the British were to invade New Spain via Texas, Douché declared, they would quickly win popular allegiance by promising freedom for commerce, freedom of conscience, and freedom from tribute for the Indians. New Spain's vulnerability to an external military attack was, in short, compounded by the internal political weaknesses caused by alienation from Spanish rule.

In the event, Douché's forebodings proved groundless. Rather than attacking Mexico, Britain was from 1775 drawn into war against its own colonial subjects, thus removing the imminent threat which Douché had feared. His warnings were not completely invalidated by this collapse of British colonial relations, however. On the contrary, the threat which he had discerned continued to be a serious preoccupation for Spanish policy makers, and the need to cope with it was to shape Spain's response to the American Revolution.

Spain and the American War of Independence

For Spain, the issues raised by the American Revolution were, first and foremost, matters of foreign and colonial policy. A decade before the start of the American Revolution, Spain and France had both suffered tremendous losses in their compact against Britain in the Seven Years' War. At the Peace of Paris in 1763, France was expelled from Canada, shattering the French vision of colonial expansion and leaving Britain as the dominant power in North America. Spain also experienced humiliating defeat and damaging losses. In 1762, the British captured Havana, a strategic stronghold which commanded the Caribbean region and acted as a crucial link in Spanish transatlantic trade. To secure its return, Spain was forced to cede Florida to Britain, and, although recompensed by France's cession of Louisiana, this transfer was a strategic setback. It removed a buffer zone between the British colonial frontier and Spain's colonies in the Gulf of Mexico, thereby exposing the viceroyalty of New Spain and the Spanish Caribbean islands – especially Cuba – to greater danger of British infiltration and attack. It also provided Britain with a position from which to prey on Spanish maritime traffic returning to Europe through the Bahama Channel, thus threatening the security of the sea lanes through which most Spanish Atlantic commerce passed on its return to Europe. The settlement at Paris had, moreover, left Spain alone to confront Britain in North America, at a time when British colonial expansion was in full flood. Not surprisingly, then, the onset of the American War of Independence posed one key question for Carlos III: how could Spain use American independence to strengthen its own empire in the Americas?

Spain's approach to this problem was shaped by several influences, not least of which was pressure from France, its leading ally. In the wake of the Seven Years' War, Louis XV's principal foreign policy aim was to restore French prestige, and the Duc de Choiseul, his foreign minister, placed America at the centre of this policy. Choiseul believed that Britain's triumph in the Seven Years' War would weaken its empire because the removal of France from North America made Anglo-Americans less dependent on Britain for defence, and he foresaw possibilities for a future alliance with rebellious British colonials against their parent power. Although he was unable to secure this before leaving office in 1770, Choiseul was nonetheless proved right in 1775, when differences between Britain and its colonies suddenly turned into armed conflict.

The first effect of the American Revolution was, then, to offer France and Spain the opportunity they had been awaiting: namely, to strike back against the victor of the Seven Years' War. The Comte de Vergennes, Foreign Minister since 1774, quickly revived Choiseul's plans, and after investigations by his agents in London and North America decided in early 1776 to seek royal approval for intervention on the side of the American rebels. In May 1776, Louis XVI duly authorised aid for the Americans, granting a million *livres* in the form of munitions to be delivered by French agents on the other side of the Atlantic.[3] France also looked to Spain for support against Britain, and Vergennes engaged in a diplomatic offensive to win the Spanish court to his side. This seemed an easy task, since Spanish ministers were equally eager to take advantage of Britain's problems. Indeed, although France is usually regarded as the major partner, there is some evidence that Spain initially took the lead in pressing for co-belligerence against Britain.

The Conde de Aranda, Spain's ambassador in Paris and a very influential voice at the Caroline court in Madrid, urged Spain to join France in war against Britain while the British were distracted by colonial rebellion, and in 1775 the Marqués de Grimaldi, Carlos III's Minister of State, backed Aranda's position. Grimaldi's enthusiasm for war with Britain was driven by his desire to strike against Portugal. For some years, the Portuguese had been infiltrating Spanish territory in South America, and to counter this threat Spain decided in 1775 to send a large military expedition to the River Plate. This was evidently a timely moment to attack Portugal, while Britain was preoccupied with its own colonial problems, and Grimaldi was so eager to seize the moment that he offered France an alliance against Britain in return for French support against Portugal, and even a share in Portuguese colonial possessions that might be won in war.[4]

Spain's readiness to exploit Britain's colonial crisis in 1775 was not immediately activated, however, because Vergennes, who was still unsure of the strength of the North American challenge to Britain, refused Grimaldi's offer. Once this moment had passed, Spain took up a more defensive stance. Grimaldi found decisions increasingly difficult, because Spanish counsels were divided – Aranda, Spain's ambassador in Paris, consistently advocated war with Britain, while Masserano, the ambassador in London, mounted equally cogent arguments against it – and because the French were unable to calm his fear that war against Britain might provoke immediate British attacks against Spain's American colonies.[5] Thus, France and Spain were unable to agree on a concerted policy and Spain settled into a calculated neutrality.

Carlos III had good cause for caution. Spain had much more to lose in the Americas than France and every reason to take its time before declaring war on Britain. Past experience showed that war with Britain badly disrupted Spanish transatlantic trade as well as exposing Spanish colonies to the risk of attack. Time was therefore needed to ensure that Spanish merchants and shippers had adequate warning and that colonial defences were strengthened. Moreover, an alliance with rebellious colonials, albeit those of a major enemy, was not to be undertaken lightly: if the subjects of the British crown were able to secure independence from a powerful metropolis, what was to prevent Spain's colonial subjects from learning by example? Carlos III's response was, therefore, to proceed covertly, exploiting Britain's problems by clandestine means. In

February 1776, José de Gálvez, an energetic proponent of war with Britain, was appointed as Minister of the Indies and, on taking office, moved to enhance Spain's colonial defences at key points while also establishing a network of informers to follow the progress of the American Revolution.[6] In May 1776, when Louis XVI authorised aid to the American rebels, Carlos III swiftly followed suit with a secret grant of an equal amount, delivered to the Americans by the same French agents who conveyed France's subsidy.

Spanish hostility towards Britain and financial support for Anglo-American rebels was, however, conducted in secret, as Spain preferred a position of neutrality. Even when Vergennes returned to Grimaldi's plan for a joint attack on Portugal, on the understanding that France would join in any ensuing war with Britain, the Spanish cabinet rejected his approach. In October 1776, Grimaldi informed Vergennes that Spain was not ready to invade Portugal, preferring not to provoke Britain until it had been further weakened by conflict with its colonies.[7] Once established, this position became more firmly entrenched when, following Grimaldi's resignation, Carlos III appointed the Conde de Floridablanca as his chief minister in November 1776.

The preference for Floridablanca over Aranda was strongly influenced by court politics, but also reflected Carlos III's wariness about Spanish intervention in the American war, for which Aranda had been a strong advocate.[8] Floridablanca's ascendancy certainly had the effect of dampening Spanish interest in war alongside France and the American rebels. He combined a European policy of accomodation with Portugal by means of negotiation and dynastic alliance, with an American policy aimed at damaging Britain by prolonging its colonial conflict. Floridablanca sustained this policy despite renewed pressure from France to join an alliance with the American rebels in 1778, and France was eventually forced to take the first step without Spanish support. After receiving news of the surrender of a British army at Saratoga in October 1777, Vergennes finally took the plunge. In February 1778, France signed treaties of alliance with the American Congress, and war with Britain followed in June 1778.[9]

The Franco-American alliance and ensuing French war with Britain changed Spain's position on the American Revolution, gradually shifting it away from neutrality. French diplomacy did much to ease the transition. Vergennes stepped up diplomatic pressure on Madrid by continuing to play on Spain's anxiety about the future of its empire: his key argument was, as always, that a war which divided Britain from its colonies would improve the security of Spain's colonies in the Americas. He also acceded to Floridablanca's demands by making more specific promises about the rewards to Spain from a successful alliance against Britain. These included the return of Minorca, the restoration of Florida and the ejection of the British from their enclaves in Central America, and even the possibility of a Spanish reconquest of Jamaica. Floridablanca also used Vergennes' desperate need for an alliance as leverage to make additional demands: that France and Spain should invade England, and that the recovery of Gibraltar from British occupation be made a central aim of war. When France agreed, Floridablanca waited only for the best circumstances in which to enter war with Britain and, after a pretence at mediation between Britain and its colonies, took Spain to war in June 1779.[10]

Spain's engagement with the American Revolution was, then, essentially through war with Britain. The French ambassador at Madrid advised Vergennes of 'how little interest Spain takes in the United States of America', and warned that such disregard would lead to complications at the end of the war.[11] The king and his ministers disliked giving open support to colonial rebellion or helping with the foundation of an independent state, for, as Floridablanca observed, 'such an event as Independence of America would be the worst example to other colonies, and make the Americans the worst neighbours, in every respect, that the Spanish colonies could have.'[12] In the end, however, Spanish geopolitical interests prevailed. Spain was prepared to use the Americans as auxiliaries in war against Britain, rather than as equals in an alliance of states, because this corresponded with the concern to reduce the British threat to Spanish America, and the ambition to recover lost territory and strengthen borders in North America.

The sense of British America as a threat, brilliantly evoked in Douché's report to Ricla, stemmed in part from the fear among Spanish statesmen and military officers that British expansion had developed great momentum from the Seven Years' War. But there was also a broader cultural context for Spanish interest in the British American colonies, formed by interest in theories of political economy and reflected in comparisons between the dynamism of the British colonial system and the older, more cumbersome Spanish empire. One of the first Spanish writers to comment explicitly on these matters was Antonio de Ulloa, whose influential and widely-read account of his travels in the Americas, first published in 1748, included an implicit comparison of Spanish and British colonies.[13]

Ulloa, like Douché many years later, based his comments on eyewitness testimony. On his return journey to Spain from South America, Ulloa's ship had been seized by British privateers and his experience as a gentleman captive, taken first to Boston and thence to England, provided him with the raw material for a commentary on British settlements in North America.[14] By outlining the history of Britain's colonies on the eastern seaboard, Ulloa recorded, first, their rapid progress; then, in his comments on New England, he singled out the causes of their prosperity. These provinces, he noted, enjoyed a high degree of autonomy: they were subject to their prince only through the rule of law; they were governed by honest officials who enjoyed the confidence of the communities which paid their salaries, and, to guarantee their liberty, they provided for their own defence without allowing any permanent garrisons in their country. Thus, they had become 'a kind of republic which, while following in part the laws of England ... had reformed or refused those which were contrary to their freedoms and their exemption from taxes, so that the same communities were their own fortresses and their citizens the troops which guard them'.[15] Thanks to the abundance of land, they lived in remarkable harmony and union, without great differences between rich and poor, and, even more astonishing, without differences between people of different ethnic origins causing conflict or threats to public order. Moreover, such was public confidence in the honesty of the officials who regulated paper money that it was used without fear of fraud; Spanish readers would, Ulloa anticipated, find this fact – that officials did not use their power for personal enrichment – 'strange and even incredible.'[16]

This admiration for the prosperity and vigour of the British American colonies was taken up by other Spaniards who, like Ulloa, favoured colonial reform. The technique of identifying the problems of empire by drawing negative comparisons with foreign models was not new, of course. In the later seventeenth-century, Spanish writers had focused on the defects of the Spanish mercantile system by comparisons with English, French and Dutch mercantilist models. However, during the eighteenth-century, such critiques developed on more systematic lines, and it became common among Spanish enlightenment writers to use foreign examples, particularly that of Britain, to reveal flaws in Spain's relationship with its colonies.[17] Pedro Rodríguez Campomanes was a particularly influential advocate of commercial reform for whom comparison with Britain and its colonies was the key to finding the solution to Spain's economic problems. In his *Reflexiones sobre el comercio español a Indias* (1762), Campomanes used the seventeenth-century English political economist Sir Josiah Child as the touchstone for a critique of Spain's economic policy, and, although he did not accept all of Child's commentary, agreed that freedom of trade was the sole means of promoting productive activities in Spain and Spanish America, and the only way to make the economies of metropolis and colonies mutually reinforcing. Campomanes' *Reflexiones* also had another notable feature: he devoted a good deal of space to describing the history of English colonisation in America and the character of Britain's American colonies, and expressing his admiration for their rapid development, 'a matter that affects us so closely and thus interests us so much.'[18]

The sense that commerce was the key to power in a world where 'the Nation that lays down the law in commerce also does so at sea and in arms,'[19] was another incentive for Spain to side with the Anglo-American rebel colonies in their war for independence. On the one hand, the British colonies were admired for their economic dynamism and presented as a model to be emulated; on the other hand, their strength made them a vanguard of military power that had to be defeated. The two images converged to form a powerful inducement for Spain to do all it could to wreck the relationship between Britain and its colonies. Even two years into the War of Independence, Spaniards still feared that Britain and its colonies might yet combine to attack Spanish America: on the eve of Spain's intervention in 1778, Juan de Miralles, Spain's unofficial ambassador to the United States, urged the king to help the Americans because, without Spain's support, they might make peace with Britain and join an attack on Spanish possessions.[20]

This continuing anxiety about the British colonies as a platform for attack on Spanish America was no doubt taken seriously by ministers most concerned with the Indies, since both had direct experience of the military threat posed by Britain in North America and the Caribbean. Ricla, the Minister for War, had personally led the military reform in Cuba after the Seven Years' War; José de Gálvez, the Minister for the Indies, had first-hand experience of Mexico as *visitador general* in 1765–71. Both were 'hawks' on the issue of war with Britain from an early stage and advocated military action that would help to sever the colonies that were Britain's bases for aggression against Spain in America. Indeed, José de Gálvez stated this agenda in typically trench-ant style. By helping the rebel colonies to secede, Gálvez affirmed, Spain and France would reduce Britain's empire to a precarious niche in India, so that Britain would be 'despoiled of its tyrannical empire of the seas'.[21]

Spain's response to the American Revolution was thus driven prima-rily by geopolitical goals and expressed in military terms. In Europe, this embraced ambitious plans to invade England and to recover Gibraltar and Minorca. In America, the key goals were to reconquer Florida, to shore up the Spanish North American frontier along the line of the

Mississippi and to strengthen Spain's position in Louisiana.[22] Behind the American plans lay several strategic imperatives: to remove the threat of a British-American overland attack on Mexico that would outflank the defences of Veracruz; to secure a Spanish frontier at the Mississippi in order to guard against future incursions by foreigner interlopers, whether from British colonies or a future United States; and to control the coasts of the Gulf of Mexico for the same ends. On the outbreak of war, Madrid had these goals firmly in sight and immediately mobilized plans prepared before the declaration of war.

The military outcome of Spain's entry into war was twofold. In August 1779, General Bernardo de Gálvez, Governor of Louisiana and José de Gálvez's nephew, launched a campaign from New Orleans against British positions in West Florida and then joined with North American and Cuban reinforcements to attack and take Mobile.[23] This campaign was followed by another, backed by an army sent from Spain, to ensure Spain's domination of the Gulf of Mexico: in 1781, General Gálvez led an army of nearly 7,500 men, drawn from an army of reinforcement sent from Spain and Cuban units, in a successful attack on Pensacola. After these achievements, Spain sought to extend the war to other British possessions, but did so with less success. The project for a joint Franco-Spanish attack intended to restore Jamaica to Spanish rule was aborted, and plans to take islands and remove the British from their foothold in Central America came to little. Nonetheless, the military victories on the Mississippi and in Florida ensured that Spain emerged from the war with solid gains. By mobilizing colonial and peninsular forces in co-ordinated operations on land and sea, Spain had not only shown that it was capable of mounting difficult military operations on the American side of the Atlantic, but had also secured valuable territory. At Versailles in 1783, Spain re-established its sovereignty over Florida and, by its territorial gains in the region, strengthened its capacity to defend Spanish sovereignty to the west and south of the Mississippi. These achievements were no doubt less than optimists had hoped for. The British threat in the Americas had been reduced but certainly not eliminated, for, although the British were forced to return Florida, they retained important colonies from Canada to the Caribbean, and thus still posed a strategic threat to Spanish America. There were also failures in Europe, where Minorca was recovered but Gibraltar remained firmly in British hands, despite the huge effort expended by Spanish and French forces. On balance, however, Spain had gained from its involvement with the American war of independence, in military victory, territorial gain, confidence and prestige.

There were, moreover, other important ways in which the American war affected the Spanish world. Most important was the shift in government policy that took place from 1776, when, after a decade of modest incremental reform, Carlos III and his ministers accelerated the pace of change.[24] The case for reform had long been made and partly implemented in the decade before 1776, but the approach of war gave fresh urgency to an agenda for economic and political reform that had been somewhat sidelined since the mid-1760s. In the shadow of impending war, the crown gave priority to reforms that aimed to bind its colonies closer. This meant reinforcing the structures of Spanish government in the Americas, improving colonial defences, and expanding Spanish transatlantic trade. After the appointments of Floridablanca as Minister of State and José de Gálvez as Minister for the Indies in 1776, reforms designed to achieve these goals were rapidly put into effect. The crown displayed its determination to strengthen royal government in the Americas by important administrative initiatives. In 1776, José de Gálvez appointed *visitadores generales* (general inspectors) for the task of overhauling government throughout South America, from the viceroyalty of New Granada in the north, through the viceroyalty of Peru and into Chile in the far south. When Spain entered war with Britain in 1779, these inspectors had all taken steps to push forward José de Gálvez's programme of administrative and fiscal reform. In 1776, the King created the new Viceroyalty of the Río de la Plata, with its capital at Buenos Aires, in order to exercise closer control over trade and territory in an increasingly strategic area of South America and the South Atlantic, where both Portugal and Britain were pressing against Spain's colonial frontiers. Political reform was, moreover, paralleled by economic reform. In 1778, the crown introduced the great *Reglamento de comercio libre* which, in one legislative sweep, cut away the restraints of monopoly and tangle of regulation that had for so long fettered Spain's Atlantic commerce.[25]

The rapid progress of colonial reform in 1776–79 suggests, then, that the American Revolution tipped the balance in favour of the reformers in the Spanish cabinet. But it also raises other questions about the ramifications of the American Revolution in Spain and the Spanish world. If preparation for a possible war with Britain triggered a reordering of economic and administrative structures, what was the broader impact of involvement in the war of American independence on society and culture in Spain or its colonies, and how did it affect relations between them?

Spain and the American Revolution

It has long been acknowledged that the American Revolution interacted powerfully with politics in Europe, disseminating ideas of liberty and equality that informed an 'age of revolution' throughout the Atlantic world.[26] The impact was strongest in France, where engagement on the side of the British American rebels helped to propagate republicanism and turn it into a serious alternative to monarchy.[27] The American Revolution also had an important impact within British political life. Despite many protestations of loyalty, the war with fellow British subjects and fellow Protestants increasingly split the country and, in its aftermath, forced Britons to start to reconsider their identity and patriotism.[28] The impact of the war and revolution in America was, by contrast, much less evident in Spain. There were some economic difficulties stemming from a contraction of commerce, but no obvious political turbulence in Spain itself, nor sign of the political damage which involvement with the American Revolution did to the monarchy of Bourbon France.

To explain why the ideas of the American Revolution found an unreceptive environment in Caroline Spain requires a brief reminder of the constraints which an authoritarian monarchy imposed on Spanish political life. While Carlos III's chief ministers sought to bring economic and social improvement to Spain, their aim was to strengthen the monarchy by reforms orchestrated from above, and, although this included some broadening of public discussion (through encouragement of the patriotic societies and a periodical press dedicated to the diffusion of 'useful knowledge'), Spanish political culture was contained within narrow boundaries, where government permitted only criticisms deemed constructive and patriotic, and where the Inquisition still had sufficient power to condemn those who espoused progressive ideas too publicly. In 1776, the year of the American declaration of independence, the Inquisition was still able to silence a leading 'enlightener' and reformer, Pablo de Olavide, by attaching the taint of heresy to his thinking, to the surprise and shock of enlightened observers in Europe.[29]

In this shielded political environment, the impact of events in North America was slight. In the first place, Spanish ministers sought to limit their visibility by drawing a veil of silence over those aspects of the war that were politically sensitive. The official emphasis was thus exclusively on the war as a struggle against Britain, with a concomitant and apparently successful appeal to patriotism. A correspondent of the Lugano gazette reported from Spain on 'the extent to which patriotism dominates the nation' even among 'women of rank, who, in imitation of the [French] ladies with whom they are allied ... prepare ships for common defence.'[30] Here, however, the similarity with France evidently ended. In Paris, fashionable society engaged in avid discussion of the revolution, romanticised its ideals, and lionised its representatives (especially Benjamin Franklin, whose image was so widely disseminated in print and on porcelain, textiles, inkwells and snuff boxes that, Franklin joked, his face was 'as well known as that of the moon').[31] By contrast, Spain's ministers were very reluctant to recognize the American representatives sent by the Continental Congress, and tried to ensure that they were kept in political and social quarantine.[32]

Printed news of the American rebellion was also carefully controlled. Two official periodicals – the *Gaceta de Madrid* and the *Mercurio Histórico y Político* – carried news of Britain's conflict with its colonies in translated extracts from European gazettes published in London, Paris, and the Hague. These were reports of events and facts rather than critical commentaries, but they would nonetheless have enabled the careful reader to follow the development of the conflict and understand its causes. For example, in 1764–65 these periodicals reported the passage of the Sugar and Stamp Acts, the colonial boycott on imports from Britain, the riots in colonial cities, the possibility that the colonies would cede from Britain, and the resolution of the conflict with the revocation of the Stamp Act. When the conflict was renewed following the Townshend Acts, the press again reported regularly on the responses of the North American colonies to Whitehall's efforts to impose its authority, including accounts of the colonial assemblies' rejection of the new legislation as unconstitutional, the establishment of the Continental Congress, and the American's self-definition as the defenders of liberty against governmental despotism.[33] Here, then, is clear evidence that between 1764 and 1776 Spaniards who read the official press had sufficient knowledge of events in North America to understand the political issues that led the British colonies to their declaration of independence.

There are no signs that such information nurtured public discussion of the American Revolution while Spain was fighting on the rebel side. During the war, censorship ensured that the press confined itself to reporting on Spanish military victories; the new private periodical *El Censor*, which was founded in 1781, did not provide an alternative source of news and comment for long: it was closed down from late 1781 until late 1783, after criticizing the superstitions of Spanish Catholics. With the establishment of *El Censor* a press that was recognisably 'modern' had come into existence, and together with the small number of other critically-inclined gazettes and periodicals that subsequently appeared in 1787–88, played an important part in creating a rich vein of enlightened, liberal criticism of Spanish social and political life.[34] However, compared to the press in France and Britain, Spain's was unimpressive: periodical publications were relatively few, had small subscriptions, brief lives, and, with only one or two short-lived exceptions, presented a bland and conformist political surface.[35]

In view of the debility of the public sphere, it is not surprising to find little deviation from the official line that Spain's engagement with the American Revolution was simply a function of fighting a patriotic war against Britain. Carlos III and his ministers signalled this position by allying with France, not the United States, and steadfastly refusing diplomatic recognition to the nascent republic. Their goal was to aggravate the division between Britain and its colonies for as long as possible, and, if possible, to separate Britain from its colonies without giving succour to a new state that might itself become a rival. The war was thus perceived as a part of Spain's ongoing struggle against British commercial and territorial aggression, and, by the same token, was regarded as a measure of the Bourbon regime's capacity to rebuild Spain's power. There was, then, very limited scope for public discussion of the ideas of the American Revolution. In 1778 and 1783, books which discussed the British colonies and their rebellion were published, but these works – by Alvarez and Covarrubias – were sanctioned by government and innocent of subversive intent or effect.[36] The imagery of 'Liberty' did not inspire the junior nobility as it had in France; the American War of Independence did not produce any Spanish equivalent to General Lafayette, the heroic aristocratic volunteer, nor a soldiery that had been exposed to republican ideas; and, above all, the Spanish nobility, unlike sections of the French aristocracy, did not find qualities in the American Revolution relevant to their own political situation.[37] In short, it seems that in Spain 'the significance of the American Revolution was virtually unnoticed, absolute monarchy was not questioned, and the Catholic Religion was still sacrosanct.'[38]

To accept this judgement is, however, to take too narrow a view. In the first place, Spain was not completely impervious to the political reverberations from the American Revolution. After the war, there was fresh and impassioned debate about the past, present and future of Spain and its empire, both in the Spanish world and among its neighbours.[39] This debate was largely contained within the boundaries of enlightened authoritarianism and expressed in a nationalist discourse that affirmed Spain's political power and cultural leadership within the Hispanic world.[40] But it also included an increasingly vocal liberal voice: descriptions and analyses of economic ideas, agrarian improvements and educational reform all used Enlightenment sources to build a critique of traditional Spain and to create a vision of alternatives.[41] Secondly, a wider perspective shows that the American Revolution affected Spain through its colonies, where the example of American independence enhanced the creoles' sense of Americanness and altered attitudes towards the metropolis.

The American Revolution in the Spanish colonies

Spanish fears that support for republican rebels in North America might inflame discontent within Spain's colonies seem to have been confirmed soon after the start of war when major rebellions broke out in Peru in 1780 and New Granada in 1781. Francisco Saavedra, the royal commissioner responsible for coordinating Spanish operations in the North American theatre of war, was convinced that there was a connection with the American Revolution and called for Spain to alter its policies accordingly:

> The face of the Indies has been altered greatly with the rebellion of the Anglo-Americans and the independence that they probably are securing; consequently it is necessary that Spain make many changes in the system that, up to this point, she has observed in her colonies ... Above all, there ought to be devised equitable trade and tax regulation, which ... no viceroy, governor, intendant etc., ought to have the authority to change by so much as a comma. As long as this maxim is not established as fundamental and invariable ... the Americans will not prosper and the mother country will run the risk of losing the colonies when least expected. The rebellion of the English colonies had its origins in taxes, that of Lima had the same beginning, and that of Santa Fe also.[42]

We now know that there was no immediate synergy between Spanish American rebellions and the American Revolution: the former knew little or nothing of the latter, and were in any case framed by cultures where notions of individual rights and representative politics were much less developed than in the 'republicanized monarchy' of Britain and its colonies.[43] Nonetheless, Saavedra was right to point out that the Spanish American rebellions bore some resemblance to the North American revolt, given that they were triggered by tax reforms and expressed political grievances among colonials who resented metropolitan arrogance. Indeed, recent historical studies have shown that the rebellions were informed by a concept of colonial autonomy which, because it called for local participation in government and policy-making, was broadly comparable to the defence of constitutional rights by North American colonials. The Comunero rebellion in New Granada affirmed the right to 'no taxation without bureaucratic representation,' and called for preference to be given to colonials in government posts.[44] The great rebellion in Peru, led by Túpac Amaru, the self-proclaimed Inca king, had similar features, with the additional dimension of Indian peasant revolt against the abuses of colonial officials and mechanisms of exploitation such as payment of tributes, forced sales of goods and coerced labour.[45] The rebellions were, then, a warning of Spain's urgent need to strengthen colonial loyalty. Indeed, on his return to Spain, Saavedra personally informed the Minister for the Indies that this was even more pressing in the wake of the American Revolution. For, he told Gálvez, there were 'many indications of emancipation in those countries, that is to say desires for independence'; he also found that the writings, proclamations and, above all, the example of the Anglo-Americans contributed to these', and that the independent United States 'would serve as the leader, inspiration and model for the rest of that part of the world.'[46]

Such warnings did not pass unheeded. Although Gálvez continued his efforts to tighten control over the colonies and to increase their fiscal and economic yield, the extension to Spanish America of the progressive cultural policies of enlightened absolutism during the 1780s and early 1790s gave creoles new scope for self expression, whether through the foundation of patriotic societies and mercantile associations dedicated to local development, or through the debate and diffusion of useful knowledge in officially-sanctioned periodical publications.[47] Closer contact with enlightened ideas did not, however, cauterize interest in the ideas and example of the American Revolution. On the contrary, the United States increasingly became a political benchmark among Spanish Americans, a foil for critiques of Spanish policy and a source of ideas for alternatives to Spanish rule.

This effect had been anticipated. The Conde de Aranda, among others, immediately saw Anglo-American independence as an example which the Spanish American colonies would follow, and he had even proposed that Spain should forestall a rupture with the colonies by transforming the empire into a friendly federation of independent kingdoms, ruled by European princes and united to Spain by dynastic ties.[48] Aranda's proposal was stillborn, but his prediction was fulfilled as Spanish Americans turned to the United States as a model for their future. Among those whom the American Revolution inspired to advocate rebellion was Juan Pablo Viscardo y Guzmán, a creole Jesuit exiled in Italy after the Jesuits' expulsion from Spain's dominions in 1767. Enthused by news of the American Revolution and the great rebellion in Peru, Viscardo informed the British consul at Livorno in 1781 that, if Britain supported them, creoles would break away from Spain and secure their independence. Although his offer to help Britain intervene on behalf of Spanish American independence was ignored, Viscardo was subsequently invited to England, provided with a pension by the British government, and resided in London from 1789 until his death in 1798. From London, he transmitted his admiration for the American Revolution into legitimation for Spanish American independence: in the *Letter to the Spanish Americans* for which he subsequently became famous, he praised the English colonies on their fight for liberty and commended the American rather than the French Revolution as the path for Spanish America to follow.[49] The *Letter* entered Spanish America a few years later, after its translation and dissemination by the Venezuelan revolutionary, Francisco de Miranda, and subsequently exerted some influence among creole dissidents.[50]

In 1781, Viscardo was far in advance of his fellow creoles. However, by the time his *Letter* circulated in Spanish America in the early 1800s, knowledge of the ideas and outcome of the American Revolution had already penetrated creole circles with subversive effect. Indeed, during the 1790s, ideas drawn from the American and French revolutions underpinned several incidents of sedition in both Spain and Spanish America. Despite Floridablanca's censorship and suppression of the periodical press, he was unable completely to insulate Spain from the revolutionary ideas which convulsed France. Seditious literature circulated in Spain and various conspiracies were uncovered, such as the 1795 plot in which Juan Picornell, a middle-class intellectual inspired by ideas from the American and French Revolutions, planned with a few accomplices to install a republic in Spain. This plot, like others, posed no real danger to the monarchy, however, and once Spaniards became aware of the excesses of the Terror, the sense of affinity with French republicanism waned, leaving opposition to the government to find other channels.[51]

In the American colonies, on the other hand, the example of the French Revolution reminded creole dissidents of the American Revolution and its relevance to their situation. In 1793, Manuel del Socorro Rodríguez, a creole intellectual in Bogotá, saw the interaction of Enlightenment ideas with the example of the United States as an unprecedented threat to Spanish authority:

> Since the establishment of the Anglo-American provinces as a free Republic, the peoples of America have taken on a character which is entirely different from that which they had. All who count themselves as enlightened are enthusiastic panegyrists for the ways of thinking of those (Anglo-American) people: the common coin of erudite discussion groups is to discuss and even to form plans around the means of enjoying the same independence that they enjoy.

And, to make matters worse, 'events in France have infused these pernicious reasonings with a new vigour' spreading 'the spirit of disloyalty on all sides.'[52] Three years later, Rodríguez reiterated his condemnation of the United States as a species of rogue state which promoted revolution and threatened the security of the Spanish empire.[53] The United States was, he affirmed, 'the meeting place from which all designs for destroying the good government of our adjacent Spanish dominions must take strength.'[54]

Although Rodriguez almost certainly exaggerated the threat of subversion, his comments indicate the ways in which the dissemination of 'enlightened' ideas during the 1780s not only sharpened creoles' commitment to engage with the 'philosophy of nature', but also enlarged their political awareness. Thus, for example, when Pedro Fermin de Vargas, a junior creole official, amateur scientist and enthusiast for enlightened reform, reported on the condition of New Granada's economy and society in 1790 and the areas which needed reform, he used the United States as his template; moroever, within a year, he took up exile there as an itinerant revolutionary. In 1794, other creoles of his class and convictions were arrested for plotting against the government, and the subsequent enquiry revealed a clandestine interest in the 'constitution of Philadelphia' and the French Assembly's Declaration of the Rights of Man, which had even been translated into Spanish for dissemination throughout New Granada.[55]

New Granada was not the only site of creole sedition. In Quito, Francisco Eugenio de Santa Cruz y Espejo, the secretary of Quito's patriotic society founded in 1792, was arrested for plotting against the government and imprisoned for sedition in 1795. Minor conspiracies were uncovered in New Spain in 1794, one aimed at independence with the aid of the United States, the other with the aid of Britain. In

Venezuela, Picornell, the Spanish republican exiled for plotting in Spain, was implicated in a conspiracy at Caracas in 1797, planned by Gual and España, two minor officials apparently inspired by the example of the American Revolution. Furthermore, a small international network of creole revolutionaries dedicated to emancipation was taking shape outside Spanish America, in Paris, London and the United States, where they invoked the example of the American Revolution and sought support from Spain's enemies.[56]

If the example of the American republic helped to promote criticism of Spain among its colonial subjects in the closing years of the eighteenth century, this was not of itself sufficient to undermine the political foundations of Spanish rule. Republican ideas presented alternatives to Spanish rule that were plausible only to a small minority of creoles and it required a crisis of old regime structures to provide the chance to convert ideas into actions, visions into institutions. This crisis came from the revolution in France and its international consequences.

Revolution and crisis in Spain

Bourbon absolutism in Spain was challenged first by the short-lived movement for constitutional monarchy in Bourbon France. The ideas of individual rights, citizenship and popular sovereignty which emanated from France fuelled Spanish interest in constitutional monarchy, and Spanish liberals made constitutionalism patriotic by propagating a version of Spanish history which harked back to the 'ancient liberties' and proto-parliaments of medieval times.[57] Most Spaniards were subsequently alienated from the French Revolution by its violence and anti-clericalism, but the constitutional ideas in which it had been born took firm root in Spain. At the same time, respect for Bourbon absolutism steadily diminished as the turbulence caused by the French Revolution reversed reformism at home and upset Spain's alliances abroad. The monarchy's deepening difficulties were further accentuated by the weakness of Carlos IV, whose trust in a royal favourite, Manuel Godoy, generated scandal and factionalism among the political elites. While Godoy tried to build consensus, avoiding the extremes of conservatism and liberalism, he achieved very little in the decade and a half in which he held a dominant position at court. During his first government he tried to revive the progressive mood of the reign of Carlos III by bringing reformers back into government. However, reformist initiatives provoked a conservative backlash and this, combined with the chronic economic difficulties brought by war with Britain after 1796, contributed to growing political instability. When Godoy returned to ascendancy in the early 1800s, the old regime in Spain entered deepening crisis, as repeated failures in the war with Britain and worsening economic and social conditions in rural and urban Spain were added to intensifying conflicts among the governing elites. Unable to cope with crisis from within, Carlos IV was overthrown by his own son Ferdinand, at the head of an aristocratic faction, in a prelude to a greater crisis. In 1808, the Bourbon regime was finally overturned by Napoleon, who would no longer tolerate the instability and unreliability of his Spanish ally.[58]

Thus it was the French Revolution in its Napoleonic expression, rather than its revolutionary republican form, that finally overcame Bourbon Spain and spread crisis throughout the Spanishmonarchy. As patriotic Spaniards reacted to Napoleon's seizure of the Spanish throne, the new constitutionalism which had emerged in the wake of the French Revolution acquired disproportionate political influence: in 1810, the first constituent Cortes was established in Cadiz; by 1812, it had produced a liberal constitution which, in the absence of the king, turned an absolutist into a limited monarchy and sought to bind the colonies to the metropolis by the affirmation of equality among all citizens.

Seen in a long perspective, this crisis of collapse at the Spanish centre may ultimately be traced back to the American Revolution, in the sense that the war of American independence had set in motion a chain of events in France that was to upset the political equilibrium on which Spanish stability depended. In the short term, however, the French Revolution had a far greater impact on the Spanish world than its American predecessor. For, while the American Revolution was rich in political relevance to Spanish Americans, it had little impact in metropolitan Spain, only slowly penetrated the thinking of the Spanish American elites, and, even then, became a political model pursued by only a small minority. The impact of republican revolution on Spain and its world thus came at a second remove from America, beginning not in 1776 but in 1789, as the overspill from political turmoil and transformation in neighbouring France. The power of the French Revolution to reshape the political life and structures of the Hispanic world was delayed during the 1790s and early 1800s, but could not be resisted indefinitely. After contributing to a gradual polarization of politics in Spain and its colonies, the French Revolution in its Napoleonic mode was to achieve what the American Revolution could not: a crisis that fractured the Bourbon state on both sides of the Atlantic and opened a way to the dissolution of Spain's empire.

Notes

1. This extensive report, of some 50 folios, is found in Spain's principal military archive. See Francisco Douché to Conde de Ricla, San Lorenzo el Real, October 25, 1772: Servicios Históricos Militares (Madrid), Guerra, Ultramar (Mexico), Caja 95.

2. On military reform in New Spain before the American Revolution, some brief biographical details on Douché, and critiques of New Spain's defences by Spanish officers, see C. Archer, *The Army in Bourbon Mexico* (Albuquerque: University of New Mexico, 1977), pp.10–20.

3. S.F. Bemis, *The Diplomacy of the American Revolution* (Bloomington, IN and London: Indiana University Press, 1957 edn.), pp.16–27.

4. Bemis, *Diplomacy of the American Revolution*, pp.42–3, argues that Grimaldi took a belligerent position in 1775. Yela Utrilla identifies the letter from Grimaldi to Aranda, dated 18 October 1775, in which he proposed the scheme for invading Portugal with French help and compensating France with conquests in Brazil: see J.F. Yela Utrilla, *España ante la independencia de los Estados Unidos* (2 vols., Lérida: Gráficos Academia Mariana, 1925)I, p.57.

5. On the differences among Spanish ministers, combined with the argument that Grimaldi took a passive position which made Spain dependent on France for the initiative, see M.P. Ruigómez de Hernandez, *El gobierno español del despotismo ilustrado ante la independencia de los Estado Unidos de América* (Madrid: Ministerio de Asuntos Exteriores, 1978), pp.174–85.

6. For a full account of Spanish spying on the British colonies in North America from 1775 to 1779, and their influence on Spanish policy, see L.T. Cummins, *Spanish Observers and the American Revolution, 1775–1783* (Baton Rouge and London: Louisiana State University Press, 1991), pp.26–139.

7. Ruigómez de Hernandez, *El gobierno español del despotismo ilustrado ante la independencia de los Estado Unidos de América*, pp.190–6.

8. On court influences, see F. Venturi, *The End of the Old Regime in Europe, 1776–1789: I. The Great States of the West*, transl. by R. Burr Litchfield (Princeton, NJ: Princeton University Press, 1991), pp.236–40.

9. For a succinct account of the treaties, see Bemis, *Diplomacy of the American Revolution*, pp.58–69.

10. *Ibid.*, pp.75–85.

11. *Ibid.*, p.86.

12. Reported by the British ambassador to Madrid in May 1777: quoted by J. Lynch, *Bourbon Spain, 1700–1808*, (Oxford: Blackwell, 1989), p.320.

13. The most recent edition of Ulloa's *Relación histórica del Viage a la América meriodional, hecho por orden de S.Mag ... [Madrid, 1748]*, published as A. de Ulloa, *Viaje a la América meridional*, ed. A. Saumell Lladó, 2 vols, (Madrid: Historia 16, 1990). All references here are to this edition.

14. Ulloa, *Viaje*, II, pp.408–433.

15. *Ibid.*, pp.429–430.

16. *Ibid.*, pp. 431–2.

17. R. Herr, *The Eighteenth Century Revolution in Spain* (Princeton, NJ: Princeton University Press, 1958), pp.47–57. On the eighteenth-century reformers and their comparisons of Spain's economic performance with that of its rivals, see A. Pagden, *Lords of All the World: Ideologies of Empire in Spain, Britain and*

France c.1500-c.1800 (New Haven, CT and London: Yale University Press, 1995), pp.120–125.

18. P. Rodríguez Campomanes, *Reflexiones sobre el comercio español a Indias*, ed. Vicente Llombart Rosa, (Madrid: Instituto de Estudios Fiscales, 1988), pp.233–95; quotation from p.253

19. Campomanes, *Reflexiones*, p.452.

20. Cummins, *Spanish Observers*, pp.135–8.

21. J. de Gálvez to Viceroy of Buenos Aires, 30 August 1779, quoted by J. Beverina, *El Virreinato de las Provincias del Río de la Plata: Su organización militar* (Buenos Aires: Círculo militar, 1935), pp.407–9.

22. On Spanish goals in North America after the declaration of war, reflected in the activities of the government's chief representative in the United States, Juan de Miralles, see Cummins, *Spanish Observers*, pp.150–61.

23. Spanish campaigns during the American Revolution have been closely chronicled, particularly the exploits of General Bernardo de Gálvez in the Mississippi and Gulf regions. For a review of this large literature, see L.T. Cummins, 'Spanish Louisiana' in L.T. Cummins and G. Jeansonne eds, *A Guide to the History of Louisiana* (Westport, CT: Greenwood Press, 1982). The standard work on Gálvez's campaigns remains that of J. Caughey, *Bernardo de Gálvez in Louisiana, 1776–1783* (Berkeley, CA: University of California Press, 1934). The crucial contribution made by Cuba is detailed in A.J. Kuethe, *Cuba, 1753–1815: Crown, Military and Society* (Knoxville, TN: University of Tennessee Press, 1986), pp.78–112.

24. On the politics and progress of Carlos III's early colonial reforms in the decade after 1763 and an explanation of the obstacles to reform, see S.J. Stein and B.H. Stein, *Apogee of Empire: Spain and New Spain in the Age of Charles III, 1759–1780* (Baltimore, MD and London: The Johns Hopkins University Press, 2003), pp.52–68.

25. There is a large literature on the Bourbon reforms. For an overview of these reforms which dates them from around 1750, but notes the acceleration of reform from 1776, see Lynch, *Bourbon Spain*, pp.340–366.

26. The pioneering works on the subject are R.R. Palmer, *The Age of the Democratic Revolution: A Political History of Europe and America, 1760–1800*, 2 vols, (Princeton, NJ: Princeton University Press, 1959, 1964), and J. Godechot, *France and the Atlantic Revolution of the Eighteenth Century, 1770–1799* (New York and London: Free Press, 1965). Gordon Wood suggests that the period might better be called the 'age of republican revolution' and argues that republicanism was the key feature to the political reordering of the Atlantic world: see G.S. Wood, *The Radicalism of the American Revolution* (New York: Knopf, 1992), pp.95–109. On war and revolution in the Americas, see P.K. Liss, *Atlantic Empires: The Network of Trade and Revolution, 1713–1826* (Baltimore, MD and London, Johns Hopkins University Press, 1983), and L.D. Langley, *The Americas in the Age of Revolution, 1750–1850* (New Haven, CT and London: Yale University Press, 1996).

27. S. Schama, *Citizens: A Chronicle of the French Revolution* (London: Viking, 1989), pp.21–49.

28. On the repercussions of the war on British political life and culture, see L. Colley, *Britons: Forging the Nation 1707–1837* (London: Vintage, 1996), pp.150–4; S. Conway, *The British Isles and the War of American Independence* (Oxford: Oxford University Press, 2000), pp.129–65.

29. Lynch, *Bourbon Spain*, pp. 288–90; Venturi, *End of the Old Regime*, I, pp. 241–6.
30. Quoted by Venturi, *End of the Old Regime*, I, p.248.
31. Schama, *Citizens*, p.43.
32. On the difficult experiences of Arthur Lee and John Jay as representatives of Congress to the Spanish court, see M. Rodríguez, *La revolución americana de 1776 y el mundo hispanico: Ensayos y documentos* (Madrid: Techos, 1976), pp.75–100; 116–32.
33. L.A. García Melero, *La independencia de los Estados Unidos a través de la prensa española* (Madrid: Ministerio de Asuntos Exteriores, 1977), pp. 58–102, 107–10, 123–8, 206–16.
34. A valuable review and catalogue of the Spanish periodical press of the eighteenth century, in its various manifestations, is F. Aguilar Piñal, *La prensa española en el siglo XVIII: Diarios, revistas y pronosticos* (Madrid: Consejo Superior de Investigaciones Científicas, 1978).
35. Herr, *Eighteenth Century Revolution*, pp.44–5; 183–94. An important exception was El Censor: see the close analysis of its contents in A. Elorza, *La ideología liberal en la Ilustración española* (Madrid: Editorial Techos, 1970), pp.208–34.
36. In 1778, Francisco Alvarez published his *Noticia del establecimiento y publicación de las colonias inglesas en la América Septentrional*, giving a history of the English colonies, and in 1783, José de Covarrubias published his *Memorias históricas de la última guerra con la Gran Bretaña*, which included a sympathetic account of the American Revolution. For comment on these publications, see Rodríguez, *La revolución americana de 1776 y el mundo hispánico*, pp.153–68. Rodríguez argues that these works show that the Spanish world knew as much about the American Revolution as northern Europe; however, as both were officially sanctioned, they might better be understood as contributions to patriotic propaganda than as analyses of the American Revolution. For further discussion of Spanish publications, see Liss, *Atlantic Empires*, pp.138–9.
37. On the impact of the American Revolution in France, see Schama, *Citizens*, pp.46–9.
38. Herr, *Eighteenth Century Revolution*, p.200; the other major work on the Spanish Enlightenment comes to a similar conclusion: see J. Sarrailh, *La España Ilustrada de la segunda mitad del siglo XVIII*, trans. A. Alatorre (Mexico and Buenos Aires: Fondo de Cultura Económica, 1957), pp.586–8.
39. For the interaction between national and international debate, and the role of the Jesuits, see Venturi, *End of the Old Regime*, pp.258–96.
40. See, for example, reaffirmation of the role of Spain in world history, analysed by J. Cañizares-Esguerra, *How to Write a History of the New World: Histories,, Epistemologies, and Identities in the Eighteenth-Century Atlantic World*, (Stanford, CA: Stanford University Press, 2001), pp.130–203.
41. Elorza, *Ideología liberal*, pp.244–57.
42. F. de Saavedra, *The Journal of Don Francisco Saavedra de Sangronis, 1780–1783*, ed. Francisco Morales Padrón, transl. by Aileen Moore Topping (Gainesville, FL University of Florida Press,1989) pp.259–261: journal entry of 29 November 1781.
43. The phrase 'republicanized monarchy' is Gordon Wood's: see his *Radicalism of the American Revolution*, p. 98.
44. For this thesis, see J.L. Phelan, *The People and the King: The Comunero Revolution in Colombia, 1781* (Madison, WI: University of Wisconsin Press, 1978) pp.79–88.

45. There is a large literature on Túpac Amaru and the great rebellion associated with his name. For recent contributions, see W. Stavig, *The World of Túpac Amaru: Conflict, Community and Identity in Colonial Peru* (Lincoln, NE and London: University of Nebraska Press, 1999), pp.207–56; C.F. Walker, *Smouldering Ashes: Cuzco and the Creation of Republican Peru, 1780–1840* (Durham, NC and London: Duke University Press, 1999) pp.16–54. For comparison of the rebellions, see A. McFarlane, 'Rebellions in Late Colonial Spanish America: A Comparative Perspective', *Bulletin of Latin American Research*, XIV(1995) 313–339.
46. F. de Saavedra, *Los Decenios (Autobiografía de un sevillano de la Ilustración)*, ed. F. Morales Padron (Seville: Ayuntamiento de Sevilla, 1995), p.207.
47. Liss, *Atlantic Empires*, pp.150–2.
48. *Memoria secreta presentada al Rey de España por el Conde de Aranda sobre la independencia de las Colonias Inglesas en America despues del tratado de Paris de 1783*, Biblioteca Nacional, Madrid: Colección de manuscritos, no. 12966/33. For a digitalized copy of this document, see http://international.loc.gov/intldl/eshtml/es_collections/scope_bne.html#espbnms. Some doubt has been cast on the authenticity of the Aranda memorandum, but there is plenty of other evidence that Aranda, and other prominent officials feared that the Spanish colonies would follow the example of the United States. For examples, see Liss, *Atlantic Empires*, pp.127–8.
49. D.A. Brading, *The First America: The Spanish Monarchy, Creole Patriots, and the Liberal State*, (Cambridge: Cambridge University Press, 1991) p.540.
50. J.P. Vizcardo y Guzmán, *Letter to the Spanish Americans: A Facsimile of the Second English Edition (London, 1810)* with an introduction by D.A. Brading. (Providence, RI: John Carter Brown Library, c2002); K. Racine, *Francisco de Miranda: A Transatlantic Life in the Age of Revolution* (Wilmington, DE: Scholarly Resources, 2003), pp.143–7.
51. Herr, *Eighteenth Century Revolution*, pp.316–36.
52. "Copia de la representación dirigida al Excmo Señor Don Pedro Acuña y Malbar, con fha de 19 de abril de 1793": Archivo General de Indias, Seville (hereinafter AGI), Estado 53, no. 84, fols. 93–99; quotations from folio 84.
53. Manuel del Socorro Rodríguez, Santafé de Bogotá, 19 September, 1796: AGI, Estado 53, no. 84, fols. 69–86.
54. *Ibid.*, fol. 70.
55. A. McFarlane, *Colombia before Independence: Economy, Society and Politics under Bourbon rule*, (Cambridge: Cambridge University Press, 1993), pp.281–93.
56. Liss, *Atlantic Empires*, pp.156–68.
57. Herr, *Eighteenth Century Revolution*, pp.346–7, 438–41.
58. Lynch, *Bourbon Spain*, pp.395–400; 408–21.

3

The American Revolution in France: Under the Shadow of the French Revolution

Marie-Jeanne Rossignol

This paper examines the effects and the legacy of the American Revolution in France from a number of angles, from the late-eighteenth century to the present day: these include the impact of the American Revolution on the French Revolution itself; its place in French political debate; and its gradual decline in French memory and historiography after the French Revolution itself was no longer central to political life. The paradoxical conclusion of the paper is that, although the American Revolution did inaugurate the Age of Revolution, it only briefly served as a major common reference for French revolutionaries and their political heirs; nor was it recognized as significant by later French historians or deemed worthy of research by them. Not only was the American Revolution considered a minor event, it was also constantly instrumentalized in French political and historio-graphical debates on the true meaning of the French Revolution. The only group currently maintaining a vivid interest in the American Revolution, the French Sons of the American Revolution, focus in fact on the War of Independence in which their forbears fought alongside the Patriots. However, examining them in a transatlantic perspective, most specifically with an emphasis on slavery (which had not been done by previous Atlantic scholars), would be a way to bring together research on the two revolutions and move beyond past controversies.

A brief historiographical survey: French historians and the American Revolution

Historians in both France and the United States have produced a great deal of scholarship exploring the relationship between the two successful revolutions at the end of the eighteenth century in those countries. Giving a thorough account of this historiography would require a full-length paper, or even a book. A spate of recent French publications on the general theme of 'Revolts and revolutions in Europe and the Americas 1773–1802' has revived interest in France in the shared context of the American and French revolutions, leading to scholarly reviews of existing publications such as Marcel Dorigny's *Révoltes et révolutions* and various similar volumes.[1] These publications take care to avoid rejuvenating the old 'Atlantic' thesis which Robert Palmer and Jacques Godechot elaborated in the 1950s and 1960s, but they certainly do bring to light the common Enlightenment context of the events and force the French Revolution out of its usual historiographical isolation. With these syntheses, the American and French Revolution are set in a wider revolutionary context, which is highly reminiscent of what Jacques Godechot had written in *La grande nation*: 'the French revolution is only one aspect of a western revolution, or rather atlantic revolution, which started in the British colonies of America shortly after 1763, continued with the revolutions of Switzerland, the Netherlands, Ireland, before it reached France .... From France it rebounded'.[2]

Focusing more narrowly on Franco-American relations is a long tradition of scholarly literature comparing the two revolutions and examining the long-standing misunderstandings between the two nations that seemed to grow out of their spectacular modern births: after Durand Echeverria tracked down the origins of mutual misunderstanding in his 1957 *Mirage in the West*, philosopher Hannah Arendt compared the two events in her *On Revolution*, while historian Patrice Higonnet drew criticism with his book *Sister Republics*, which he published on the occasion of the French bicentennial.[3] In addition to this literature are works dealing with anti-Americanism in France or Francophobia in the United States, and the ways that both nations refer to their revolutionary past in order to justify today's international positions or local policies, thus leading each to oppose the other on the basis of their divergent revolutionary political heritages. One major publication in this field is Philippe Roger's *L'ennemi américain: généalogie de l'anti-américanisme français*.[4]

In contrast to these comparative studies, French publications on the American Revolution *per se* have been few and far between, with Elise Marienstras's original contributions standing out in the 1970s and 1980s.[5] André Kaspi, a major historian, published a small book in 1976 on the occasion of the bicentennial of the American Revolution – which obviously did not trigger an explosion of French publications – while Bernard Cottret, otherwise a specialist of Protestantism, has probably published the most recent history in French with *La revolution améri-caine: la quête du bonheur.* Claude Fohlen, another major specialist of American history, published *Les pères de la revolution américaine* in 1989. With the notable exception of Marienstras, these few historians do not present or grapple with the considerable revisions and questions that have defined the historiography of the American Revolution in the United States in the past thirty years. Authors like Ronald Hoffman or Gary Nash, who insisted on the racial dimension of the revolution and considered it as 'a social movement', have not been translated into French.[6] Neither have Alfred F. Young, a key proponent of the 'radical' history of the American Revolution, nor Edward Countryman, who penned one of the rare scholarly syntheses in English.[7] In fact there is no point in drawing up an exhaustive list of American scholars and their histories, as it is a fact that the French academic world has remained impervious to these new interpretations of the American Revolution by 'red-diaper babies'.[8] Typical of this trend is Serge Bianchi's otherwise stimulating synthesis *Des révoltes aux revolutions* in which the short bibliography on the American Revolution stops in the early 1970s, just when the radical historians started writing.[9]

Grounded in original research and a thorough knowledge of relevant secondary sources in both French and English, Elise Marienstras's work is thus an exception in French, partly because she acknowledges the debt due to this generation of American historians: 'Thus I owe a major debt' she writes 'to the historians of America, and most particularly those, like Ira Berlin or Ronald Hoffman, who specifically guided me to sources they had access to.'[10] Focusing on the broad revolutionary period from the angle of rising American nationalism, Marienstras did not write a history of the American Revolution *per se*, but *Nous, le people* (1988) retraces the history of the colonies from migration to the Revolution and the post-revolutionary settlement, borrowing first from anthropology and social history to study how national sentiment could slowly be forged in the daily lives of ordinary Americans; in later chapters, Elise Marienstras insists that the new nation's unity and con-sensual ideology was challenged by the poor, and by those the Revolution crushed in its colonial thrust, such as American Indians. Once the Revolution was over, its enduring mythology was turned into the ideological mainstay of the new nation.

In a previous book, Marienstras had already dealt with the revolutionary period. *Les mythes fondateurs* (1976) was grounded in the American his-toriography that preceded the vast production of the 1970s and 1980s, yet it challenged the self-satisfied consensus histories of the American

Revolution that historians in the United States were just beginning to question, portraying the event, its leaders and their many writings to the French public in ways that were both erudite and stimulating. This particular book has been outstandingly successful in France, going through many editions, and leading to the vocations of a number of American Studies specialists, like myself, but had far less effect on historians of eighteenth-century France. Once again, one cannot but wonder why. Like her Italian counterpart, Loretta Valtz-Manucci,[11] Marienstras was able to let these scientific cooperations with American historians bloom into a few joint conferences and follow-up publications in France, but by the mid-1990s, the impetus for joint research on the American Revolution across the Atlantic had waned and Marienstras herself focused more and more on research centred upon native Americans.[12]

From commonalities to differences: the changing view of the American Revolution in France in the late eighteenth century

In order to understand why historians in France have paid so little attention to the American Revolution, one first needs to turn to the revolutionary period itself. However insensitive French historians may have become to the history of the American Revolution, one indisputable fact is that contemporary observers were acutely aware that the two revolutions were closely linked within the general framework of the Enlightenment and the challenge it posed to established absolute regimes. As Patrice Higonnet writes: 'Many of the same people figured in both events, either as actors or witnesses ... The two events embodied many similar principles, to the annoyance of many Americans ... Both revolutions stood for popular sovereignty, nationalism, the rights of man, no taxation without representation, Republicanism, and suspicion of established religion.'[13] That the American Revolution had a direct and immediate impact on the French Revolution is undeniable and well-known. The French scholar Bernard Faÿ developed all the facets of what he called 'the revolutionary spirit in France and America' in his PhD dissertation published in 1924 and went on to publish separate studies on specific transatlantic figures of this connection, such as Benjamin Franklin.[14] Writing mainly during the interwar period, another scholar who emphasized the commonalities and the links between the two revolutions within the Enlightenment context was Gilbert Chinard.[15]

As the bicentennial of the French Revolution approached, there was a renewed focus on the influence of the American Revolution on the French one, this time from the point of view of political thought. French political scientists such as Marcel Gauchet, Denis Lacorne, and Philippe Raynaud all elaborated on the gradual intellectual transition from the American Revolution to its successor.[16] The nature and limits of the American influence are conveniently detailed in Lacorne's 1991 book, in which he asks if the American revolution was a model for the French. Lacorne explains that the French were well-informed about events and ideas coming from across the Atlantic before their own Revolution, in part because of the American War of Independence, which was supported and subsidized by the French state. The American war actually deepened the French debt to such an extent that the Estates General were called in 1789 in what was to be the first step toward the Revolution in France.

Thus the 1780s were years characterized by the liberal elite's interest in the newly independent United States: François-Jean de Chastellux published his *Travels in North America* in 1785; Mably, Condorcet, Dupont de Nemours, Turgot, Brissot, and the abbé Raynal all published works on North America, eulogizing the American model, which could serve as an inspiration for the whole of mankind, but also give a concrete illustration of their progressive ideas.[17] Brissot and Clavière created the 'Société gallo-américaine' in 1787, while philosopher Condorcet defined himself as an 'American citizen' on the eve of the French Revolution in 1788.[18] The American model was very specifically a political one, of course, and the French could rely on the 1783 translation of the Declaration of Independence and the various state constitutions in order to fuel their own discussions. Subversive ideas were heavily censured in eighteenth-century France, but that ban could not apply to texts coming from an allied nation as historian Joyce Appleby earlier argued.[19] Benjamin Franklin had been instrumental in making the publication of these documents possible, as he had personally contributed to turning the American Revolution into a popular event in France in general, transcending aristocratic circles. The simple life he embodied was widely appealing to Frenchmen from all educated circles and was reflected in 1784 in the successful publication in France of J. Hector St. John de Crévecoeur's *Letters from an American Farmer*.[20] Simon Schama says of Franklin's popularity that 'it ... was so widespread that it does not seem exaggerated to call it a mania ... [He] was of course the designer of his own particular celebrity, and by extension, the Patriot cause, on both sides of the Atlantic'. The Patriot cause, or fighting for

Liberty, was thus seen as a noble cause, amongst young liberal aristocrats in particular; this was partly due to the American Revolutionary War in which a number of them had fought, but generally speaking the American Revolution reverberated positively with those young aristocrats who were disenchanted with absolute monarchy. The fact that many of them eventually joined the Third Estate in June 1789 certainly has its roots in their class reactions to the American experience.[21]

Since its main value was deemed to be political, the American model was central to the late eighteenth-century French debate on how to reform French political institutions: Lacorne refers to Mably's publication of his correspondence with John Adams (1787), the many articles on the United States in the *Encyclopédie méthodique* and the fact that Thomas Jefferson had originally published his *Notes on the State of Virginia* in French.[22] Jefferson himself was consulted by La Fayette on the Declaration of Rights which the French eventually produced in the summer of 1789, and the wording of one proposal Jefferson put to paper certainly suggests that he had been involved in the discussions and was keenly aware of the specific French stakes.[23] Furthermore, the orators of the Constituante, the French assembly that sat between 1789 and 1791, very often referred to the American model.

However what this American political model meant, and to what extent it could be adapted to the French context, was from the first a matter of some debate among its French interpreters. Joyce Appleby thinks that admirers mainly supported the American model, because it embodied opposition to Britain and its institutions: the 'américanistes', she writes, gathered around Turgot, the Minister of Finance, and were friends of Franklin, and then Jefferson. They included Dupont de Nemours, Condorcet, Mirabeau, the dukes of La Rochefoucauld, and were joined in 1789 by Roederer, La Fayette, and others such as Talleyrand.[24] One encouraging feature in the early state constitutions were unicameral legislatures, such as was present in the 1776 Pennsylvania constitution. Unicameral legislatures were seen as offering an alternative model to British mixed government. But unicameralism eventually proved to be the exception, not the rule, in the new American institutions, 'a problem', Appleby notes, 'that was aggravated by the new Federal constitution for the United States in the eyes of French observers.[25]

Lacorne confirms that the American preoccupation with a balance of powers was seen as a legacy of British institutions and thus considered as inadequate by many in France. One such opponent was Turgot, whose critique of American government prompted John Adams to publish an apology of mixed government in *A Defence of the Constitutions of*

Government of the United States of America, against the Attack of Mr.Tugot (1787–1788);[26] but others included key players in the early years of the French Revolution, such as Condorcet and Dupont de Nemours, who opposed such division of powers. Like Sieyès, they insisted that national sovereignty could not be divided. As Adams's work was being published in London, the French opponents of mixed government took up an American pamphlet that argued against Adams, John Stevens's *Observations on Government, including some Animadversions on Mr. Adams's Defence*, which they quickly translated and had published to counter the influence of Adams's ideas.[27]

Thus the American model, and American ideas, fuelled debate in France, but the French américanistes were mainly preoccupied with borrowing from the Americans those arguments, ideas, and actual models, that could serve their own political purposes. Because bicameralism rather than unicameralism became established in the United States as the years went by, the relevance of the American model weakened and certainly could not be long upheld as the French Constituante eventually 'overwhelmingly chose a unicameral legislature' in the fall of 1789.[28] Consequently 'the American experience ... seemed from the first insufficiently radical, unduly influenced by English tradition' and institutions.[29]

Not only did the two constitutional traditions eventually prove incompatible, but the central notion of rights also emerged as a source of differences between the two political cultures. The French did uphold the notion of rights, but did not confer the same interpretation on it as the Americans had in their earlier bills of rights. Lacorne explains that American rights were primarily extra-legal protections against unjust legislation, while French rights were embedded in the law.[30] Political philosopher Marcel Gauchet insists that the same intellectual discourse (which he calls 'civic humanism') underlay discussions of rights in both countries, and that the French also wanted to preserve citizens from excessive central authority. But the Americans grounded their defence of men's rights in a general fear of all political power, while the French turned the protection of rights over to the law, which was now supposed to be under the control of the people. Both nations, then, would not have disavowed the inspiration of the 1689 English Bill of Rights, but as Marcel Gauchet argues, this earlier British model suffered a radical transformation in the case of the French Revolution.[31]

Because it fused rights and power, and did not keep them apart, the French Declaration of Rights was gradually seen by its champions as having more universal appeal than the American declarations, and

Robespierre claimed that the French Revolution was the first to be based on a theory of the rights of mankind.[32] This claim was probably lost on their American contemporaries who also thought that they had started a universal movement and considered their principles as applying to the whole of mankind.[33] Yet from that moment on, the French Revolution gradually left its American 'model' behind, with its most ardent promoters believing that their's was the one and only revolution, and that with it, mankind had started a new history.[34] The historical and ideological origins of present-day French disinterest in the American Revolution can be dated from this period.

Other reasons during the 1790s contributed to downplaying the importance of the American Revolution and its commonalities with the French Revolution. One of them was the economic debate between France and the United States. The French had considerably increased their national debt while supporting and fighting with the American insurgents, and as France itself became beleaguered by antirevolutionary neighbours, the new French leadership looked to the United States for rapid repayment of the debt and for full economic cooperation. They were sorely disappointed, however, when they saw that the new American republic remained under the economic influence of Great Britain after the war, and Jay's Treaty (1794) appeared to French observers to demonstrate that the Americans had reverted to their colonial status. Despite the efforts of Thomas Jefferson and other Democratic – Republicans such as James Monroe, then minister in France, to maintain good relations between the two countries, including the speedy start of debt reimbursement, economic differences compounded the growing sense of political alienation between the two countries.[35]

From a more global perspective, one has also to admit that the American Revolution's star was bound to wane in the revolutionary sky once the French Revolution broke out. Not only were they geographically distant, but to Europeans the former British colonies were also peripheral to the European status quo in their comparatively egalitarian New World society and relatively democratic voting system. When France started its own revolution and scrapped the feudal system and the absolute monarchy that had characterized it, these actions had a far greater impact on the rest of Europe than the American Revolution. France was the biggest and wealthiest country in Europe, with the largest population (25 million to the four million in the United States): the complete upheaval of its social system and institutions was bound to have an impact far beyond that of the American events, relegating them to a sort of mild revolutionary pre-history. European observers felt that the French Revolution occupied center stage in Europe for much of the next generation, spreading its ideological message far and wide, becoming a haven for revolutionaries of all nationalities and causing far stronger negative reactions than the American one had: Burke had initially supported the American Revolution but opposed the French one, for instance.[36] Thus the American 'model' naturally faded away during the more radical years of the French Revolution (also marked by bitter wars in Europe); during these years, former revolutionaries such as Thomas Jefferson felt rejuvenated by the energy unleashed by the French Revolution: even if the revolutionary movement had begun in North America, it returned to the United States with a vengeance to question the revolutionary generation's lasting commitment to democratic values, and caused a bitter political debate in the United States.[37]

From instrumentalization to exclusion: the American Revolution in French Politics and revolutionary history 1800–1989

After Napoleon assumed power in 1799, French politics no longer embodied the democratic hopes of mankind, and even Thomas Jefferson lost interest in the Franco-American connection that had symbolized revolutionary sisterhood to him. The Treaty of Mortefontaine (1800) confirmed the termination of the special relationship that had begun in 1778. But that did not mean that the American Revolution no longer had any impact on French politics.

Elise Marientras and Naomi Wulf have studied the continued legacy of the Declaration of Independence over the nineteenth and twentieth centuries in a seminal study, concluding that 'at the time of the two great revolutions, French debates on the American founding documents were lively bearers of political action. In the nineteenth and twentieth centuries, attention to the Declaration of Independence and other American documents dwindled, to be revived again according to the political and ideological needs of French history'.[38] Yet both French liberals and conservatives were divided over the significance of the American Revolution; but it was mainly appreciated for what was seen as its moderation, which implied a renewed interest in the constitutional model the revolution offered.[39] French interest in the American example thus revived at times of and in reaction to political upheaval in the 1830s and then at the time of the 1848 Revolution in France. The most famous example of this renewed focus on the former allies was de Tocqueville's *La démocratie en Amérique*. But *La démocratie* proved to have a short-lived influence in France, Marienstras and Wulf remind readers, reviving only with the advent of the Cold War as a founding theoretical document for French conservative liberalism. Typically, just as we noted for the early years of the French Revolution, Marienstras and Wulf conclude that references to the American Revolution in the nineteenth- and twentieth-centuries were mainly ways to address French problems and fuel French political debates. They argue that this can be seen clearly in the work of historians writing about the French Revolution and contrasting it with the American one: Augustin Cochin, working in the early twentieth century, eulogized the American Revolution as a model of moderation, while more progressive historians condemned it as an incomplete revolution, merely political, and not social.[40] Thus it appears that any study of the impact of the American Revolution in France necessarily has to acknowledge, and risks being overwhelmed by the French Revolution and its central role in French history, society, and politics. Undoubtedly the American Revolution in France has always suffered from the temporal proximity to the French Revolution, causing constant comparisons in terms of value and quality, and politicizing the historical debate.

To conduct readers through the complex history of the French Revolution in French historiography, a better specialist than myself would be required and I will thus tread cautiously on this sensitive ground, and with an acute awareness of my limitations. What follows is of necessity a very personal view of this major subject in French life. As the founding event of modern France, the French Revolution has triggered a large number of monumental histories, often written by key figures in French politics. This was the case mainly in the nineteenth-century with François Guizot, a major minister in the 1830s and 1840s, who wrote a vast history of France and the Revolution; Jean Jaurès, the father of French modern socialism, also wrote a 'socialist' history of the French Revolution in the early years of the twentieth-century.[41] During the nineteenth-century, the left-wing historian Michelet had written about the French Revolution with reverence, as he saw it as the founding moment of a popular and republican regime still under threat in his own time.[42] Writing about the French Revolution was a way of commemorating the event, of communing with it, and of insisting on its continued relevance to contemporary debates: the enterprise involved patriotic commitment together with the writing of history.[43] As is obvious with Jaurès, it was also a way of combining one's political convictions with one's interest in what was perceived as the dominant event in modern French history.

With the rise of socialism at the end of the nineteenth century, then the Russian Revolution and the ensuing polarization of French political life, writing about the French Revolution became a conduit for capturing its patriotic and radical aura for the benefit of Marxist activism in France, most particularly the Communist party, which enjoyed a broad popular base in France from the 1920s to the early 1980s, with particular support from a large spectrum of influential intellectuals. Vovelle recalls that Jaurès re-discovered Robespierre, the leader of the Montagnards during what is often called the 'reign of terror' in the years 1792–1794, seeing in him the embodiment of the social democracy which he wanted to promote: 'Robespierre is characterized as the supporter of the people in all his statements and in an attitude that was stressed since the beginning of the Assemblée Constituante in 1789. He speaks for the people, the poor, but also all those who were dispossessed, excluded, the Jews, actors, slaves, soldiers and their families'.[44]

But French historian François Furet set out to denounce this appropriation of the French Revolution by Marxists in the 1960s and 1970s, after penning a new history of the French Revolution with Denis Richet that described the Terror as a mistake rather than the most far-seeing moment in the revolutionary period.[45] Furet said he wanted the Revolution to be read as a 'cold' historical object, no longer as a 'hot' topic for political discussions, in the better interest of research.[46] According to him, the Marxists had treated it as a 'hot' subject, appropriating the French Revolution in several ways: first, as Robespierre had claimed that the French Revolution was the first truly universal revolution, Marxists considered that discussing its history implicitly provided adequate foundations for contemporary political debates on human rights and other politically charged subjects. Not only was the French Revolution universal, unlike others, but it was also unique and eternal, forever embodying the fight for liberty.[47] Thus Marxist activists could transpose the passionate political opposition between the Republic and the monarchy, which had emerged during the French Revolution and survived through nineteenth-century political conflicts (after all France became a Republic only in 1875) to the contemporary conflicts between communism and anticommunism.[48] As a result, Marxist historians even applied revolutionary concepts to their current political convictions, as Michel Vovelle revealed in an interview in 1989, explaining 'why we are still robespierrists'.[49] More generally, the Marxists read the French Revolution as heralding the coming of later communist revolutions, in a way that Furet considered to be a severely confused and inaccurate historical understanding of the French Revolution itself.[50] Second, these

contemporary historians laid great emphasis on the social and economic transformations which occurred during the French Revolution,
insisting on the revolutionary disjunction in these two fields: as Furet
himself summarized Marxist historians' ideas 'before there was feudalism, after came capitalism'.[51] But of course, as Furet spent much of his
career arguing 'the events of 1789 must be replaced within a much
longer chronology. Their distant origins are to be traced to the crisis
which the society of ancient medieval France underwent in the fifteenth
and sixteenth centuries'.[52]

Whatever their differences, neither the Marxist historians nor Furet
had much use for the American Revolution. Following in the wake of
Jaurès, historians Albert Mathiez, Albert Soboul and George Lefebvre
produced massive historical works, painting the French Revolution as
mainly economic and social.[53] Intellectual debates over political philosophy were certainly not seen as equally important: and thus highlighting
the link with the American Revolution was made difficult, which
explains why the indexes of these books contain very few references to
the American events.[54] Praising the inspiring effect of an 'American'
upheaval would probably have been politically difficult for these
Marxist historians, too, and they preferred to focus on how dramatic a
rupture in history the French Revolution had proved to be.

However critical of the Marxist approach François Furet may have
been, he too proved unwilling to assert the American Revolution's original contribution to political modernity, recalling the Patriots' belief in
their rights as Englishmen, not their profound sense of having broken
with the deeper principles of European political culture: 'In their case
[the American one], was it the crucial, philosophical moment of all, the
moment of the contract? They do not claim unknown rights ... On the
contrary they "state" rights they have been considering as fundamental
since their arrival ... America is a new world, still close to nature, with
few inroads by inequality, and the "Declarations" do not contain any
subversive dynamics'.[55] Therefore the American Revolution finds itself
depicted as a moderate event, fit for conservatives. In the same way that
he wanted to re-establish the French Revolution in a longer historical
continuum, Furet insisted on the continuities between English institutions and the American Revolution, neglecting to see it as a complex
and highly modern movement which necessarily had its roots in the
past.[56] However, as Marientras and Wulf note, Furet at least showed
interest in the American founding documents in various publications.[57]
But for both Marxist and non-Marxist historians in France, the American
Revolution remains peripheral to the French narrative, though for

different reasons. In both cases the French Revolution is presented as an exceptional event, in its size and complexity, signalling the birth of democracy for the rest of western civilization.

The present situation: the irrelevance of Revolution in France?

At the time of the bicentennial of the French Revolution in 1989, Michel Vovelle was put in charge of the intellectual commemoration as head of the prestigious Institut d'Histoire de la Révolution Française, thus overseeing the myriad conferences which were held to celebrate this major event. Yet by this time, as Steven L. Kaplan has artfully shown, Furet's views on the French Revolution and the Terror had become dominant and Vovelle's obsolete in French political and civic culture. The crumbling of the Berlin Wall, the concomitant decline of French communism in the 1980s and 1990s, and the ensuing lack of credibility of Marxist theses were the cause. Attacks against Vovelle's supposed lack of intellectual leadership in renewing interpretations of the French Revolution during and after the bicentennial hit him hard and led him to react strongly in publications such as *Combats pour la Révolution*.[58] But he kept treasuring his earlier views: writing in 2003, he was still insisting on the legitimacy and relevance of the social paradigm to explain the French Revolution: 'Although it is opposed by some today, the social history of the French Revolution, as it has groped its way, and strengthened its hypotheses, from Jaurès to Mathiez, to George Lefebvre and their successors, offers one of the best frameworks in order to understand what made men move'.[59] Vovelle hammered home the message that the French Revolution gave 'its modern meaning' to 'revolution' in general, and thus dismissed the American Revolution, which he says must be interpreted primarily as a movement of national independence, and whose founding documents were 'pragmatic' in their approach to the rights of man, 'with no pretence at universality'.[60] Although he was aware of the American experiment in revolution and republicanism, Vovelle considered that the successful connection between the two in France constituted a 'French exception': other related events paled in comparison.[61]

Marienstras and Wulf consider that with the coming of the bicentennial the American Revolution gained renewed acceptance and enjoyed a measure of interest again in French left-wing intellectual circles, noting that the universalist underpinnings of American founding documents were thus once again stressed. However, as we saw earlier, that does not mean that research on the American Revolution *per se* gained more prominence in historical research or political discourse in France. On the contrary, as its fate in France had always been closely associated with that of the French Revolution, there was no way the American Revolution could prosper as a point of reference and as an area of research after the French Revolution declined as a central fixture of the right/left political debate: the American Revolution simply could not replace the French Revolution. It appeared as if François Furet had been too successful: providing the educated French public with a new narrative of the French Revolution that no longer took sides for or against the Terror as the core of democratic belief in France, but also emptying research on the French Revolution of what had made it such a vibrant area.

To such an outside observer as myself, just coming back from one year in the United States, the 1989 grandiose public commemorations of the French Revolution in France were sometimes frankly puzzling, with great shows coordinated by celebrities from the art world; but they never were truly popular as they might have been had the French Revolution still resonated as a strong patriotic symbol with the population as a whole. Maybe this personal malaise was indicative of the national identity crisis which only became obvious in the early 2000s. Indeed it climaxed in November 2005 when minority demonstrators declared that the French Republic's enduring motto 'liberty, equality, fraternity', a legacy of the Revolution, was no longer relevant for them: they considered contemporary French society was riven by discriminations in spite of its self-satisfied belief in 'republican integration' for immigrants.

Academic commemoration of the bicentennial of the French Revolution failed to launch a wide array of new research, in spite of the best efforts of historian Michel Vovelle. The French Revolution was now definitely a 'cold' historical subject, though some exciting research still continued as Antoine de Baecque's cultural history studies proved.[62] As a result, the American Revolution also vanished from French political debate as a major reference for conservative liberals, while the American 'model', now understood as the Republican Party's interpretation of American democracy in the late twentieth century, started holding greater sway with the French right than it probably ever had. Consequently, the Paris monuments to American Revolutionary leaders such as George Washington, and the various buildings where the American envoys resided and worked during their negotiations with the French, form a historical trail only to the curious American visitor, and they do not resonate in the context of a vibrant passion for a common revolutionary heritage for the average French passer-by.[63]

Paradoxically, though less importantly, a sincere interest in the American Revolution has been entertained continuously since the late nineteenth century by the French Sons of the American Revolution. Members of this group comprise the only interested public group, an audience whose *raison d'être* is mainly their ancestors' participation in the American Revolution. Often dismissed by French American Studies specialists as too conservative – which is in fact not the point – the French Daughters and Sons, organized in two distinct associations, like their American counterparts, are a fascinating group to those interested in the diffusion of the American Revolution among the French public. Thus they provide an intriguing angle of approach for whoever is interested in the American Revolution in France.

The French Sons date back to 1897, a high point of cooperation between the two nations – and a low point for anti-americanism – when American Sons living in France started a chapter of the American Association, which had been started in 1889 in the wake of the first centennial of the Declaration of Independence; the current French association, formally created in 1927, is a chapter of the American association. In contrast with the American Sons and its over 26,000 members in 470 chapters over the world, this is a small group of around 400 members, who are mainly interested in the military events of the War of Independence; even more strictly than the American Sons, an association which has a very broad understanding of its possible membership, the French Sons are in fact a private club, connecting the descendants of the aristocrats who fought in the war far more than those of the common soldiers.[64] The central figure is Lafayette, at whose tomb they gather every year on 4 July. Another highlight is their yearly celebration of Yorktown. They publish a newsletter *Société en France des Fils de la Révolution Américaine*, number 11 of which has just come out, and they have a website at http://sarfrance.net.

Unlike the American Sons, a strongly patriotic society with keen interests in present-day American society, the French Sons are far more committed to the French past than to the present. The fact that so many of them are descended from the former French aristocracy may account for this: after all, it was the French monarchy who came to the rescue of the American insurgents. The French Sons are hardly relevant to French society today then, as they are a minority group who stay away from contemporary issues, and their vision of the American Revolution is a memorial one, more strictly focused on a number of military engagements and personal sacrifices.[65] They, too, cannot but deplore the increasing irrelevance of revolution in France, even though they understand the American Revolution mainly as a war of independence.

Conclusion

This may appear to be a fairly dispiriting essay, yet studying the American Revolution and the French Revolution is necessary in France, both for the historical significance of the two revolutions and for the democratic principles both undeniably embody. Neither the French nor the American Revolutions can be relegated to the confines of fading public memory and it may prove counter-productive to treat them as 'cold' historical subjects. On the other hand, French historians seem to be firmly opposed to a return to the 1950s 'Atlantic' paradigm. However the Atlantic World as it has been defined by English and American historians in the past twenty years could prove a fertile concept for the incorporation of the French and American Revolutions within the larger framework of slavery and abolition – a promising research perspective – without losing sight of their specific differences and their respective weight in world histories.[66] Such a framework could prove to be an opportunity to revitalize research in France on both revolutions by focusing, not on how much they accomplished, but on how much democratic change they promised to all members of their domestic and colonial societies without having delivered.

For the time being, Anglo-American historians have taken the lead in that field, bringing together the complex strands that connect the American, French, and Haitian revolutions.[67] But research on French revolutionary abolitionism has been rejuvenated in the past fifteen years by a group of scholars under the leadership of Yves Bénot, Marcel Dorigny and Florence Gauthier: they have constantly connected their work to that of Elise Marienstras and other French specialists of Colonial British America and are aware of the fact that research on Caribbean colonies is the new frontier of revolutionary studies, as European and American reactions to slave resistance and revolution in the area put to the test the promises of the Enlightenment.[68] In the new world of Atlantic research, the American Revolution will no longer be under the shadow of the French Revolution, and all of the Atlantic revolutions will be joined in a common search for the democratic, yet flawed beginnings of our modern societies.

Notes

1. M. Dorigny, *Révoltes et révolutions en Europe et aux Amériques (1773–1802)* (Paris: Belin, 2004); Marc Bélissa, *Révoltes et révolutions: en Europe, Russie comprise, et aux Amériques de 1773 à 1802: approches de la question* (Paris: Hachette, 2004); S. Bianchi, *Des révoltes aux révolutions. Europe, Russie, Amérique (1770–1802)* (Paris: Presses Universitaires de Rennes, 2004). Others might be mentioned.

2. J. Godechot, *La grande nation. L'expansion révolutionnaire de la France dans le monde de 1789 à 1799*, 2nd edn. (Paris: Aubier, 1983).
3. D. Echeverria, *Mirage in the West. A History of the French Image of American Society to 1815* (Princeton, NJ: Princeton University Press, 1957); H. Arendt, *Essai sur la révolution*, transl. M. Chrestien (Paris: Gallimard, 1967); P. Higonnet, *Sister Republics: the Origin of French and American Republicanism* (Cambridge, MA.: Harvard University Press, 1988). See also S. Dunn, *Sister Revolutions: French Lightning, American Light*. (New York: Faber and Faber, 1999).
4. P. Roger, *L'ennemi américain: généalogie de l'anti-américanisme français* (Paris: Seuil, 2002). There are many other such publications on the subject, both scholarly and popular, including the recent bestseller by J.-F. Revel, *L'obsession anti-américaine: son fonctionnement, ses causes, ses inconséquences* (Paris: Plon, 2002).
5. E. Marientras, *Les mythes fondateurs de la nation américaine: essai sur le discours idéologique aux Etats-Unis à l'époque de l'indépendance: 1763–1800* (Paris: Maspéro, 1976). E. Marienstras, *'Nous, le peuple': les origines du nationalisme américain* (Paris: Gallimard, 1988). E. Marienstras and B. Vincent, eds, *Les Oubliés de la Révolution américaine: femmes, Indiens, Noirs, quakers, francs-maçons dans la guerre d'Indépendance* (Nancy: Presses Universitaires de Nancy, 1990).
6. I. Berlin and R. Hoffman, eds, *Slavery and Freedom in the Age of the American Revolution* (Charlottesville, VA: University Press of Virginia, 1983); P.J. Albert, *The Transforming Hand of Revolution:Reconsidering the American Revolution as a Social Movement* (Charlottesville, VA: University Press of Virginia, 1996); G.B. Nash, *Race and Revolution* (Madison, WI: Madison House, 1990).
7. A.F. Young, ed., *The American Revolution:Explorations in the History of American Radicalism*, (DeKalb, IL: Northern Illinois University Press, 1976); E. Countryman, *The American Revolution*, rev.edn. (New York: Hill and Wang, 2003). This synthesis, which was recently revised, contains a long historiographical essay, which has not yet been translated.
8. For a general view of these American historians, see Marienstras in 'Autour de la Révolution américaine', in M.-J. Rossignol and N. Wulf eds, *Transatlantica 2006* (forthcoming issue of the electronic journal of the French Association of American Studies).
9. Bianchi, *Des révoltes aux révolutions*, pp.56–7.
10. Marienstras, *'Nous, le peuple'*, p.19.
11. Loretta Valtz-Mannucci, Italian specialist of the revolutionary period, organized ten bi-annual conferences in Milan between 1980 and 2000, bringing together European historians and American specialists of the Revolution. When she retired, it proved hard to find a new impetus for the conferences. See the web site of the Milan group, at http://www.dssi.unimi. it/dipstoria/mg/introduction.htm
12. B. Karsky and E. Marienstras, eds, *Autre temps, autre espace. Etudes sur l'Amérique pré-industrielle* (Nancy: Presses Universitaires deNancy, 1986); B. Karsky and E. Marienstras, eds, *Travail et loisir dans les sociétés pré-industrielles* (Nancy: Presses Universitaires de Nancy, 1991).
13. Higonnet, *Sister Republics*, p.1.
14. B. Faÿ, *L'esprit révolutionnaire en France et aux Etats-Unis à la fin du XVIIIè siècle*. (Paris: Edouard Champion, 1924). Books by Faÿ, a French academic, were quickly translated into English as was the case with his *Benjamin Franklin* (1930).

15. Gilbert Chinard published around two dozen volumes on Jefferson and his French friends, Lafayette and the physiocrats, on America and French literature in the seventeenth and eighteenth centuries, focusing among other things on French travellers to America.

16. M. Gauchet, *La Révolution des droits de l'homme* (Paris: Gallimard, 1989).

17. Amongst which one could refer to: G. Bonnot de Mably, *Observations sur le gouvernement et les loix des Etats-Unis d'Amérique* (Amsterdam and Paris: Hardouin, 1787); J.-A.-N. de Caritat Condorcet, *De l'influence de la révolution d'Amérique sur l'Europe* Repr. From Œuvres de Condorcet, vol. VIII (Paris: Firmin Didot, 1847); E. Clavière et J.-P. Brissot de Warville, ce Royaume et des Etats-Unis, des avantag *De la France et des Etats-Unis ou de l'importance de la révolution d'Amérique pour le bonheur de la France; des rapports de ce royaume et des Etats-Unis, des avantages réciproques qu'ils peuvent retirer de leurs liaisons de commerce et enfin de la situation actuelle des Etats-Unis* (London: s.n., 1787); G.-T. Raynal, *Révolution de l'Amérique* (London: L. Davis, 1781).

18. D. Lacorne, *L'invention de la république. Le modèle américain* (Paris: Hachette, 1991), pp.19, 78.

19. J. Appleby, 'America as a Model for the Radical French Reformers of 1789', *William and Mary Quarterly*, 3d. ser., XXVIII (1971) 267.

20. A.E. Stone, 'Introduction', in J. Hector St John de Crèvecoeur, *Letters from an American Farmer* ... (New York: Penguin Books, 1987), p.12.

21. S. Schama, *Citizens. A Chronicle of the French Revolution* (New York: Knopf, 1989), pp.43, 40.

22. Lacorne, *L'invention de la république*, pp.78–80.

23. J. Appleby and T. Ball, eds, *Jefferson: Political Writings* (Cambridge University Press, 1999), pp.349–51.

24. Appleby, 'America as a Model', p.274.

25. *Ibid.*, p.276.

26. Lacorne, *L'invention de la république*, pp.171–3.

27. Appleby, 'America as a Model', p.277.

28. *Ibid.*, pp.283–6.

29. P. Reynaud, 'Révolution américaine', in F. Furet and M. Ozouf eds., *Dictionnaire critique de la Révolution française*, vol. II, *Idées* (Paris: Flammarion, 1992), p.441.

30. Lacorne, *L'invention de la république*, p.192.

31. Gauchet, *La Révolution*, pp.37, 38–9.

32. *Ibid.*, P. iv.

33. The first text selected by S.P. Newman in his anthology of documents by American observers of the French Revolution is a letter from George Washington to Thomas Jefferson in which Washington says that the American Revolution has made better known the rights of man, those of the people and the true principles of liberty better known and accepted. J.-P. Dormois and S.P. Newman, eds, *Vue d'Amérique. La Révolution Française jugée par les Américains* (Paris: France-Empire, 1989), p.29.

34. Higonnet, *Sister Republics*, p.7.

35. A. Potofsky, 'G.A. Ducher and the Collapse of "Doux Commerce" during the American Revolution', in L. Bergamasco and M.-J. Rossignol, eds, 'L'Amérique: des colonies aux républiques', *Cahiers Charles V* n°39 (Paris: Université Paris 7-Denis Diderot, 2005).

36. Bianchi, *Des révoltes aux révolutions*, pp.149 and 469. Some major syntheses of the 'age of revolution' used to begin in 1789: see, for example, E. Hobsbawm, *The Age of Revolution: Europe, 1789–1848* (London, Abacus, 1977) and J. Godechot, *La grande nation: l'expansion révolutionnaire dans le monde, 1789–1799* (Paris: Editions Montaigne, 1956); R.R. Palmer naturally broadened this perspective to include the North American Revolution in *The Age of Democratic Revolution: a political history of Europe and America, 1760–1800* 2 vols. (Princeton, NJ, Princeton University Press, 1959–1964). But one had to wait for L. Langley's synthesis of the American revolutions to see these analysed as a coherent and complex group: *The Americas in the Age of Revolution, 1750–1850* (New Haven, CT: Yale University Press, 1996).

37. M.-J. Rossignol, *The Nationalist Ferment. The Origins of U.S Foreign Policy, 1789–1812* (Columbus, OH: The Ohio State University Press, 2003), pp.25–65.

38. E. Marienstras and N. Wulf, 'The Declaration of Independence in France', *Journal of American History*, LXXXV (1999) 1316.

39. *Ibid.*, 1316–8.

40. *Ibid.*, 1320.

41. *Ibid.*, 1320. J. Jaurès's *Histoire socialiste de la révolution française* in 2 volumes was initially published over a century ago: (Paris: J. Rouff, 1901).

42. J. Michelet, *Histoire de la révolution française* (Paris: Chamerot, 1847–53).

43. F. Furet, *Penser la révolution française* (Paris: Gallimard, 1978), p.30.

44. M. Vovelle, 'Pourquoi nous sommes encore robespierristes' in M. Vovelle, ed., *Les aventures de la raison: entretiens avec Richard Figuier* (Paris: Belfond, 1989),pp. 157–60.

45. Furet, *Penser*, p.20. François Furet and Denis Richet justified their criticism of the French revolutionary events starting in 1791 as a deviation from the true liberal course of the French Revolution in *La révolution française* (Paris: Hachette, 1965): 'The point was … to replace the episodes caused by the war, the forms of dictatorship and terror assumed by the Revolution by contrast with the accomplishments of the members of the Assemblée constituante and later ones in the nineteenth century' (my translation), p.10.

46. Furet and Richet, *La révolution française*, p.7.

47. F. Furet, ed., *L'héritage de la Révolution française* (Paris: Hachette, 1988), p.13.

48. Furet, *Penser*, p.20.

49. M. Vovelle, 'Pourquoi nous sommes encore robespierristes'. Vovelle started his publications on the French Revolution in 1972 with *La chute de la monarchie: 1787–1792* (Paris: Seuil, 1972), but also published a six-volume history of the French Revolution in the 1980s *La Révolution française* (Paris: Messidor, 1986).

50. Furet, *Penser*, p.20.

51. *Ibid.*, p.27.

52. Furet and Richet, *La Révolution française*, 2nd edn (Paris: Fayard, 1973), p.8.

53. A. Mathiez, *La révolution française*, 3 vols, originally published in the 1920s (Paris: Armand Colin, 1951). Mathiez devoted his life's work to the French Revolution and one of his main focuses was Robespierre himself. George Lefebvre also devoted his life's work to the French Revolution, with a specific focus on peasants during the French Revolution: see *Les paysans du Nord pendant la Révolution française* (Lille: O. Marquant, 1924), and *La Révolution française, la chute du roi* (Paris: Centre de documentation universitaire, 1940).

54. A. Soboul, *La civilisation et la Révolution française. Vol. 1 la crise de l'Ancien Régime* (Paris: Arthaud, 1970) contains no reference to either George Washington or Thomas Jefferson. No chapter or sub-chapter contains a reference to the American Revolution or its possible influence. I have not conducted an exhaustive search in the works of this or other writers of this group. Apart from *La civilisation et la Révolution française*, in three volumes, Soboul also devoted his life's work to the French Revolution, and he wrote a specific book bearing that title: *La Révolution française* (Paris: Gallimard, 1964).
55. Furet, *L'héritage*, p.19.
56. Recent syntheses of the political history of the American Revolution, from republicanism to liberalism, are to be found in L. Bergamasco and M.-J. Rossignol, eds, 'L'Amérique: des colonies aux républiques', *Cahiers Charles V n°39* (Paris: Université Paris 7-Denis Diderot, 2005). These include L. Bergamasco, 'Le Républicanisme: Thème historique, paradigme historiographique', pp.15–43 .and A. Léchenet, 'La République, "un habit neuf"?', pp.79–95.
57. Marienstras and Wulf, 'The Declaration of Independence in France', 1320–1321. Furet and Richet, in their *La révolution française* (Paris: Hachette, 1965), do briefly refer to the American Revolution: 'Chronologically there is no French priority. As early as 1776, the British colonies of America define their independence in a great liberal and egalitarian text that was to set the whole of enlightened Europe dreaming.' (my translation), p.24.
58. M. Vovelle, *Combats pur la Révolution* (Paris: La découverte, 1993), pp.7–10.
59. M. Vovelle, *La Révolution française 1789–1799* (Paris: Armand Colin, 2003), p.4.
60. *Ibid.*, pp.47, 52, 94–5.
61. M. Vovelle ed., *Révolution et république. L'exception française* (Paris: Kimé, 1994) in which, however, two articles on the American events are to be found, by Denis Lacorne and Bernard Vincent.
62. A. de Baecque, *La caricature révolutionnaire* (Paris: Presses du CNRS, 1988); *Body Politic: Corporeal Metaphor in Revolutionary France, 1770–1800* (Stanford, CA: Stanford University Press, 1997); A. de Baecque, *Glory and Terror: Seven Deaths under the French Revolution* (New York: Routledge, 2001).
63. D. Jouve, *Paris, Birthplace of the USA. A Walking Guide for The American Patriot* (Paris: Gründ, 1995).
64. For the definition of its membership, see the American SAR web site: http://www.sar.org/about/about.htm
65. This account is mainly due to conversations with Jacques de Trentinian, a member of the French Sons, to whom I must express my heart-felt thanks.
66. See a recent reflection on the renewed concept by one of its main promoters, B. Bailyn, *Atlantic History: Concepts and Contours* (Cambridge, MA: Harvard University Press, 2005).
67. This is the case in particular of David Barry Gaspar, and David Patrick Geggus whose most recent publications on the subject include Gaspar and Geggus, eds., *A Turbulent Time. The French Revolution and the Greater Caribbean* (Bloomington and Indianapolis: Indiana University Press, 1997); see also Geggus, *The Impact of the Haitian Revolution in the Atlantic World* (Columbia, SC: University of South Carolina Press, 2001). Also to be noted are the two volumes by Laurent Dubois published in the year of the bicentennial of Haitian independence: *Avengers of the New World: the story of the Haitian*

Revolution (Cambridge, MA: Belknap Press of Harvard University Press, 2004), and *A Colony of Citizens: Revolution and Slave Emancipation in the French Caribbean, 1787–1804* (Chapel Hill, NC: University of North Carolina Press, 2004).

68. For a broad survey of literature by Bénot, Dorigny and Gauthier and others on the subject, see M.-J. Rossignol, 'In the Wake of the Bicentennial of the French Revolution: a New Colonial and Revolutionary Perspective, Focusing on the Haitian Revolution and the Atlantic Paradigm', paper given at 'African American and Diasporic Research in Europe: Comparative and Interdisciplinary Approaches', a conference in honour of Michel Fabre and Geneviève Fabre, 15–18 December 2004, Université de la Sorbonne Nouvelle-Paris III, organized by the W.E.B Du Bois Institute for African American Research, Harvard University, Cercle d'études afro-américaines.

4
British Historians and the Changing Significance of the American Revolution

Simon P. Newman

Writing as the United States entered the Second World War, the eminent Cambridge historian Sir Denis Brogan (1900–74) began a book about American law and politics by paying homage to what he regarded as the most hallowed shrine in the American national capital.[1] For Brogan this was not the White House, Capitol Hill or even the Lincoln Memorial, but rather the Rotunda of the National Archives, whose darkened, church-like interior both moved and inspired him. Within this secular shrine are preserved the 'The Charters of Freedom', and each year hundreds of thousands of people pass before the Declaration of Independence (1776), the Federal Constitution (1787) and the Bill of Rights (1791), 'inspecting – and revering', as Brogan put it, 'these fundamental documents of the American nation'.[2]

These founding documents represented far more than a national commitment to rights and liberties by the people of the United States. Writing in Cambridge in 1942, after fascism and communism had overwhelmed continental Europe, Brogan looked westward to the United States as he articulated both his hope and his belief that the promises within the preambles to the Declaration and Constitution (as well as the entire Bill of Rights) were universal rather than particular. 'The American nation, at its birth', wrote Brogan, 'proclaimed not merely its own local rights or grievances, but asserted that it held "these truths to be self evident, that all men are created equal, that they are endowed by their Creator with certain unalienable Rights, that among these are Life, Liberty and the pursuit of Happiness."'[3]

Brogan reflected and helped lead a change in popular British perceptions of the United States, and this emerging new impression of the

United States was embodied in a Philip Zec editorial cartoon that he drew for the *Daily Mirror*, entitled 'Liberty Lights the Way', in which the bright flame held aloft by the Statue of Liberty illuminated the way to a darkened Europe.[4] Convoys of ships were heading towards Britain, but Zec was not simply presenting the United States as the source of military hardware. Rather, he was articulating a sentiment that would gain currency throughout Britain during the war and in the years that followed, namely, that the United States embodied and protected liberty and democratic government not just at home but all over the world.

Historians, perhaps more than any other group of British academics and intellectuals, played a pivotal role in helping to fashion this image of the United States and its role and significance in the world. In the wake of the Second World War the attitudes of Brogan and his contemporaries were institutionalized as American History and American Studies developed at universities all over the United Kingdom. More and more Britons encountered – and often embraced – the notion of a universal American Revolution, which heralded the dawn of enlightened government of the people, by the people and for the people. The American republic came to occupy a unique place, as perhaps the first nation in history whose founding principles sanctified liberty and free and representative government for people beyond its own national borders.

Half a century later American history, literature, politics, media and law are taught more widely to more students in British schools and universities than ever before. However, in the opening years of the twentieth century it is clear that events in the United States have challenged both academic and popular British interpretations of the nature and the contemporary significance of the American Revolution and the values enshrined in the Declaration of Independence, the Constitution and the Bill of Rights. This essay will begin by laying out the American context for the interpretation of the Revolution and its great texts, and will then explore how, why and with what significance two major British historians led the way in extolling the virtues of 'The Charters of Freedom' and all that they represent. The essay will then conclude with a discussion of recent changes in the United States that have undermined the admiration for the American Revolution and the ideals of its founding documents that once characterized British scholarship and popular attitudes.

The late eighteenth-century Founders of the American republic certainly believed that they spoke for and to people beyond the borders of the new United States, by establishing their new nation on the Enlightenment premise of the rights and liberties of the common citizen. The Founders spoke in absolute and universal terms, not in the parochial voices of citizens of a single nation. Washington rejoiced that the American Revolution had strengthened 'the rights of mankind, the privileges of the people and the true principles of liberty' in Europe.[5] 'Nothing then is unchangeable but the inherent and unalienable rights of man' wrote Thomas Jefferson, for 'the principles of government ... [are] founded in the rights of man'.[6] Jefferson's political adversary Alexander Hamilton agreed, declaring that 'the sacred rights of mankind ... are written ... in the whole *volume* of human nature'.[7] These are absolute articles of faith, not merely the building blocks of the American Revolution and republic, but rather the principles upon which the rights of all humanity rest.

In the centuries since the American Revolution, Americans have recognized the founding principles of their nation as what Abraham Lincoln regarded as a 'sacred trust', and Brogan referred often to Lincoln's Gettysburg Address, in which the President had spoken so powerfully and effectively of the desperate struggle to ensure that 'government of the people, by the people, for the people shall not perish from the earth'.[8] A century later John F. Kennedy faced the new problems of the Cold War by, just like Lincoln, turning to the founding ideals of the American republic. 'We dare not forget today that we are the heirs of that first revolution', announced Kennedy in an inaugural address in which he articulated an American unwillingness 'to witness or permit the slow undoing of those human rights to which this nation has always been committed, and to which we are committed today at home and around the world.'[9]

American history demonstrates, however, the difficulties that Americans have experienced in living up to the rhetoric of individual rights and liberties. During much of American history the liberties espoused by the nation's founding documents were restricted and ignored by government and citizens alike, and a meaningful national commitment to liberty at home and abroad was in many ways a twentieth-century construction. John Adams, who signed both the Declaration of Independence and the Constitution, also signed the Alien and Sedition Acts of 1798, which savagely curtailed individual liberties and the freedom of the press. Deeply concerned by the radicalism of the French Revolution abroad, and the political beliefs and practices of the Jeffersonian Republicans at home, the Adams administration stamped upon the liberties of immigrants and native-born Americans who opposed the government. Those found guilty of writing, printing or uttering 'false, scandalous, and malicious' words that would 'defame' the United States, the President or Congress faced up to two years in jail and a fine of as much as two thousand dollars.[10]

Slavery provided the clearest evidence of the discrepancy between the rhetoric and reality of American liberty. Perhaps the greatest defender of states' rights against the federal government was the antebellum South Carolinian Senator John C. Calhoun, who was in no doubt that

> It is a great and dangerous error to suppose that all people are equally entitled to liberty. It is a reward to be earned, not a blessing to be gratuitously lavished on all alike; – a reward reserved for the intelligent, the patriotic, the virtuous and deserving; – and not a boon to be bestowed on a people too ignorant, degraded and vicious, to be capable either of appreciating or of enjoying it.[11]

And while Abraham Lincoln, the Great Emancipator himself, spoke as effectively as any American ever had on the nation's commitment to liberty, as president he did not hesitate to suspend *habeus corpus*.[12] Similarly Woodrow Wilson took the United States into the First World War, declaring that 'the World must be made safe for democracy', and dedicating America to 'the rights of nations great and small and the privilege of men everywhere to choose their way of life'. Yet his administration ruthlessly censored and imprisoned political opponents, including Rose Pastor Stokes who was jailed for ten years for declaring that 'I am for the people and the government is for profiteers.'[13]

It was the reaction against governmental attacks upon civil liberties during the First World War that began the twentieth-century creation of a modern understanding and appreciation of civil liberties. During the war both the government and sections of the population attacked and imprisoned socialists, German Americans, Irish Americans and others; banned books and censored the press; and outlawed the teaching of the German language. The situation worsened after the war, when the Russian Revolution, domestic labour unrest, economic turbulence and political radicalism fuelled the Red Scare. The Palmer Raids of 1920 resulted in the illegal and usually unwarranted arrest of thousands of Americans, and were followed by waves of vigilante attacks. During these years freedom of speech, freedom of association and freedom from arbitrary arrest all but ceased to exist, and in their thousands Americans were attacked, arrested, imprisoned and even deported or murdered for their presumed beliefs or because of their ethnicity.[14]

Americans' traditional suspicion of the federal government encouraged a negative reaction to the Palmer Raids, lead by Republican opponents who championed civil liberties in their attempts to discredit the Wilson administration and destroy Attorney General A. Mitchell Palmer's presidential ambitions. Moreover, activists such as the settlement-house worker Roger Baldwin created the National Civil Liberties Bureau in 1917, which in the wake of the Palmer Raids was renamed the American Civil Liberties Union (ACLU), attracting the support of major public figures such as Jane Addams, Clarence Darrow, John Dewey and Felix Frankfurter. With growing popular support, the ACLU began using the courts to attack governmental assaults on the constitutional rights and liberties of the American people. Finally, Oliver Wendell Holmes, Jr. helped lead a growing movement within the federal judiciary to 'be eternally vigilant against attempts to check the expression of opinions that we loathe.'[15]

These reactions against the repressions of 1917–20 helped ensure that civil rights were far better protected within the United States during the Second World War, and Americans enjoyed and on occasion exercised the right to articulate attacks on the policies and personnel of the federal government. Dissenters were tolerated, rather than being attacked by the authorities and vigilantes, with the obvious exception of the Japanese Americans who were interned. Following the War the anti-communist witch hunts of the McCarthy era showed the weaknesses of constitutional protections for the left: however, against the backdrop of the subsequent black civil rights movement, the Supreme Court and American society as a whole repudiated the witch hunts, and the 1950s and 1960s saw a remarkable growth in popular, judicial and political commitment to a new understanding of the meaning and application of the rights and liberties guaranteed in the Constitution and Bill of Rights.

These same years saw a parallel transformation of American foreign policy, as the United States abandoned its traditional isolationism and embraced an internationalism that was in part premised on a belief that American liberty and democracy could enrich and improve not just the United States but the entire world. Henry Luce, writing in support of this new internationalism on the eve of American entry into the Second World War, famously described the twentieth century as 'the American Century'. Defending America transcended the protection of American territory, Luce argued, for he believed that the United States was already 'in a war to defend and even to promote, encourage and incite so-called democratic principles throughout the world.'[16] Acclaiming America's destiny as the twentieth century's foremost superpower, Luce believed that the American Century promised a different kind of rule and power than the world had ever seen, for American internationalism would be grounded in 'a sharing with all peoples of our Bill of Rights, our

Declaration of Independence, our Constitution'.[17] What he derided as the 'sneers, groans, catcalls, teeth-grinding, hisses and roars' of the Fascists contrasted vividly with Luce's championing of an American 'determination to make the society of men safe for the freedom, growth and increasing satisfaction of all men'.[18]

Speaking shortly before America's entry into the Second World War, Franklin Roosevelt insisted that the Four Freedoms to which he and the United States were committed – of speech and worship, and freedom from want and fear – were the rights of people 'everywhere in the world'. His wife Eleanor Roosevelt helped draft the Universal Declaration of Human Rights, which was adopted by the United Nations in 1948, symbolizing the institutionalization of the liberties proclaimed by the Declaration of Independence and the Bill of Rights as international rather than national.[19] During the twentieth century, then, Americans succeeded in consolidating their own rights and liberties, while simultaneously developing a sense of these as universal rather than as particularly American.

From relatively early on, British historians and intellectuals who were interested in the United States were fascinated by the ideology of the American Revolution and the founding of the republic. Lord Acton (1834–1902) was the first major British historian to visit the United States, in 1853 at the age of 19.[20] He turned regularly to the history of that nation as he thought and wrote about liberty, which he regarded as the foremost goal of human progress, but his ideas about the American Revolution changed dramatically during the second half of the nineteenth-century. His first major essay on the subject appeared in *The Rambler* in May of 1861, and was entitled 'Political Causes of the American Revolution'. It was a striking essay, which began with a lengthy study of the Constitutional Convention of 1787, arguing in explicitly Madisonian terms against the tyranny of the majority, and proposing that the Constitution had succeeded in protecting liberty by restraining the rampant democracy and majority rule of Jeffersonian radicalism:

> It is a most striking thing that the views of pure democracy, which we are accustomed to associate with American politics, were almost entirely unrepresented in that convention. Far from being the product of a democratic revolution, and of an opposition to English institutions, the Constitution of the United States was a powerful reaction against democracy, and in favour of the traditions of the mother country.[21]

Acton did not believe, however, that the Federal Constitution was a perfect document, regarding it as flawed by a series of compromises over slavery, federalism, states' rights and other key issues. The result was the American Revolution referred to in his essay's title, which was in fact the secession of the Confederate states a few months earlier.

> For the dissolution of the Union is no accidental or hasty or violent proceeding, but the normal and inevitable result of a long course of events, which trace their origin to the constitution itself.[22]

This was a remarkable conclusion. Over the course of the war, a growing proportion of Britons would come to associate the Union with liberty and republican government, while identifying the Confederacy with slavery and oppression. Yet at the beginning of the conflict one of Britain's greatest historians of liberty justified secession (although not slavery) as a necessary check on the unrestrained absolute rule of the Northern majority, and thus as the last best hope for the preservation of freedom in America. Acton concluded that 'the spurious democracy of the French Revolution' had infected American political culture, and had 'destroyed the Union, by disintegrating the remnants of English traditions and institutions'.[23]

Over the course of his career, however, Acton's views changed. Two decades later he published in the *English Historical Review* a lengthy review of James Bryce's *The American Commonwealth*, in which he appeared to reverse his earlier position and embrace the radicalism of the Declaration of Independence and Jeffersonian republicanism. The American Revolution was, he declared 'the supreme manifestation of the law of resistance ... the abstract revolution in its purest and most perfect form.'[24]

Rising to his subject, Acton praised the revolutionary Patriots, whose example

> teaches that men ought to be in arms even against a remote and constructive danger to their freedom; that even if the cloud is no bigger than a man's hand, it is their right and duty to stake the national existence, to sacrifice lives and fortunes, to cover the country with a lake of blood, to shatter crowns and sceptres and fling parliaments into the sea. On this principles of subversion they erected their commonwealth, and by its virtue lifted the world out of its orbit and assigned a new course to history.[25]

This paean to the Patriots and their Revolution represented a dramatic reversal, as Acton applauds American revolutionaries for their dedication to abstract liberty. Gone are his worries about unrestrained majority rule, replaced by an enthusiasm that echoes Jefferson's passionate avowal of perpetual revolution.

Acton developed his position in later lectures. In his Inaugural Lecture as the Regius Professor of Modern History, delivered at Cambridge University in June of 1895, Acton celebrated the forward march of liberty as exemplified in the creation of the United States. But while a quarter-century earlier he had regarded American achievements as being crucially linked to British constitutional precedents, he now set the American Declaration of Independence, the Constitution and the Bill of Rights on a higher plane:

> with our indigenous constitution, not made with hands or written upon paper ... we can have nothing equivalent to the vivid and prolonged debates in which other communities have displayed the inmost secrets of political science to every man who can read. And the discussions of constituent assemblies ... above nearly all those of the most enlightened States in the American Union, when they recast their institutions, are paramount in the literature of politics, and proffer treasures which at home we have never enjoyed.[26]

Coming from the man who had been appointed by the Crown as the most senior historian at Cambridge, this was a remarkable assertion. Less than two decades earlier the *Cambridge Chronicle* had railed against the creation of a series of lectures on the history and politics of the United States, warning that they would 'indoctrinate in the youth of the governing classes a love for democratic principles and democratic institutions ... producing discontent and dangerous ideas among persons less educated than themselves, over whom they would naturally exercise some considerable influence'.[27]

Acton further refined his arguments in a lecture on 'The American Revolution', delivered at the university in 1901, a year before his death. This time the Revolution was not confused with the American Civil War, and Acton sought to reconcile his earlier views with his more recent enthusiasm for the radicalism of the American Revolution. He suggested that the Patriots were not oppressed, and that they resisted and then rebelled against Britain on the basis of a higher principle, namely, liberty. Referring to the Boston Tea Party Acton proposed that:

> The dispute had been reduced to its simplest expression, and had begun a mere question of principle. The argument from the [colonial]

Charters, the argument from the [British] Constitution was discarded. The case was fought on the ground of the Law of Nature ... On that evening of 16th December 1773, it became, for the first time, the reigning force in history. By the rules of right, which had been obeyed till then, England had the better cause. By the principle which was then inaugurated, England was in the wrong, and the future belonged to the colonies.[28]

However, and this is where Acton's earlier ideas resurfaced, he contended that while the Declaration of Independence and the revolution it heralded were premised upon liberty, they failed to secure it. The Federal Constitution was the result, and its federalism 'was the most efficacious restraint on democracy that has been devised; for the temper of the Constitutional Convention was as conservative as the Declaration of Independence was revolutionary'.[29] Just as he had argued forty years earlier, Acton contended that by failing to deal properly with potential threats to federalism, the Constitution was flawed. But this time he argued that it was strong enough to endure and to protect liberty, for 'by the development of the principle of Federalism, it has produced a community more powerful, more prosperous, more intelligent, and more free than any other which the world has seen'.[30] At the dawn of the twentieth-century, Acton had come to believe that the United States could represent a great force for liberty, but his celebration of America remained qualified.

A half-century later Sir Denis Brogan assumed Lord Acton's mantle as the Cambridge historian of the United States and the principles upon which the republic was based. Gone were Acton's reservations and qualifications, and Brogan played a leading role in the development of American Studies in post-World War II Britain. While Acton had been unusual in his reverence for the ideals on which the American republic was founded, Brogan and his peers worked in a far more congenial era. As early as 1941 an article in the London *Times* entitled 'Studying America' had applauded the fact 'that substantial facilities exist for the teaching of American history in several British universities', suggesting that 'the study of American history, American institutions, and above all American traditions is of prime importance'. Harold Laski was quoted with approval as suggesting 'It has become more important for Englishmen to understand the spirit of American politics ... than at any period since the revolution of 1776'.[31] During the Second World War, the governments of both nations believed that they could enhance the nascent special relationship by encouraging the study of the United States in Britain.[32] The Cold War furthered the educational exchange, with the passage of the Fulbright Act in 1946, and the allocation of generous grants to emerging American Studies departments at British universities.

During the latter half of the twentieth century, Britons began learning more about the history of the United States, first in high school and then in American Studies courses at university. Courses on the American Revolution became relatively common, and students read and discussed Jefferson's paeans to 'the inherent and unalienable rights of man', and his vigorous assertions that the 'freedom and happiness of man ... [are] the sole objects of all legitimate government', John Adams' warning that the 'only Maxim of a free Government, ought to be to trust no Man living, with Power to endanger public Liberty', and Thomas Paine's fiery assault on monarchy and aristocracy and his defense of a democratic and republican form of government.[33] As it was taught in more and more universities, and then even in schools, the American Revolution and the founding documents fascinated British students. The Revolution's heroes are, like all heroes, flawed, yet their struggle to create not only a new and better society, but to point the way to a new and better world, enthralled students as much as it had their teachers.

Arguing that republicanism, democracy and liberty, both inside and outside of the United States, have built upon the American foundations of 1776 and 1787, Brogan and other European scholars of the United States kept faith in the American experiment. In an essay published in the wake of the trauma of Civil Rights, during the height of the Vietnam War unrest, and shortly after the assassinations of Martin Luther King, Jr. and Robert Kennedy, Brogan movingly recalled Lincoln's plea to preserve the United States as 'the last best hope of earth'.[34] This essay was written shortly before his death, and in a more emotive style than was characteristic, Brogan recalled his first impressions upon visiting the United States, remembering not just the size and strength of the nation, but also an overwhelming impression of 'hopefulness'.[35] This is not to suggest that such scholars were uncritical: just like Acton, Brogan thought of the United States as a work in progress, describing the nation and its history as 'an experiment of overwhelming historical significance'.[36] Brogan regarded the experiment as ongoing, pointing out that the preamble to the Constitution 'sets out as the main object of that document the creation of "a more perfect union" ... it is not yet perfect or complete'.[37]

Brogan's faith in the ideals on which the American republic had been founded was shared by other Britons who came to the United States in the course of the 'American century'. Like Brogan they believed that the United States was vital to the preservation of liberty and democratic government in the western world. Even as he lamented the commercialism and materialism of modern America, G.K. Chesterton marveled that 'America is the only nation in the world that is founded on a creed. That creed is set forth with dogmatic and even theological lucidity in the Declaration of Independence; perhaps the only piece of political writing that is also theoretical politics and also great literature.'[38] Jefferson's founding document inspired Briton's who studied and taught American history, and William Brock declared that 'it is hard to imagine better precepts for sane government'.[39] Peter Parish believed that 'The Declaration of Independence enshrined the high ideals for which America stood, and defined the object of the great experiment', and he applauded the 'marvelous blend of precision and ambiguity' achieved by the Constitution.[40] When Herbert Nicholas published a short history of the United States in 1948 for the increasing number of British undergraduates taking American history courses, he drew that history to a conclusion by suggesting that the United States was now the 'last, best hope' not just for the Union, but for 'world civilization'.[41] William Brock echoed this in the introduction to his study of Reconstruction, suggesting that 'The present history of the United States in the world makes their history the concern of all peoples'.[42] Thus Radical Republicans in the 1860s 'hoped that the preamble to the Declaration of Independence should become the new formula for national existence': the tragedy of their failure, Brock concluded, 'transcends the particular circumstances of the post-war era and belongs to the whole condition of modern man'.[43] Studying American history was an act of faith amongst British academics in the decades following the Second World War, who believed that Americans 'have much to give, materially and spiritually: a well-founded optimism about their own possibilities; a well-founded belief that some of the problems of unity ... have been solved in the American experience'.[44]

Leo Marx, one of the founders of American Studies, recalled that 'Somewhere back of the American Studies idea there once lurked an amorphous conception of the United States as the embodiment of a social ideal'.[45] If Acton and Brogan had been early prophets of this idea in Britain, during the second half of the twentieth century an increasing number of British academics and students followed them. Many never lost this faith and enthusiasm, reiterated by Howard Temperley and Malcom Bradbury in the introduction to the 1997 edition of their

Introduction to American Studies, first published in 1981:

> The American Revolution was implicitly a transformation of Europe –
> more than an American event. And among other things it transformed
> the image of America from a static, paradisal Brave New World to a
> historically active power, a 'Beacon of Freedom'.[46]

At the dawn of the twenty-first century, however, American actions
and legislation have occasioned a growing sense of disenchantment
with the United States, and the regretful conclusion that the principles
of 1776 and 1787 have been betrayed. Almost all of the enthusiasm of
British academics, and indeed the British and European public at large,
for the promise of the American Revolution for the world as a whole has
disappeared. 'We are all Americans' declared *Le Monde* in the wake of the
terrorist attacks on September 11, 2001, in a front page article that articulated not just sympathy and support, but also a sense that an attack on
the United States was an attack on the rights and liberties of all people.[47]
Subsequently, however, the domestic and foreign policies of the
American government have appeared to many to threaten a complete
reversal of American Century attempts to establish and protect individual
rights and liberties throughout the world. Former Vice President Albert
Gore noted that the September 11th attacks had inspired 'sympathy,
goodwill and support [for the United States] around the world', but that
a year later American policies had 'replaced that with fear, anxiety and
uncertainty'.[48] Fearing further terrorist attacks the United States has
reacted strongly, not just against perceived enemies abroad, but also
against them at home, and the perceived betrayal of liberty and freedom
within the United States is as alarming as American policies abroad.

The twenty-first century has witnessed the largest, most comprehensive
and most dangerous assault ever mounted upon the liberties articulated
in the founding documents enshrined in the National Archives. The full
horror of the terrorist attacks prompted many Americans to support
strong governmental actions that necessarily involved the abrogation of
individual liberty, and even the guardians of these liberties could do
little to protect them. Speaking at New York University Law School several weeks after the Twin Towers had fallen, Associate Supreme Court
Chief Justice Sandra Day O'Connor predicted the scale and significance
of the assault on the twentieth-century constructions of the liberties
articulated in the Declaration of Independence, the Constitution and
the Bill of Rights, lamenting that 'We're likely to experience more

restrictions on our personal freedom than has ever been the case in our country.'[49] The full power of the federal government has been brought to bear, supported by a largely compliant American media and population, with the result that both in law and in popular practice, domestic opposition to the Federal government and its policies has become unacceptable, and individual rights and liberties are under serious threat.

Opposition to this historic reversal was enormously difficult. Attorney General John Ashcroft warned members of the Senate Judiciary Committee in December 2001 not to oppose the policies of the Bush administration, castigating those who 'scare peace-loving people with phantoms of lost liberty' by arguing that their defense of constitutional rights and liberties 'only aid terrorists – for they erode our national unity and diminish our resolve'. Ashcroft was quite explicit in condemning such naysayers as foolish and unpatriotic people who 'give ammunition to America's enemies'.[50]

This process began with the Patriot Act, signed into law on 26 October 2001. 'Patriot' stands for 'Provide Appropriate Tools Required to Intercept and Obstruct Terrorism'. The Patriot Act of 2001 vastly expanded Federal government power and authority over its citizens in retaliation against past and possible future attacks. Under threat were the rights to freedom of religion, assembly, speech and the press; protection against unreasonable search and seizure; guarantee of due process of law; the right to a speedy trial by jury, with the right to confront witnesses; and protection against excessive bail and cruel and unusual punishments, all of which were rights codified in the Bill of Rights and in twentieth-century Supreme Court interpretations of the Constitution and the rights that it guarantees.

When President George W. Bush signed the Homeland Security bill into law he explained that ever since the terrorist attacks of September 11th, 'America has been engaged in an unprecedented effort to defend our freedom'. The nation's new Department of Homeland Security would, President Bush continued, 'focus the full resources of the American government on the safety of the American people,' taking 'every possible measure to safeguard our country and our people'.[51] In the biggest reorganisation of the American government since the Second World War, the act consolidated the work and the employees of a number of existing federal departments and agencies within a new Department of Homeland Security with just under 200,000 employees. More significantly, the law massively expanded the power of the federal government over its own citizens, limiting their liberties as never before.

As a result, the Homeland Security Act drew criticism from both the left and the right. Conservative *New York Times* columnist William Safire led the charge with an outraged editorial entitled 'You Are a Suspect'. Wryly noting that the Latin motto over the office of the Director of the government's Information Awareness Office 'reads "Scientia Est Potentia" – "knowledge is power" ', Safire condemned the 'Total Information Awareness' that would enable the federal government to add 'Every purchase you make with a credit card, every magazine subscription you buy and medical prescription you fill, every Web site you visit and e-mail you send or receive, every academic grade you receive, every bank deposit you make, every trip you book and every event you attend' to the information already held.[52]

A proposed follow-up law, the Domestic Security Enhancement bill, was drafted in late 2002 and early 2003 in order to broaden law enforcement powers, including domestic intelligence gathering, surveillance, and the authorization of secret arrests, while decreasing public access to information and judicial review authority. According to Anthony Romero, Executive Director of the American Civil Liberties Union (ACLU), these massive expansions in the power of the Federal government over its own citizens 'won't make us safer, but it will make us less free'. According to the ACLU, these laws 'launched one of the most serious civil liberties crises our nation has ever seen,' and in April 2003 the organisation published full-page advertisements in newspapers all over the United States. The advertisement featured a 'while-you-were-out' post-it sticker on a front door, listing all of the things government agents could now do in and to an American citizen's home without his or her knowledge.[53] After the bill was leaked to the press in February 2003, the outcry was so pronounced that the proposed legislation was withdrawn.

The Patriot Act and the Homeland Security Act significantly increased the power of the executive branch of the government of the United States, and in so doing they constituted the most comprehensive assault upon civil liberties in American history: the constitutional protections of freedom of speech, association, religion and the press; protection against unreasonable search and seizure; and the guaranteed right to due process, equal protection, and a fair and speedy trial have all been diminished.[54]

From the start there was opposition to this assault on individual liberty. Casting a lone vote against the Patriot Act in the United States Senate, Wisconsin Senator Russell Feingold warned that 'Preserving our freedom is one of the main reasons that we are now engaged in this new war on terrorism. We will lose that war without firing a shot if we sacrifice the liberties of the American people.'[55] Some protests have come from unlikely sources: beginning early in 2003, for example, thousands of public librarians all around the nation ended each day by shredding all of the handwritten requests for books, reference information and computer access that had been submitted to them. The laws passed since 2001 meant that the federal government could – without subpoena or judicial authorisation – review the business records of its own citizens, including their library records. As one California librarian lamented, 'I am more terrified of having my First Amendment rights to information and free speech infringed than I am by the kind of terrorist acts that have come down so far.'[56]

Adopting a defiantly patriotic stance, the ACLU web page declared that 'An immutable characteristic of our nation is freedom. If we allow the interests of "national security" to take away our freedoms, we surrender what it is to be an American.'[57] When rights and liberties are curtailed and even suspended within the United States, and when power is expanded and exercised in this manner abroad, then the American government risks betraying its own Founders and the ideals on which they built the republic.

The early twenty-first century assault on constitutional liberty may at first glance appear to be simply one more of many steps backward to have occurred since 1787. The first assault on the civil liberties enshrined in the American Constitution was also provoked by 'terrorism', for that was the word used by John Adams to describe the activities of the Jeffersonian Republicans that inspired his Federalist administration and Congress to pass the Alien and Sedition Acts of 1798.[58] But this is more than a case of history repeating itself. During the twentieth-century the individual rights and liberties promised by the Declaration of Independence, the Constitution and the Bill of Rights were re-imagined and re-applied both inside and outside of the United States. The Alien and Sedition Acts of 1798, Lincoln's suspension of *habeus corpus* during the American Civil War, and the routine abridgement of individual rights and liberties during the later-eighteenth, the nineteenth and the early-twentieth centuries were consigned to the past by an American Century that witnessed a striking commitment by Americans to the extension of the liberties enshrined in their founding documents, first to all citizens of the United States, and then to people all over the world. What is most striking about the McCarthy era's witch hunts is how quickly they passed and were repudiated, just as the violent opposition to Black Civil Rights was overwhelmed more speedily and effectively than many with a memory of three centuries of racial slavery could ever have predicted.

Consequently, in the early years of the twenty-first century the United States faces more than just another of the periodic curtailments of individual liberty that have occurred throughout American history, but rather a systematic reversal of the internationalism of a commitment to universal liberty enshrined in Luce's American century. The American Century had been premised in part upon a powerful new incarnation of John Winthrop's ideal of the city upon a hill, with Americans hoping that the United States would succeed in becoming the greatest defender of liberty the world had ever seen. American historians, both in the United States and beyond, wrote and taught about the American Revolution and the republic that it founded in international as much as national terms, agreeing with Tomas Paine that the 'cause of America is in great measure the cause of all mankind'.[59] However, the curtailment of liberty at home and the use of American power abroad has undermined the City on a Hill, and in stark contrast with the past the process has been all but unchecked in the United States. In 1866 the Supreme Court, declaring Lincoln's suspension of *habeus corpus* to have been unconstitutional, proclaimed that 'No doctrine, involving more pernicious consequences, was ever invented by the wit of man than that any of [the Constitution's] provisions can be suspended during any of the great exigencies of government'. Such a doctrine would inevitably lead to despotism, argued the Court, for 'the theory of necessity on which it is based is false; for the Government, within the Constitution, has all the powers granted to it, which are necessary to preserve its existence'.[60] No such judicial decision or congressional action appears likely in the early twenty-first century.

As a result, the enthusiasm of British historians and the public at large for the rights and liberties enshrined in America's founding documents has dwindled. To many Britons, the European Convention on Human Rights, the European Court of Human Rights in Strasbourg, and the World Court in the Hague are more visible, more powerful and more articulate defenders of universal liberties than are the governmental institutions of the United States. Before the Second World War few Britons knew much about the Declaration of Independence, the Constitution and Bill of Rights, and the events and ideals of the founding of the American republic. But during the second half of the twentieth century Brogan in his newspaper columns and radio pieces, Alistair Cooke in his 'Letters from America', and the academics who created and taught American Studies enhanced understanding and significantly increased knowledge of the history and political ideals that had defined the United States.

This deeper understanding and knowledge has allowed profound criticism of the United States to emerge in Britain in the early-twenty-first century. Nicholas Garland's editorial cartoon in the *Daily Telegraph* on 5 July 2005, the day after Americans had celebrated the anniversary of the Declaration of Independence, illustrates a radically different view of the United States than the awed and hopeful vision of the Statue of Liberty drawn by Zec in 1941. Garland's cartoon showed President George W. Bush, Vice-President Dick Cheney, Donald Rumsfeld and Condeleeza Rice, all in eighteenth-century dress. President Bush was presented in such a way as to evoke the image of George Washington, and the four contemporary American leaders were gathered together around his desk in the posture of the signers of the Declaration of Independence who had gathered to commit themselves to liberty. However, the caption to Garland's editorial cartoon completely undermined the implication that President Bush and his colleagues were committed to the same cause as the eighteenth-century Patriots, reading 'We hold these "truths" to be self-evident hogwash'.[61]

This cartoon representation would have meant little to many Britons a century earlier. Garland's cartoon worked because newspaper readers had sufficient knowledge of the opening sentence of the Declaration of Independence, of John Trumbull's early-nineteenth-century painting of the signing of the Declaration of Independence, and of portraits of George Washington to understand the betrayal implied in the cartoon and its caption. In short, the pioneering work of such scholars as Acton and then Brogan, and the development of American Studies had helped create a far greater awareness of the creation of the American republic, and the ideals enshrined in the founding documents. Such knowledge had at first led to a significant degree of admiration and respect for the United States, but it meant too that the United States was then judged according to the remarkably high standards set in its founding documents, and at present British academics and the British public at large are enormously critical of a perceived failure of the United States to live up to its own principles. A few months after publishing his cartoon Garland announced to an audience of American historians at London's British Library that 'The Bush administration hurtled into the American Dream and sent it flying.'[62]

The American historian Richard Hofstadter once observed that 'It has been our fate as a nation not to have ideologies, but to be one.'[63] From the mid-nineteenth to the later-twentieth century, a succession of British historians held the ideology that was the United States in high regard, seeing the United States as a nation that in the principles embodied in its founding transcended all others. Acton and Brogan typified the awe with which these historians regarded the Declaration, the Constitution, the Bill of Rights and the men who created them. Today such beliefs have all but vanished from the British academy, and the reverence and awe of Acton and Brogan can no longer be found in the histories written by British historians today.

This is not to say, however, that the study of the United States is in decline, but rather that its tone has changed. In April of 2005 the British Association for American Studies (BAAS) celebrated its fiftieth anniversary, a milestone for the nation's American Studies community. As Chair of BAAS I reported to the assembled membership that 'American Studies in Britain is stronger than ever, and this fiftieth anniversary conference bears witness to the strength and depth of our vibrant research culture and teaching provision'. BAAS represents a large and vibrant group of scholars and postgraduate students, who are researching and teaching more broadly in American history, literature, politics and culture than any preceding generation of Britons.

Two weeks before the conference I had personally experienced the continuing attraction of American history for British students when I led a group of seven undergraduate students from my University of Glasgow course on the American Revolution on a research trip to Philadelphia. After a year of reading and discussing the Declaration of Independence, the Federal Constitution, the Bill of Rights and a host of related documents and sources, we were in the city where the Charters of Freedom had been created. The students saw a copy of the Declaration of Independence in Jefferson's own handwriting, an edition of Paine's *Common Sense* featuring his own marginalia, and the building where the Declaration and the Constitution were debated and passed. These students' excitement, and their sense of enthusiasm for the ideals on which the American revolution had been premised was as real and as profound as that experienced by Acton more than a century ago, by Brogan more than a half-century ago, and by other leading British historians during the second half of the twentieth century. Yet this excitement and enthusiasm was tempered by a persistent sense of misgiving, a feeling of confusion, and an unhappy yet strong conviction that there has never been so great a disjunction between the ideals of 1776 and 1787 and contemporary American governmental policies. These students, like their teachers in Britain, could not help but wonder if the full promise of a nation evoked by F. Scott Fitzgerald as 'the last and greatest of all human dreams,' and of a republican democracy defended by Lincoln as 'the last best hope of earth,' was being fatally undermined by 'the last and greatest betrayal of the last and greatest of human dreams'.[64]

How, then, will future British historians and their students approach the study of the American Revolution and the republic that the Patriots created? This essay has demonstrated that British analysis of the American past is contingent upon American actions in the present, and how those actions measure up against the standards set in 1776 and 1787, and reaffirmed by Lincoln during the Civil War. During the late-nineteenth and most of the twentieth-century, British historians from the far left and the far right had little interest in the United States, and it was liberals – including Lord Acton, Sir Denis Brogan, Peter Parish, Esmond Wright, Malcolm Bradbury, Marcus Cunliffe, and others – who celebrated what America represented. In the present, and most likely in the future, the confidence of such liberals in the ability of the United States to live up to the promise embodied in the founding documents may well have eroded to such an extent that the last remnants of American exceptionalism will cease to resonate in the writings and teaching of British historians. In a symbolic as much as a literal sense, the American Century is over.

Notes

1. With a profusion of newspaper articles in the London *Times* and the Manchester *Guardian*, and regular appearances on BBC radio programmes, Denis Brogan illuminated the society and institutions of the United States for many Britons. Born in Glasgow in 1900 and educated at the University of Glasgow, Brogan was fascinated by the United States from an early age, and was particularly interested in its democratic and republican form of government. Following his postgraduate education at Cambridge and Harvard Brogan taught at University College London and then at Oxford, before in 1939 becoming Professor of Political Science at Cambridge, and in the years after the Second World War, Brogan emerged as the first of the Oxbridge dons to combine scholarly distinction with a broad popular appeal. In books such as *The American Political System* (London: H. Hamilton, 1933); *U.S.A., An Outline of the Country, its People and Institutions* (London: Oxford University Press, 1941); *American Themes* (London: H. Hamilton, 1948); and *America in the Modern World* (New Brunswick, NJ: Rutgers University Press, 1960), but especially in his newspaper writings and media appearances, Brogan did as much as any other Briton to explore and explain the significance of the strange inhabitants, customs and political practices of the people of the United States. Background information has been drawn from the London *Times* obituary, in *Obituaries from the Times, 1971–1975*, ed., F.C. Roberts (Reading: Newspaper Archive Developments Ltd., 1978), pp.70–1.
2. D. Brogan, *Politics and Law in the United States*, (Cambridge: Cambridge University Press, 1942), p.1.
3. *Ibid.*, p.3.

4. P. Zec, 'Liberty Lights the Way', *Daily Mirror*, 5 September 1940.
5. George Washington to Thomas Jefferson, 1 January 1788, in J.C. Fitzpatrick, ed., *The Writings of George Washington* (Washington: The United States Printing Office, 1944), XXIX, p.350.
6. Thomas Jefferson to Major John Cartwright, 5 June 1824, in A.A. Lipscomb, ed., *The Writings of Thomas Jefferson* (Washington, DC: Thomas Jefferson Memorial Association, 1904), XVI, pp.48, 51.
7. A. Hamilton, 'The Farmer Refuted', 23 February 1775, in H.C. Syrett, ed., *The Papers of Alexander Hamilton* (New York: Columbia University Press, 1961), I, p.122.
8. A. Lincoln, 'Message to Congress in Special Session', 4 July 1861, and 'Address Delivered at the Dedication of the Cemetery at Gettysburg', 19 November 1863, in R.P. Basler, ed., *The Collected Works of Abraham Lincoln* (New Brunswick, NJ: Rutgers University Press, 1953) IV, p.490, V, p.19.
9. J.F. Kennedy, Inaugural Address, 20 January 1961, in T.C. Sorensen, ed., *'Let the Word Go Forth': The Speeches, Statements, and Writings of John F. Kennedy* (New York: Delacorte Press, 1988), p.12.
10. J.M. Smith, *Freedom's Fetters: The Alien and Sedition Laws and American Civil Liberties* (Ithaca, NY: Cornell University Press, 1956), pp.441–2.
11. J.C. Calhoun, 'A Disquisition on Government' (1851), in C.N. Wilson and Shirley B. Cook, eds, *The Papers of John C. Calhoun* (Columbia, SC: University of South Carolina Press, 2003), pp.37–8.
12. J.M. McPherson, *Battle Cry of Freedom: The Civil War Era* (New York: Ballantine Books, 1989), pp.288–90.
13. W. Wilson, 'An Address to a Joint Session of Congress', 2 April 1917, in A.S. Link, ed., *The Papers of Woodrow Wilson* (Princeton, NJ: Princeton University Press, 1983), XXXXI, p.525. Stokes, editor of the Socialist *Jewish Daily News*, uttered these words during an after-dinner speech to the Women's Dining Club of Kansas City. See Z. Chafee, *Free Speech in the United States* (Cambridge, MA: Harvard University Press, 1941), pp.52–3
14. For an excellent discussion of this point, see A. Brinkley, 'A Familiar Story: Lessons from Past Assaults on Freedoms', in R.C. Leone and G. Anrig, Jr, eds, *The War on Our Freedoms: Civil Liberties in an Age of Terrorism* (New York: The Century Foundation, 2003), pp.23–46.
15. Justice O.W. Holmes, Jr., 'Dissenting Opinion on Abrams v. United States (1919)', in A. Lief, ed., *The Dissenting Opinions of Mr. Justice Holmes* (New York: Vanguard Press, 1929), p.50.
16. H.R. Luce, 'The American Century', *Life*, 17 February 1941, 62.
17. *Ibid.*, 64.
18. *Ibid.*, 65.
19. See W. Schulz, *Tainted Legacy: 9/11 and the Ruin of Human Rights* (New York: Thunder's Mouth Press, 2003), p.42.
20. Biographical information is drawn from R. Hill, *Lord Acton* (New Haven, CT: Yale University Press, 2000).
21. J.E.E.D. Acton, 'Political Causes of the American Revolution', in Acton, *Essays on Freedom and Power*, ed., G. Himmelfarb (Boston, MA: Beacon Press, 1949), p.200.
22. *Ibid.*, p.199.
23. *Ibid.*, p.250.

24. Review of Acton, *The American Commonwealth*, by J. Bryce, *English Historical Review*, IV (1889) 395.
25. *Ibid.*, 395.
26. Acton, 'Inaugural Lecture on the Study of History', in Acton, *Lectures on Modern History*, ed., J.N. Figgis and R.V. Laurence (London: Macmillan, 1906), p.6.
27. From the *Cambridge Chronicle*, 10 February 1866, quoted in G. Martin, 'The Cambridge Lectureship of 1866: A False Start for American Studies', *Journal of American Studies*, VII (1973) 24.
28. Acton, 'The American Revolution', in *Lectures on Modern History*, eds, Figgis and Laurence, p.311.
29. *Ibid.*, p.314.
30. *Ibid.*
31. 'Studying America', *The Times*, 17 June 1941, 5.
32. D. Reynolds, 'Whitehall, Washington and the Promotion of American Studies in Britain during World War Two' *Journal of American Studies*, XVI (1982) 165–88.
33. Jefferson to John Cartwright, *op cit.*; Jefferson to Thaddeus Kosciusko, 26 February 1810, in *Writings of Thomas Jefferson* XII, pp.369–70; J. Adams, 'Notes for an Oration at Braintree, Spring 1772', in L.H. Butterfield, ed., *Diary and Autobiography of John Adams* (Cambridge, MA: Belknap Press, 1962), II, p.59; T. Paine, *Common Sense* (1776), (New York: Penguin, 1986).
34. A. Lincoln, Annual Message to Congress, 1 December 1862, quoted in D. Brogan, 'The Last Best Hope', *Spectator*, 29 August 1970, 212.
35. Brogan, 'The Last Best Hope', 212.
36. *Ibid.*, 212.
37. D. Brogan, 'A Separation of Powers', *London Calling: Overseas Journal of the BBC*, 9 June 1955, 4.
38. G.K. Chesterton, *What I Saw in America* (New York: Dodd, Mead and Company, 1922), p.7.
39. W.R. Brock, *The Character of American History*, 2nd edn (London: Macmillan, 1965), p.62.
40. P.J. Parish, *The American Civil War* (London: Eyre Methuen, 1975), p.20.
41. H.G. Nicholas, *The American Union: A Short History of the U.S.A.* (London: Christophers, 1948), p.303. I am indebted, for this reference, to M. Heale's essay 'The British Discovery of American History and the Atlantic Connection', delivered at the 50th anniversary conference of the British Association for American Studies, Cambridge, April 2005.
42. W.R. Brock, *An American Crisis: Congress and Reconstruction, 1865–1867* (London: Macmillan, 1963), p.vii.
43. *Ibid.*, p.34.
44. D. Brogan, *The American Character* (1944), (New York: Knopf, 1950), p.169.
45. L. Marx, 'Thoughts on the Origin and Character of the American Studies Movement', *American Quarterly* XXXI (1979) 400.
46. H. Temperley and M. Bradbury, 'Introduction', *Introduction to American Studies*, 3rd edn, (Harlow: Addison Wesley Longman, 1998), p.6.
47. J.M. Colombani, *Le Monde*, 12 September 2001.
48. 'Gore Comes Out Swinging on Iraq: San Francisco, September 23, 2002', CBS News.com, http://www.cbsnews.com/stories/2002/09/23/politics/printable523030.shtml

49. Sandra Day O'Connor, quoted in L.Greenhouse, 'A Nation Challenged: The Supreme Court', *New York Times*, 29 September 2001, B5.
50. Quoted in 'Ashcroft: Critics of New Terror Measures Undermine Effort', CNN.Com, 7 December 2001, http://www.cnn.com/2001/US/12/06/inv.ashcroft.hearing/
51. 'Remarks by the President at the Signing of H.R. 5005, the Homeland Security Act of 2002', The White House home page, http://www.whitehouse.gov/news/releases/2002/11/20021125-6.html
52. W. Safire, 'You Are a Suspect', *New York Times*, 14 November 2002.
53. 'ACLU's Latest Ads Highlight New Law Enforcement Powers To Conduct Secret "Sneak and Peek" Searches of Private Homes.' News Release, 15 April 2003, ACLU web site, http://www.aclu.org/SafeandFree/SafeandFree.cfm?ID=12380&c=206
54. N. Chang, 'How Democracy Dies: The War on Our Civil Liberties', in C. Brown, ed., *Lost Liberties: Ashcroft and the Assault on Personal Freedom* (New York: The New Press, 2003), pp.33–51.
55. R. Feingold, 'On the Anti-Terrorism Bill', quoted in Chang, 'How Democracy Dies', p.34. For other works chronicling opposition to the government measures prompted by the 9/11 attacks, see W. Schulz, *Tainted Legacy: 9/11 and the Ruin of Human Rights* (New York: Thunder's Mouth Press, 2003); N. Hentoff, *The War on the Bill of Rights and the Gathering Resistance* (New York: Seven Stories Press, 2003); and D. Cole, *Enemy Aliens: Double Standards and Constitutional Freedoms in the War on Terrorism* (New York: The New Press, 2003).
56. D.E. Murphy, 'Some Librarians Use Shredder to Show Opposition to New F.B.I. Powers', *New York Times*, 7 April 2003, A12.
57. ACLU 'National Security' web page, ACLU web site, http://www.aclu.org/NationalSecurity/NationalSecurityMain.cfm
58. John Adams to Thomas Jefferson, 30 June 1813, in L.J. Cappon, ed., *The Adams-Jefferson Letters: The Complete Correspondence Between Thomas Jefferson and Abigail and John Adams* (Chapel Hill, NC: University of North Carolina Press, 1959), II, pp.346–7.
59. Paine, *Common Sense*, p.63.
60. Ex parte Milligan, 71 U.S. 2 (1866).
61. N. Garland, Opinion Cartoon, *Daily Telegraph*, 5 July 2005.
62. N. Garland, 'UK Political Cartoonists Observing America', lecture delivered at conference on 'Cartooning the USA: American Through the Pen of Political Cartoonists', organized and hosted by the Eccles Centre for American Studies, the British Library, London.
63. Quoted in S.M. Lipset, *American Exceptionalism: A Double Edged Sword* (New York: Norton, 1996), p.18.
64. F.S. Fitzgerald, *The Great Gatsby* (1926), (Harmondsworth, Middlesex: Penguin, 1978), p.187; W.S. Burroughs, 'Thanksgiving Day, Nov. 28, 1986', *Tornado Alley* (Cherry Valley, NY: Cherry Valley Press, 1989), p.2.

5

The Relevance of the American Revolution in Hungarian History from an East-Central-European Perspective

Csaba Lévai

The American Revolution has not always played a significant role in East-Central-European history, but at certain key points in the last two and a quarter centuries it has served as an important point of reference.[1] Just like western Europeans, the inhabitants of East-Central-Europe have always interpreted the American Revolution according to their own beliefs and needs. On the one hand they have regarded the Revolution as not just an important chapter in the history of the United States of America, but also in the history of all mankind. Thus Hungarian historians of the eighteenth-century have examined how the American Revolution, as an integral part of world history, has indirectly affected Hungarian history. However, this is the standpoint of an outsider, and while it does not mean that historians from East-Central-Europe develop more objective or detached opinions of the American Revolution than do their American colleagues, these historians are less involved with or connected to the events and consequences of the Revolution than are scholars in the United States.

On the other hand, historians from East-Central-Europe have on occasion argued for the existence of far more direct and consequential links between the American Revolution and their own countries. In this case they mostly interpret it from the point of view of a given problem or situation in East-Central-European history. These historians feel a far greater sense of connection with the American Revolution because most seek to use it as a positive example for their own countrymen and women.

In practice, most East-Central-European historians have employed elements of both approaches. However, this essay will focus on the latter approach, and will explore how and why the American Revolution has been viewed in different ways and for different reasons in Hungarian history in particular, and in East-Central-European history more generally. This essay will explore six periods (the eighteenth-century, the first half of the nineteenth-century, the second half of the nineteenth century, The First World War and the interwar period, and the era of the communist regimes), but with a particular focus on the first two periods.[2]

The eighteenth century

If one compares the position of Hungary within the Habsburg Empire with the position of the mainland colonies in North America within the British Empire during the eighteenth-century, many interesting similarities can be found. Before the reforms of Maria Theresa (1740–80) and especially Joseph II (1780–90), Hungary enjoyed a relatively high degree of autonomy and self-government within the empire. The current ruler of the empire was also the monarch of Hungary, a nation that had its own legislative body, the Hungarian Diet. The mainland colonies in North America also enjoyed high levels of self-government within the British Empire. The British monarch was the ruler of the colonies, but they also had their own legislative bodies. While the imperial governments in Vienna and London enjoyed ultimate authority over these local legislative bodies, it was in the interest of the imperial governments to rule benignly through them. Thus until the reforms of Maria Theresa and Joseph II in Hungary, and of George III's government after 1763 in North America, imperial rulers and local populations enjoyed a relatively harmonious and mutually beneficial relationship. The North American colonies, as well as Hungary, profited from participation in the imperial structures. Both needed imperial military assistance for example, against the Turks and the French respectively. These similarities existed despite enormous differences between political structures. In the Hungarian Diet only the traditional estates (the nobility, the Catholic clergy, and the inhabitants of the so-called royal free towns) were represented, and they constituted a small minority of the total population. While it is true that local elites had considerable power over the colonial assemblies of British North America, these governments were nonetheless far more representative.[3]

Both empires were deeply involved in the international conflicts of the eighteenth-century and once again Hungarian and North American elites shared common views of these imperial wars. Both supported the war efforts of the empires, but always with their own local needs and objectives in mind. The consequences of the Seven Years' War were also similar in Hungary and North America. The British government initiated a new policy towards the colonies at the end of the war in order to reorganize the structure of the enlarged empire. The Viennese court experimented along very similar lines in order to mobilize the resources of the empire in an effort to secure victory in ensuing conflicts. Both states became severely indebted, and in order to raise revenue, post-war imperial governments tried to invent more efficient governmental structures. In doing so, the Viennese and British governments kept in view the ideal of a more centralized and unified empire, reconstructed and organized for the benefit of the imperial centres.[4]

The economic policies of both empires were inspired mainly by mercantilism. In mercantilist theory, the value of an empire was defined by its utility as both a supplier of raw materials and a market for finished products. To these ends, the British government had introduced several measures to regulate colonial economy during the seventeenth and the first half of the eighteenth centuries.[5] But such official policies had been weakened as a result of the 'salutary neglect' of the colonies by successive British governments, with the result that executive power was occasionally lax and always selective in the enforcement of legislation. This meant that the colonists enjoyed the benefits of British protection and the advantages of trade within the imperial system, while they avoided enforcement of many of the restrictions aimed at them.[6]

The Hungarian economy was in a similar position within the Habsburg Empire during the first half of the eighteenth century. The expulsion of the Turks in 1699 provided Hungary with a chance to rebuild its economy. The growing demand for foodstuffs in the more densely populated manufacturing regions of the Western Habsburg provinces stimulated Hungarian agricultural production, and this strengthening of the Habsburg Empire suited the ambitions of the Viennese court. Thus the Habsburg government, just like the British government in North America, tried to promote the sectors of Hungarian economy that seemed to be the most useful from the point of view of the imperial center. The Viennese court promoted the introduction of better methods of cultivation and animal husbandry in Hungary, and most cultivated lands were in the hands of the nobility and the Catholic Church. These developments proved to be very profitable for the privileged estates of Hungarian society. Under these circumstances local elites were ready to cooperate with the Habsburgs, and to accept the integration of the country into the empire.[7]

But under the pressure of the urgent need to reorganize the structure of their empires, both imperial governments dissolved elements of the mutually beneficial compromises of earlier years. The Viennese court introduced new tariff regulations in 1754, and made preparations for reform of the tax system. The London government also introduced new methods of raising revenue in the colonies, and began tightening imperial control of the colonies.[8] And in stark contrast to earlier periods, decision-makers in Vienna and London made it clear that they were determined to enforce the new regulations.

On both sides of the Atlantic, then, the relationship between the imperial peripheries and centers fluctuated during the eighteenth-century. The swing of the pendulum depended upon the actual balance of power between local elites and their imperial rulers. The accession of George III in 1760 and the subsequent passing of the Declaratory Act in 1766 and the Townshend Acts a year later was mirrored in the Habsburg Empire by the accession of Joseph II to the throne in 1780 and his institution of a series of reforms, clear signs that both imperial governments were determined to continue the administrative reforms that they had begun: the pendulums were swinging towards the imperial centres.

On the North American mainland the colonial assemblies were the bastions of local self-government, and thus the centers of resistance against the encroachments of the British government. In Hungary, local government and administration were managed by the county assemblies, in which the nobility alone were represented. These assemblies worked both to prevent the encroachments of the Habsburgs and also to defend the traditional privileges of the nobility. Little wonder, then, that one of the principal aims of Joseph II was to eliminate the counties from the administrative system of the country. To replace more than sixty counties he created ten districts, which were headed by loyal royal commissars. The twofold aim of this measure was to rationalize and modernize the administration of the empire, and to undermine the resistance of the Hungarian nobility. The British government also tried to weaken the North American colonial assemblies, and loyal colonial governors had conflicts with the assemblies that mirrored those between the royal commissars and the counties in Hungary.[9]

Nevertheless, not all Hungarians were hostile towards the measures of Joseph II, and the Hungarian Josephists formed a small but significant group of devoted followers. The Josephists acknowledged the relative backwardness of their homeland, and as faithful disciples of the enlightenment they had confidence in the progressive policies of an enlightened monarch. As royal commissars and other civil servants appointed directly by Joseph, Hungarian Josephists played a crucial role in Hungarian state administration during his reign, and they were shocked by the resistance of their compatriots against Joseph's 'benevolent' reforms. But they were also Hungarians who were worried about some measures of the ruler, especially the language decree and the subordination of the interests of Hungary to the ideal and reality of a centralized monarchy. The American loyalists were following the same path in revolutionary North America. They too tried to reconcile their loyalty to the mother country and to their homeland. On the other hand, loyalists constituted a much larger proportion of colonial society than the tiny fraction of Hungarian Josephists.[10]

The Hungarian nobility had a split personality. On the one hand they were eager to maintain their traditional privileges and their rule over their social inferiors, but on the other hand, they were the defenders of the country's independence against the absolutistic tendencies of the Habsburg emperors. In some ways, this kind of split personality also characterized the American colonial elite. They dominated the colonial assemblies and they were the leaders of the resistance against the new measures of the British, yet they too were eager to maintain their privileged position and thus they opposed the radicalization of the revolution.[11] In both Hungary and North America, colonial assemblies argued that they were simply defending their ancient rights and liberties against the tyrannical intrusions and innovations of their respective rulers. They emphasized that they wanted nothing more than a return to the peaceful status quo of former times.[12]

Resistance against the encroachments of the imperial centres proved to be a major catalyst of the birth of modern nationalism and national consciousness in both Hungary and British North America. Opposition to Joseph's language decree gave a major impetus to the movement for the modernization of the Hungarian language, helping to set the scene for the birth of modern Hungarian literature and science. Along similar lines, the breach with Britain forced the American colonists to try to redefine their identity. At first they had emphasized that they were the true heirs of English liberties, but after independence the colonists began to construct an American culture and context for these rights and freedoms.[13]

The resistance to the measures of Joseph II brought Hungary to the brink of an open revolt, but in contrast to the mainland colonies in North America this dissatisfaction with the policy of the imperial centre never led to an open rebellion. Under the pressure of international and domestic events, the disillusioned and mortally ill Joseph gave in. Four weeks before his death, at the end of January 1790, Joseph revoked all but a few of his decrees. His successor, Leopold, was a more tactically astute politician. Soon after his succession to his late brother's throne Leopold II (1790–92) summoned the Hungarian Diet, and their deliberations ended with a compromise based on the pre-Josephine status quo. The Hungarian estates reaffirmed the rule of the Habsburg dynasty in Hungary, while a law passed by the Diet and adopted by the king described the country as a 'free and independent kingdom', to be governed by its own laws only. Diets were to be summoned every three years and had the exclusive legislative power over taxes and recruitment.[14]

To what degree were contemporary Hungarians aware of the striking similarities between themselves and Britain's North American colonists? The popular press provides useful evidence to help answer this question. The first regular newspaper in Hungarian, the *Magyar Hírmondó* (*Hungarian Herald*) began twice-weekly publication in 1780. Between 1780 and 1782 Mátyás Rát (1749–1810) edited the newspaper in the spirit of the enlightenment. The *Magyar Hírmondó* published quite a lot of information about the final events of the War for Independence, drawing most of this information from the reports of foreign, especially German newspapers.[15]

Rát was keenly interested in the economic aspects and consequences of the war too. Owing to strict censorship he could not draw a direct parallel between the economic situation of the North American colonies and Hungary, and he used the example of Ireland and Britain's North American colonies to do no more than subtly imply that Hungary was similarly subordinated. Thus Rát explained to his readers that before the war for independence 'the Northern Americans were obliged to purchase everything exclusively from England'. He did not mention Hungary, but it was clear to readers that Hungary faced a similar situation. Rát observed that with independence the Americans had secured the opportunity to sell their goods to France or to other nations without restriction. Rát sympathized with the cause of the American revolutionaries, and while he could not express this openly, his opinions were revealed in various veiled references. When the position of the patriots was improving in the second half of 1781, Rát wrote with clear approval that 'The rebellious population of North America is not willing to surrender to England, since they were not ready to do that when their situation was not so favourable'.[16]

The universal popularity of leading American revolutionaries allowed Hungarians to express sympathy for the American cause and what it represented to them. Benjamin Franklin was far and away the best known American in contemporary Europe. Franklin had a Hungarian correspondent, János Zinner (or Czinner), a professor of statistics and world history at the Royal Academy of Kassa (Kosice, now Slovakia). In a private letter in French, Zinner could express more openly his enthusiasm for the American cause. He wrote that 'I cannot express to you the joy I feel when I hear or read about your progress in America. To confess the truth, I regard you and all the leaders of your Republic as angels whom the heavens have sent to lead and console mankind.' A few months before, Zinner tried to contact William Lee (1739–95), the first emissary of the United States to the courts of Berlin and Vienna. William Lee was received by some leading officials of the Habsburg government only as a private traveller, and the Habsburg Empire neither recognized the United States nor concluded a treaty of commerce with it. Zinner had asked for Franklin's help to support two of his works in progress on America, both in Latin. He received some materials from the 'doctor', and in order to reach a wider audience he decided to publish his work in German. Zinner's work contains forty-eight documents, with his own glosses and short biographies of the most important figures. He incorporated into his collection, not only biographies of the most famous figures as Benjamin Franklin, George Washington, Thomas Jefferson, Benedict Arnold, John Hancock, or Lafayette, but also those of less well-known persons, such as Israel Putnam and Arthur St. Clair. It is remarkable that Zinner also included in his collection an excerpt from *Common Sense*, the inflammatory radical pamphlet by Thomas Paine, although he mistakenly attributed it to Samuel Adams.[17]

While it is true that for the sake of impartiality Zinner included some British documents, in many cases these papers simply served to emphasize the greatness and the heroic efforts of the American Patriots. Zinner's assessment of the actual fighting and of the treatment that American prisoners received revealed his true sympathies: in his commentary he stressed that the British treated their American prisoners as criminals, and he described in detail how they used savage Indians against the Americans. He observed that 'civil wars are generally fought with desperate cruelty. In this war the English thought that threats and destruction would lead to victory. The Americans paid greater attention to human rights'.[18]

Zinner was one of the Hungarian Josephists who faced the dilemma of how to reconcile their desire for reforms with loyalty to their homeland. This was also true for Gergely (Gregory) Berzeviczy (1763–1822), the outstanding economic theorist of his age. By the end of the 1780s his faith in the benevolent reforms of Joseph had been shaken, and after the king's death Berzeviczy and the enlightened nobility had high hopes for the reign of Leopold, who summoned the Hungarian Diet for the first time in a quarter century. In preparing for the Diet, both the traditional nobility and the enlightened reformers tried to set the agenda. Berzeviczy was no exception. On 12 May 1789, a few months before Joseph's death, Berzeviczy delivered a speech at the Freemasons Lodge at Buda. Referring to Joseph's policy he noted that 'It is the characteristic of human nature that it takes advantage of unrestrained power, and often use it with cruelty. England, the home of liberty, where humanity and law are held in high esteem, still treated its American colonies with oppressive tyranny. I do not wish to sink into an analysis ... of whether or not what the Americans did was just. The results are validated. For us, the Americans are the embodiment of a courageous free people.' It is clear again that Berzeviczy used the example of the oppression of the American colonies by Britain as an analogy of the subordination of Hungary to the interests of Austria.[19]

He repeated this argument in another lecture delivered at the same Freemasons Lodge a few months later. In this speech Berzeviczy used the theory of the social contract to condemn Joseph's policies. According to Berzeviczy, Hungary was a free country, which tolerated Habsburg rule only on certain conditions. But, he argued, the Habsburgs had repeatedly abused and usurped Hungary's traditional rights and privileges. A 'long train of abuses and usurpations' had been brought to a head by Joseph's rule, for the monarch allegedly had destroyed the foundations of the contract between himself and the Hungarian nation. Consequently, Berzeviczy concluded, the contract was now null and void, and Hungary was no longer obliged to defer to and obey the Habsburg monarch. The logic of Berzeviczy's argument precisely parallels that of the American Declaration of Independence, a copy of which he owned in the handwriting of one of his friends.

After the death of Joseph II, Berzeviczy felt that Hungary would seize the opportunity to end the rule of the Habsburgs in Hungary. He composed a detailed analysis of the rule of the Habsburgs in Hungary in which he repeated his former arguments. Moreover, he included the American colonies on a historical list of similarly oppressed nations that included England under the Stuarts and Sweden under the rule of the Wasa dynasty. Berzeviczy pointed out that all of these countries had defended themselves successfully against the encroachments of tyranny.[20]

József Hajnóczy (1750–95) was an even more typical representative of Hungarian Josephists, but by the time of Joseph's death Hajnóczy had lost all confidence in the ruler. The ensuing constitutional debate and the convocation of the Diet also encouraged Hajnóczy to summarize his views, and in the summer of 1790 he wrote a short essay in Latin. Regarding the problem of religious tolerance, which as a Lutheran Hajnóczy considered to be of fundamental importance, he pointed out that 'political liberty cannot exist without the freedom of religion, and the first and most fundamental requirement of political liberty is the free confession of religion'. Hajnóczy had the American example in mind, since he recommended that the Hungarian Diet should adopt 'that law in its entirety, which the United States of America promulgated in 1786. It was from them that we received corn and tobacco, and lo, our native land can produce them as well. There is no doubt that this law, breathing of humanity, could take root here just the same as there, that is, it can strengthen our civic unity'.[21]

In 1791, when the Diet was in session, Hajnóczy published a detailed tract, also in Latin, about the constitutional position of Hungary. He repeated his earlier proposal concerning religious freedom almost verbatim, but now 'for the sake of those readers who don't know it' he attached the full text of the American document, which he had also translated into Latin. The Continental Congress had passed no law concerning religious freedom, and the statute referred to and translated by Hajnóczy was in fact Thomas Jefferson's Statute for Establishing Religious Freedom, enacted by the General Assembly of Virginia in 1786.[22]

Despite this error it is clear that Hajnóczy had a deep interest in the political system of the American republic. In the library of Count Ferenc Széchényi, Hajnóczy's mentor, there was a copy of János Zinners's collection of American documents. Hajnóczy was not only the Count's secretary but also his librarian, charged with the compilation of a library catalogue and the ordering of new books. In all likelihood, it was actually Hajnóczy who had ordered Zinner's collection. We also know that he asked one of his friends in Vienna to send him a book about the American constitution in 1789, and it is quite likely that Hajnóczy received such a collection, probably in French, and that he based his translation of Jefferson's statute on a French translation in that volume.[23]

The parallels between Hungary and the North American colonies were far from unique in East-Central-Europe, and while the situation in eighteenth-century Poland was quite different there were also some similarities between the two territories. Three emerging great powers (Russia, Prussia, and the Habsburg Empire) had emerged on the borders of the historic Polish-Lithuanian state. The result was three partitions of

Poland between these powerful nations in 1772, 1793 and 1795. Like Hungary, Poland had lost its independence and come under the rule of foreign powers. But in the case of Hungary, the territorial integrity of the country had been preserved, and the country could maintain some kind of semi-independent status within the Habsburg Empire. This was not the case with Poland, which simply disappeared from the map of Europe after 1795.[24]

Another important difference is that there was far more direct participation by Poles in the American Revolution. Tadeusz Andrzej Bonaventura Kosciuszko (1746–1817) proved to be one of the major military figures of the American Revolution, and he was also the leader of the Polish uprising of 1794. Kazimierz Pulaski (?1748–79) also played an important role as the organizer of his own cavalry unit, the 'Pulaski legion', and he gave his life for American independence at the siege of Savannah in 1779. In contrast, Colonel Mihály Kováts (1724–79) was the only Hungarian who played a significant role in the War for Independence. He was appointed training officer of the cavalry by George Washington, after which he joined the 'Pulaski legion'. He too gave his life for the American cause at the defense of Charleston, in the same year as Pulaski.[25]

The first partition of their country had shocked Polish intellectuals, and some of them reacted by attempting to modernize the governmental structure of Poland. The reformers introduced a new constitution in the Polish parliament, which was approved on 3 May 1791. The new constitution established a more representative body instead of the old Diet in which only the nobility and the Catholic clergy had been represented. The king remained the head of the legislative branch, but only as a kind of prime minister. Government ministers were responsible, not to the ruler, but to the legislature, and the king was required to sign the executive orders sent to him by governmental ministers. The new constitution also introduced religious tolerance. But the constitution was heavily opposed by Russia, Prussia, and by some members of the Polish aristocracy. Members of the latter made an agreement with Russia concerning military intervention, and Russian troops invaded Poland. On 23 January 1793, Russia and Prussia signed an agreement concerning the second partition of Poland. The result of the second partition was a Polish insurrection in 1794 under the leadership of Kosciuszko. But the overwhelming superiority of the Russian and Prussian troops led to the defeat of the Polish army, and the fate of the country was sealed. In October 1795, Russia, Prussia, and the Habsburg Empire wiped Poland from the map of Europe.[26]

Just as in Hungary, the American Revolution had very real resonance for Polish reformers and nationalists. During this period the *Gazeta Warszawska* (*The Warsaw Gazette*) was the only daily newspaper published in Warsaw. In the first years of the American War for Independence, the *Gazeta* gave accurate accounts of the American position, and also published translations of some important documents, such as the Declaration of the Causes and Necessity for Taking up Arms. The editor of the *Gazeta* was Stefan Luskina, who gradually came to support the American cause, and who played a major role in disseminating the political and philosophical arguments of the American patriots.[27]

Polish authors were fascinated by the governmental structure of the new United States. The Articles of Confederation were criticized by Poles whose experience of the weak central government of Poland under the old regime led them to conclude that the Continental Congress was also too weak. But representatives of different parties interpreted the lessons of the American government differently. For some 'America' was the symbol of revolt and resistance, but others used the United States to support national expansion, an improved standard of living, or even the prosperity of cities. Reformers, as well as conservatives, cited different American examples to support their political opinions. With regard to the federal constitution of 1787, Polish writers were mostly interested in the model of a functioning legislative body, and they virtually ignored the executive branch. This was probably because from the sixteenth century on the Polish parliament (in effect the nobility) had elected the monarch, a system that proved to be the source of significant political instability, and had presented neighbouring powers with greater opportunities to intervene in Polish politics. Consequently, by the eighteenth century many Poles believed that hereditary monarchy guaranteed greater stability and continuity in politics than elective leadership. One of the fundamental aims of Polish reformers was the establishment of a stable hereditary monarchy modeled on Great Britain. Consequently, many of them could not understand why the Americans had separated from a country with such good and free political institutions.[28]

During the debates in the Polish Diet about the new constitution some reformers raised the issue of a republican form of government, and they pointed to the example of the American republic. However, the majority of them argued for the advantages of the British system. As Stanislaw Malachowski, speaker of the Diet explained to his colleagues 'We have two famous republican governments in this century, that is, the English and the American, the latter improving on the faults of the former. But what will be enacted today will be better, for it takes from both what is best and most suitable to our needs.'[29]

The first half of the nineteenth century

After the outbreak of the French Revolution and the French Revolutionary and Napoleonic Wars, the compromise made by the Hungarian estates and the Habsburgs worked very well. The Habsburgs needed the revenues and the military contribution of Hungary to sustain their war efforts against France, and they summoned the Hungarian Diet five times between 1796 and 1811. The Hungarian nobility was also satisfied with the compromise of 1791, since it guaranteed their traditional privileges, and because the imperial army was in urgent need of foodstuffs produced by Hungarian agriculture. But after the final defeat of Napoleon the Habsburgs no longer required Hungarian assistance, and the Hungarian Diet was not summoned until 1825 when Francis I (1792–1835) required Hungarian recruits and taxes to suppress the revolutionary upheavals in Italy and Spain.[30]

From the last decades of the eighteenth century, the transforming hand of the industrial revolution began to change the economic and social life of Western Europe. Manufacturing and industry started to play a more and more important role in the economies of Britain, France, Germany and the United States. In most of these rapidly modernizing nations, constitutional political systems had replaced absolutist governments, but in Hungary the traditional feudal estates retained significant political power. The Hungarian economy was still dominated by the seriously underdeveloped agrarian sector, and serfdom still existed. The most enlightened members of the nobility, and also many intellectuals, realized that there was an urgent need for social, political and economic reforms. They were eager to find examples to follow, and the dynamic young American republic was a very obvious candidate for that role. The first travelogues about the United States were published in Hungarian, and the two and a half decades between 1825 and the outbreak of the Revolution of 1848 proved to be the golden age of the American Revolution and the United States as significant examples for the people of Hungary.

One book played a crucial role in the formation of the ideas of Hungarian reformers about the American Revolution and the United States: Sándor Bölöni Farkas's *Utazás Észak-Amerikában* (*Journey in North America*), which was published in 1834. Bölöni (1795–1842) visited the United States at the same time as his famous French contemporary

Alexis de Tocqueville (1805–59). Both authors were impressed by the egalitarian nature of American society and politics, but the approaches of the two travelers were quite different. Tocqueville arrived from France, one of the well-developed countries of Western Europe, which enjoyed a constitutional monarchy and a representative political system, and was benefiting from the beginnings of industrialization. Although universal male suffrage did not yet exist in France, the extension of the suffrage to the lower strata of society was one of the hotly debated issues of the era. According to Tocqueville, the extension of suffrage to all male members of society was an irresistible historical process, and as a direct result of the American Revolution the United States enjoyed a world-leading role in this process. As a result, he concluded that the mass democracy of Jacksonian America would be the destiny of European countries. As it is well known, Tocqueville criticized some effects of mass democracy, such as what he termed the 'tyranny of majority'. Tocqueville realized that Europeans should also learn from the negative side effects of American mass democracy, using the United States as a laboratory in which to study the consequences of an egalitarian political system. In stark contrast, Bölöni arrived from an underdeveloped East-Central-European country, with a semi-feudal social and political order. To him, a representative democracy seemed to be in the distant future of his and similar countries. Consequently, he praised and applauded the political democracy of the United States as a shining but not immediately relevant example for his countrymen, and he made few critical remarks, even with regard to slavery.[31]

Since the American Revolution 'gave birth' to the political system of the United States, Bölöni was deeply interested in the history of the great event. His intent was to discern the revolutionary origins of America as 'the shelter for liberty and the rights of man'. His travelogue always highlighted his arrival at an important scene of the revolution, and he devoted a whole chapter to the revolution's history. He gave detailed descriptions of the causes of the rebellion, mainly based upon the works of such American historians as David Ramsay (1749–1815). Bölöni sympathized fully with the Patriots, and he presented the American Revolution as an example for his compatriots. He published in his book the first Hungarian translation of the Declaration of Independence, and he compared this American document with various charters issued by European kings and emperors. In his opinion, the latter were simply concessions on the part of the rulers, but the American Declaration 'summons Americans to a political creation, to the framing of a just government. The language of the Declaration is not the language of diplomacy but the language of natural law.' The real significance of the Declaration to Bölöni was made clear in his private diary, in which he revealed that the 'Declaration of Independence was the most important for me in my book of three hundred and forty six pages. All the other parts are simply a frame around it.'[32]

As examples of American constitutionalism, Bölöni also published the full text of the constitution of New Hampshire and large sections of the federal constitution of 1787. His high esteem of the latter is clear from the following story. While aboard a ship on Lake Erie he met a Hungarian immigrant called Ferenc Müller, who was full of enthusiasm for his new homeland. In his book Bölöni printed in italics Müller's heartfelt wish that 'if only the American Constitution could be planted in Hungary, then it would be the happiest land on earth.'[33]

Bölöni also visited Mount Vernon, and while contemplating the burial place of George Washington there 'flashed through my mind America's sufferings and struggle, its triumphant happy present, and rich legacy to mankind. I felt my heart pound. The man in front of whose earthly remains we stood played enormous role in all this. Only the cool counsel of reason kept me from prostrating myself before his grave'. He had the same feelings at the monument to Kosciuszko at West Point, and his words clearly express the significance of the great East-Central-European martyr to liberty: 'Rest in peace, Kosciuszko, ye guardian of Liberty and humanity. Your memorial is simple. Yet looking at it, the traveler feels his heart beat faster, for he remembers liberty and the rights of man.'[34]

Bölöni's work proved to be a tremendous success in contemporary Hungary. The one thousand copies of the first edition sold out in a few months, as did the additional thousand copies of the second edition that were published a year later. But after the second edition the work was placed on the index of prohibited books. Nevertheless, the author was elected a member of the Hungarian Academy, and many if not all of the significant Hungarian reformist liberal politicians read it, including count István Széchenyi (1791–1860), the first leading theorist and political figure of the Age of Reforms (1825–48).

In Széchenyi's opinion, Bölöni's book 'is filled to the brim with such excellence and communicated to the reader with such interest and lucidity and care that the blessed seed which sprouts from it would blossom endlessly in far worse soil even than ours'.[35] He had a very high opinion of the 'blossoming child', as he labeled the young American republic. In fact Széchenyi brought up the subject of the United States in company so often and so passionately that he was referred to as 'der Americane' behind his back.[36]

Széchenyi was mostly impressed by the rapid economic progress of the United States, but he also made very interesting direct references to the American Revolution. He ranked Washington and Franklin among the most important figures of history. In Milan an Italian manufacturer once referred to him as 'the Hungarian Washington': Széchenyi was deeply touched by these words and replied 'I wish it could be true, Sir'. As a young man he was especially attracted by the life and work of Franklin. Referring to the works of the 'doctor', he noted that 'In a flowering and fruitful country the life of an industrious citizen is indeed a wonderful life, because all his actions on behalf of his homeland are praised and rewarded ... I was not granted such a homeland'. But Széchenyi knew the works of other leaders of the American Revolution too. He included Jefferson's manual on parliamentary procedure among the books he wanted to read, and it became a much well thumbed volume in his library. He applauded the ideas of John Adams as well, who he believed was 'fired by an enthusiasm towards public good.'[37]

Lajos Kossuth (1802–94), who in the 1840s took over the lead of the liberal reformist movement, was also an admirer of Bölöni's book. He used the example of American institutions in connection with the reform of the administrative system of Hungary, and when considering taxation. He admired the separation of state and church as a particularly important consequence of the American Revolution. In the Hungarian Diet only the Catholic Church had official representation, in a country of which 30 per cent of the population belonged to Protestant denominations, and Kossuth himself was Lutheran. He approvingly noted that 'With respect to constitutional law ... it is undeniable that the American laws have drawn a rather healthy limit on the power of the Church'.[38]

The European revolutions of 1848 gave an opportunity for the Hungarians to establish an independent country with a liberal, representative government, and the shared common ruler remained the only tie between the country and the Habsburg Empire. But Habsburg troops launched an attack against Hungary in September 1848. After desperate months of retreat, the Hungarian army launched a successful counterattack in the spring of the following year. During the days of the revolution and war for independence, many Hungarians made repeated references to the example of the American Revolution, including members of a radical republican minority. The power and significance of the American Revolution for Hungarians became clear to see in the influence that the American Declaration of Independence had on the birth of the Hungarian Declaration of Independence in the spring of 1849.[39]

The circumstances leading to the creation of these two declarations were somewhat similar. The Second Continental Congress as well as the Hungarian Parliament was divided in respect to the question of independence. However, in the end these documents were adapted unanimously, although in both countries some delegates voted for it with less than full confidence in the outcome of their cause. The circumstances of war and the pressure of the masses helped the supporters of independence in both countries to convince some of the delegates to vote for it, or at least to abstain.[40]

It was far from a coincidence that, just like the Second Continental Congress, the Hungarian Parliament nominated a committee of five to compose the text of their declaration of independence. And just as in the case of the American declaration, the Hungarian document was largely the work of one man. In the case of the American colonies that person was Thomas Jefferson, while it was Lajos Kossuth who drafted the text of the Hungarian declaration.[41]

There are striking similarities in the structure, construction and language of the two documents. The Hungarian declaration roughly follows the logic of its American counterpart. One can divide both documents into three parts. The first sentence of the Declaration of Independence declared that 'a decent respect to the opinions of mankind requires that they should declare the causes which impel them to the separation'. The Hungarian parliament also felt it necessary 'to declare the reasons of our resolution before the decent world'. The Second Continental Congress based its argument for independence on the theory of natural law. So too did the framers of the Hungarian document, who declared that the fundamental aim of the declaration was to 'give back to Hungary its unalienable natural rights'.[42]

In the second and longest part of the Declaration of Independence, Congress sought to establish the legality of their separation from Britain by enumerating the 'long train of abuses and usurpations' committed by the British king and government. The framers of the Hungarian declaration did very much the same, enumerating the crimes that the Habsburg dynasty had committed against the Hungarian nation. The only difference was that Kossuth compiled an even longer list of 'abuses and usurpations' than his American colleague, because he could go back to the origins of the rule of the Habsburg dynasty in Hungary in the sixteenth century. Independence was finally declared in the third part of the American document. The Hungarian Parliament did the same, and the Hungarian legislators referred again to the 'unalienable natural rights' of Hungarians. This part of the Hungarian declaration is longer than the corresponding section of the American document, in part because the Hungarian Parliament was not just removing Hungary's king, but dethroning the entire Habsburg dynasty.[43]

Kossuth and the leaders of the Hungarian Revolution were very well informed about the political system of the United States. Besides the publication of the Hungarian translation of the Declaration of Independence, Bölöni had described the cult of the document as he had experienced it throughout the United States. In addition, in May 1848 a new translation of the Declaration of Independence and the full text of the federal constitution were published in Hungary. Many of the leaders, including Kossuth himself, could speak English, and there is no doubt that Kossuth tried to make use of both the structure and the logic of the American Declaration of Independence. The similarity between the two documents was so striking that Kossuth's political opponents accused him simply of adapting the text of the American document. It is surely significant that Kossuth felt it necessary to send a copy of the Hungarian declaration to Zachary Taylor (1784–1850), the president of the United States of America.[44]

But despite the similarities between these two documents, they fared very differently. The Hungarian War for Independence was defeated by the joint effort of the imperial armies of Austria and Russia. Consequently, in contrast to its American counterpart, the Hungarian declaration failed, and thus could not become the sacred founding document of an independent nation. Furthermore, the controversial circumstances surrounding its adoption made it even more unlikely that a cult of the Hungarian Declaration of Independence would develop along the lines of the American one.

While the situation in Poland was quite different to that in Hungary, some Poles also looked to the American Revolution for inspiration. Napoleon helped to revive the Polish state in the form of the short-lived Grand Duchy of Warsaw, but after the defeat of the French emperor it was not in the interests of the victorious great powers to restore the independent kingdom of Poland. The only concession they made was the creation of a semi-autonomous Kingdom of Poland within the Russian Empire. By the late-1820s, however, their Russian rulers were undermining what little autonomy the Poles enjoyed, which helped trigger the Polish insurrection of 1830–31.[45]

Some Polish writers tried to learn a lesson from the defeat of their revolt in 1794, and they highlighted the successful American Revolution as an example of how to avoid such defeat. One of them was József Pawlikowski, whose work was published after the outbreak of the insurrection in 1830. For him, the American Revolution was a shining example of a successful popular insurrection. He suggested that just like the American Patriots, the Poles could take advantage of the international conflicts between the great European powers, and that like the Americans they could exploit the conflict between France and Britain.[46]

Julian Ursyn Niemcewicz had been one of Kosciuszko's aides during the insurrection of 1794 and had accompanied the general on his voyage back to the United States. Like Bölöni, Niemcewicz was attracted by the egalitarian nature of American society and politics. Referring to his visit to the governor of Connecticut, Niemcewicz echoed Bölöni by stating that 'This visit allowed me to understand the genuine simplicity of the customs, the real equality that exists in a free country. The governor, the highest official in the state, tills his land himself. Would that our contemporary democrats followed his example.'[47]

The Polish insurrection of 1830–31 and the Hungarian Revolution and War for Independence in 1848–49 had certain features and consequences in common, including popular disillusionment occasioned by the failure of the liberal great powers to help the oppressed people of East-Central-Europe. In the case of Hungary this disillusionment rarely extended to the United States, since the Hungarian public was aware of the fact that the United States sympathized with the Hungarian cause, although the American government was not in the position to give any kind of assistance. Hungarians also knew that many participants in their own revolution subsequently found refuge in the United States where they were well received, like Kossuth himself during his famous tour in America in 1851–52. However, Kossuth eventually left America somewhat more disheartened, since the American government and people were more focused on and diverted by slavery than they were interested in supporting the Hungarian cause. According to Eugene Kusielewicz, Poles were more likely to be disillusioned by the United States, despite the fact that 'many prominent Americans, including Samuel F. B. Morse, Ralph Waldo Emerson and Samuel Gridley Howe, did what they could to assist the insurrectionists'. Nevertheless, such major figures as the famous poets Adam Mickiewicz (1798–1855) and Cyprian Norwid (1821–83) gave voice to this bitterness and disenchantment. The values of the two societies appeared to be quite different, and many Polish immigrants came to the conclusion that Americans were much more interested in business than the liberation of oppressed people.[48]

The second half of the nineteenth century

The declining power of the Habsburg monarchy in international politics in the decades after the Hungarian revolution forced the leaders of the empire to once again reach a compromise with the Hungarians. The result was the birth of the Austro-Hungarian Monarchy in 1867. Hungary became an equal partner with Austria in this dual state, and a parliamentary monarchy with a liberal, representative government was established. The economy also started to grow, and for many Hungarians these developments promised the fulfillment of the fundamental goals of the Age of Reform and the Revolution of 1848. Most of the political exiles returned to Hungary, except for Kossuth and a handful of others. Consequently, the American Revolution became less relevant for most Hungarians. As the nineteenth century progressed, the American Revolution became ever more distant, both in time and as an intellectual and ideological influence. In the eyes of the younger generation the American Revolution in particular and indeed revolutions in general became all but irrelevant.[49]

However, the beginning of the mass emigration of Hungarians to North America in the 1880s once again drew attention to the United States. America became increasingly attractive to many Hungarians and other inhabitants of the Kingdom of Hungary, but these people were inspired mainly by economic opportunities and not by the ideals of the American Revolution. Furthermore, many Hungarian intellectuals and politicians criticized heavily the mass emigration. However, there were a few occasions in this period when the inheritance of the American Revolution played an important role in the development of American-Hungarian relations. More and more Hungarian Americans were eager to identify themselves with their new homeland, but they also tried to preserve their Hungarian identity. And one of the key and most revealing ways in which they expressed this dual identity was in the erection of a monument to the great hero of the American Revolution, George Washington, in Budapest. They began fund-raising in the United States, and the statue was unveiled in a prominent position in the City Park in 1906. It is clear that for them, George Washington represented the embodiment of both American ideals, and of the ideals of Hungarians on both sides of the Atlantic.[50]

In Poland, despite disillusionment following the defeat of the insurrection of 1830–31, the lack of an independent Polish state meant that a romantic, idealistic approach to America and the American Revolution did not disappear. Stefan Buszczynski is a good example. In a work commemorating the centenary of American independence, he declared that the American Declaration of Independence had 'opened a new chapter in the history of man'.[51]

Then came the defeat of the insurrection of 1863 and as a result the so-called Polish positivists came to the conclusion that armed revolt was not the solution to the problems facing their country. They thought that the systematic economic and cultural development of the nation was more important than the waste of life occasioned by rebellions. Consequently, like many of their Hungarian contemporaries, they became mainly interested in the economic development and the social structure of the United States. The letters of the famous writer Henryk Sienkiewicz (1846–1916), written from America between 1876 and 1878, are very good examples of this approach. As Eugene Kusielewicz put it, for him 'the merit of the Revolution was that it had established not merely a democratic state but also democratic customs, based on respect for all forms of socially useful work'. Sienkiewicz had a positive opinion of the United States that emphasized a wider array of virtues of American life than had his more romantic predecessors.[52]

The First World War and the interwar years

The First World War had very different consequences for Hungary and Poland. For Hungarians it meant not only the collapse of the Austro-Hungarian Monarchy, but also the disintegration of the one thousand years old historical Kingdom of Hungary. The Peace Treaty of Trianon (1920) deprived Hungary of two-thirds of its former territory and nearly 60 per cent of its population, including 30 per cent of ethnic Hungarians. In stark contrast, the defeat of the Central Powers and the outbreak of the Russian Revolution provided the opportunity for the Poles to re-establish the independent Polish state. The United States was the ally of victorious France and Britain, and President Woodrow Wilson was one of the three major players at the Versailles peace conference.

Wilson sought to impose his interpretation of the founding ideals of the American republic on post-war Europe. In his famous Fourteen Points he used the ideal of national self-determination to argue for the re-establishment of the Polish state on the one hand, and for independence and self-determination for the nations of the former Austro-Hungarian monarchy on the other hand. Consequently, Wilson, and his recapitulation of the ideals of the American Revolution were applauded in Poland. In 1917 Tadeusz Korzon, a well-known representative of the Polish Positivists, organized a celebration honouring the hundredth anniversary of Kosciuszko's death. He declared that 'if the principles of the American Revolution were not espoused generally the causes of the tragedy of World War I would never be eliminated'. The Hoover Relief Commission provided significant aid in the establishment of Poland, and many Americans supported the war efforts of the young Polish state against Soviet Russia. Not surprisingly, then, the accounts of the American Revolution written by Polish historians during the interwar-period were very positive. Henryk Mosicki for example, delivered a speech on the one hundred and fiftieth anniversary of American independence in 1926, in which he argued for a direct connection between the American Revolution and the ideas of President Wilson that had resulted in the re-establishment of Poland. This positive attitude did not change after the *coup d'état* of Józef Pilsudski (1867–1935) in the same year, but more emphasis was subsequently laid on the conservative, less democratic features of the American Revolution, such as the constitutional convention of 1787.[53]

In contrast, Wilson appeared to be a villain to many in Hungary who believed that he had played a crucial role in the disintegration of their nation. As a result of a bloodless revolution in the autumn of 1918, liberal politicians came into power who criticized vehemently the political system of the Austro-Hungarian Monarchy, and the participation of Hungary in the war on the side of Germany. Naturally, they attached great hopes to a fair peace promised by the American president. They could not solve the tremendous social, political and economic problems of the country, and as a result a pro-Soviet regime came into power in the March of 1919. But it proved to be very short-lived, and the troops of Admiral Miklós Horthy (1868–1957) overthrew it with the help of the armies of the allied powers. Horthy and his supporters blamed the revolutions for the loss of the war and the collapse of the historic kingdom. This was compounded by the propaganda of the victorious counter-revolutionaries who suggested that the Peace Treaty of Trianon had been imposed upon Hungary as a punishment for the revolutions, the leaders of which were condemned as Wilsonians. Even though France and Britain overruled Wilson in their reshaping of the Treaty of Versailles, the Hungarians nonetheless held the American president responsible and grew disillusioned with the ideas he had articulated. The American Revolution, and all that it represented, became almost completely irrelevant in inter-war Hungary.[54]

The two countries played different roles again in the Second World War. Poland was eliminated by the Soviet Union and Nazi Germany in 1939, but Hungary was able to regain some of its territories through the help of the Axis powers. Consequently, Hungary lost the war as an ally of Germany while Poland finished it as a victorious country. Hungary was the enemy and Poland the ally of the United States. But in the end this mattered little, since both nations fell under the influence of the Soviet Union, and by the end of the 1940s the communist parties ruled both Hungary and Poland.[55]

The rise and fall of the communist regimes

During the Cold War the American republic became the leading power of the so-called free world, and as a result, gradually re-emerged as a positive example and symbol of those ideals that were inaccessible to Hungarians. Due to the oppressed position of the people, and the serious lack of information, Hungarians started to develop a fundamentally positive but highly idealized picture of the United States, despite communist propaganda that suggested, for example, Coca Cola was a dangerous drug employed by bourgeois imperialists to keep American youth under control.

The American Revolution did not play a significant role during the anti-communist insurrection of 1956, and the rebels considered the Hungarian Revolution of 1848–49 as their prime inspiration. The United States did not help the Hungarian freedom fighters, and the defeat of the revolt caused some disappointment with the failure of the world's most powerful nation to help Hungarians achieve freedom and self-determination. But during the ensuing thirty years America once again became the embodiment of the free world. In Western Europe Coca Cola and McDonalds became the symbols of American imperialism, and political and military hegemony. But in Hungary they were considered as emblems of freedom. The first public sales of Coca Cola in Hungary at the end of the 1960s, and the opening of Hungary's first McDonald restaurant in Budapest in 1986 were thus important cultural and even political events. While Coca Cola was not the dangerous drug that communist propaganda had claimed, young Hungarians felts that they tasted freedom when they consumed the same drink as Elvis Presley, and listened to American pop and rock music.[56]

From the beginning of the 1950s it was forbidden to publish evaluations of the American Revolution that did not strictly follow the Marxist-Leninist interpretation of the great event. The problem for Hungarian and Polish Marxist historians was that it was not easy to fit the American Revolution into this ideological framework. Was it, like the French Revolution, a 'bourgeois revolution' that destroyed feudalism and created the preconditions for capitalist development, or was it the first anti-colonialist uprising? But there was no feudalism in North America in the European sense of the word, so there was no ancien regime to bring down. And if it was fundamentally a movement for independence, led by colonial bourgeoisie to make them free from exploitation by British capitalists, what kind of role had the mass of working people played? Marxist historians struggled to find solutions to these dilemmas, mainly with the help of the Marxist interpretation of the French Revolution, according to which the Jacobins represented the most progressive political movement because they worked hardest to destroy the structure of feudalism. The moderate bourgeoisie had been terrified by the active political role of working people, and they had brought down the Jacobin regime and thus consolidated capitalist rule.

In the case of the American Revolution, Marxist historians applied a similar logic, arguing that Shays Rebellion in Massachusetts had been the final example of revolutionary political activity by the masses, which had terrified the moderate bourgeoisie. A counter-revolutionary reaction forced the new federal constitution on the masses, excluding them from political power and consolidating capitalist rule. This interpretation was laid out in a two-volume history of the United States written by Soviet authors in the late 1950s, which was published in Hungarian in 1964. This approach was then echoed in a volume by the Hungarian historian László Solti, who analyzed the different interpretations of the constitutional convention of 1787. The approach of these Marxist historians to the American Revolution was essentially positive, since they considered it to be a fundamentally progressive event in the history of mankind, which established a pure capitalist economy and society in the United States, and thus helped to create the preconditions for socialist revolution. From the different schools of American historiography the progressive approach of Charles A, Beard proved to be the closest to this Marxist interpretation, and Beard's greatest work was applauded by Solti, and published in Hungary in 1988.[57]

Until the collapse of the socialist regime at the end of the 1980s this remained the official interpretation of the American Revolution in Hungary. Nevertheless, a gradual change was evident from the late 1960s onwards. On the bicentennial of American independence in 1976, a small volume by Ervin Szuhay-Havas was published. The author followed the official interpretation, but he tried to avoid ideological issues and concentrated on such topics as the military history of the revolution or the everyday life of the colonist. Aladár Urbán published a collection of fundamental texts of American history in Hungarian in

1981, including such important documents of the revolution as the Declaration of the Causes and Necessity of Taking Up Arms, The Treaty of Alliance with France and many others. The Hungarian publication of Charles A. Beard's classic mentioned above, was also the sign of this gradual change. By giving Hungarian students the documents that had expressed the revolutionary ideals of the Patriots, these historians enabled Hungarians to develop their own opinions about freedom, liberty and popular rights.[58]

According to Eugene Kusielewicz, post-war Polish historians faced a similar dilemma. There was a debate in Polish historiography over just how revolutionary the American Revolution had been. Wladislaw Rusinski argued that 'the American War of Independence wrought no change in the existing economic and social structure of the country.' Similarly, Slawomir Sierecki suggested that George Washington was not the leader of a social revolution, but rather of an anti-colonial war for independence. On the other side of the debate, Henryk Katz argued that there was a real 'upheaval in political, economic and social relations occasioned by the war ... Thanks to these changes, the lower and middle classes in the United States were freed from the insupportable burden of lay and spiritual feudal authority'. But overall, just like their Hungarian colleagues, Polish historians' interpretations written during the socialist regime 'on the whole have been fairly favorable, even in the writings of Marxist historians'.[59]

For many leading intellectuals, the American Revolution once again became revolutionary during the collapse of the communist regime in Hungary. The American Revolution came to be seen as representing a moderate change of regime in contrast with the violence of the French and the Russian Revolutions. In Hungary, the reformist wing of the communist party, as well as the opposition, strove for a peaceful constitutional transformation. Consequently, the example of the birth of the United States, and especially the processes of constitution-making was compelling. Hungarians had to face the same problem the American Founding fathers had confronted two centuries earlier: how to establish a functioning democracy? The Declaration of Independence, the Federal Constitution of 1787 and various other documents had already been translated into Hungarian, and these were now joined by several essential texts of early American political thought including the Articles of Confederation and the Federalist Papers, as well as key writings by leading figures of the American Revolution such as Thomas Jefferson, John Adams, James Madison and Alexander Hamilton. Three general histories of the United States were published in four years, and Aladár Urbán wrote the first detailed account of the political history of the American Revolution written by a Hungarian historian. Several doctoral students decided to write their dissertation about the history of the American Revolution, and classes about the colonial era and the revolutionary period were packed with students.[60]

But now, fifteen years after the collapse of the communist regime this early enthusiasm has faded, and most history students consider the American Revolution as an important, but not especially relevant event. The younger generation have grown up in, and thus do not find remarkable, a democratic and pluralist society and culture. Furthermore, the United States is no longer as popular in East-Central-Europe as it was fifteen years ago. Due to the two Gulf Wars and the discriminatory visa policy of the American government, the United States appears to many Hungarians as the symbol of globalization, worldwide imperialism and greed. Hollywood movies such as *The Patriot* or *National Treasure* could attract some interest in the Founding period of the American republic, but most Hungarian spectators are more interested in adventure and the films' stars than they are in the events and ideals of the American Revolution, events and ideals that over the past two and one-quarter centuries have had real and important effects in Hungary.

Notes

1. According to Jenő Szűcs, East-Central-Europe consists of the territories of the historical kingdoms of Hungary, Bohemia and Poland, and the German lands east of the river Elbe. East-Central-Europe integrates into a coherent unit some elements of the historical development of Eastern Europe (Russia and the Balkans) on the one hand, and Western Europe on the other. J. Szűcs, 'The Three Historical Regions of Europe: An Outline', in J. Keane, ed., *Civil Society and the State: New European Perspectives* (London: Verso, 1988) pp.291–332.
2. For the best account of the relevance of the American Revolution in East-Central-Europe see: B.K. Király and G. Bárány, eds, *East-Central-European Perceptions of Early America* (Dordrecht: The Peter De Ridder Press, 1977).
3. J.P. Greene, *Peripheries and Center: Constitutional Development in the Extended Politics of the British Empire and the United 1607–1788*, (New York: W.W. Norton, 1990), pp.7–76. I.K. Steele, 'The Anointed, the Appointed, and the Elected: Governance of the British Empire, 1689–1784', in P.J. Marshall, ed., *The Oxford History of the British Empire: The Eighteenth Century* (Oxford: Oxford University Press, 1998), pp.105–27.
4. C. Bonwick, *The American Revolution* (Charlottesville, VA: University Press of Virginia, 1991), pp.69–77; P. Lucas, *American Odyssey, 1607–1789* (Englewood Cliffs, NJ: Prentice-Hall, 1984), pp.212–18.
5. For example the Navigation Acts of 1651, 1660, 1663, 1673, the Wool Act of 1699, the Trade Act of 1705, the Hat Act of 1732, the Molasses Act of 1733,

and the Iron Act of 1750. On British mercantilist policy see J. Hughes, *American Economic History* (Boston, MA: HarperCollins, 1990), pp.65–81.

6. On mercantilism and salutary neglect see, Lucas, *American Odyssey*, pp.57–72, 127–42.

7. L. Kontler, *Millennium in Central Europe: A History of Hungary*, (Budapest: Atlantisz, 1999), pp.191–2, 197–201, 209–11.

8. For example: the Proclamation of 1763, the American Revenue or Sugar Act of 1764, and the Stamp Act of 1765.

9. On the colonial assemblies see for example, Greene, *Peripheries and Center*, pp. 19–76. Lucas, *Amereican Odyssey*, pp.169–76. On the role of the counties in Hungary see: Kontler, *Millennium*, pp.215–17.

10. On the Hungarian Josephists see Kontler, *Millennium*, pp.212–13. In 1784 Joseph II ordered that German was to become the official language of the empire, except the Austrian Netherlands, Italy and Galicia. In Hungary German was to be introduced to the central adminsitration immediately, to the counties after a year and to other offices and courts within three years. Any public servant unable to master it within the given period would be dismissed. On the language decree see T.C.W. Blanning, *Joseph II* (London and New York: Longman, 1996), p.70. On the role of colonial governors see, Greene, *Peripheries and Center*, pp.21–2, 34–42, 46–7.

11. Bonwick, *American Revolution*, pp.38–42, 45–8, 61–5, 112–14, 126–9, 197–198. On the Hungarian nobility see, Kontler, *Millennium*, pp.198–200.

12. B. Bailyn, *The Ideological Origins of the American Revolution*, (Cambridge, MA: Harvard University Press, 1967); G.S. Wood, *The Creation of the American Republic 1776–1787*, (Chapel Hill, NC: University of North Carolina Press, 1969); G. Barany, 'Hoping Against Hope: The Enlightened Age in Hungary', *American Historical Review*, LXXVI (1971) 319–57.

13. J.P. Greene, 'Empire and Identity from the Glorious Revolution to the American Revolution', in P. J.Marshall, ed., *Oxford History of the British Empire*, pp. 208–30; Kontler, *Millennium*, pp.215–16.

14. Kontler, *Millennium*, pp.217–20.

15. Gy. Kókay, *A magyar hírlap és folyóirat irodalom kezdetei 1780–1795* (Budapest: Akadémiai, 1970) pp.68–177.

16. Kókay, *A magyar hírlap*, pp.104.

17. Jean Charles Zinnern to Benjamin Franklin, 26 October 1778, in Claude A. Lopez, ed., *The Papers of Benjamin Franklin, Volume 27, July through October 31, 1778* (New Haven, CT: Yale University Press, 1988) pp.646–48. On Zinner see G. Závodszky, *American Effects on Hungarian Imagination and Political Thought, 1559–1848* (Highland Lakes, NJ: Atlantic Research and Publications, Inc., 1995) pp.19–25; K. Halácsy, 'Benjamin Franklin's Image in Hungary', *The New Hungarian Quarterly*, XVII (1976) 121–5. On the mission of William Lee, see K.A. Roider, 'William Lee: Our First Envoy to Vienna', *Virginia Magazine of History and Biography*, LXXX (1978) 163–8; P. S. Fichtner, 'Viennese Perspectives on the American War of Independence', in Király and Bárány, eds, *East-Central-European Perceptions of Early America*, pp.19–29.

18. Závodszky, *American Effects*, p.21.

19. On the life and works of Berzeviczy see: É.H. Balázs, *Berzeviczy Gergely a reformpolitikus 1763–1795* (Budapest: Akadémiai, 1967). The original title in German is *Bemerkungen über Mauerey*: see Balázs, *Berzevicy Gergely*, pp.313–16.

20. The original title in German is *Über Oesterreichs Grundsätze in der Regierung Ungarns*: see Balázs, *Berzevicy Gergely*, pp.317–26.
21. The original title in Latin is *Ratio proponendarum in comitiis Hungariae legum*. On the life and works of Hajnóczy, see A. Csizmadia, *Hajnóczy József közjogi-politikai munkái*, (Budapest: Akadémia, 1958), pp.5–25, 91–2; Kontler, *Millennium*, pp.213, 219–21.
22. Csizmadia, *Hajnóczy József*, pp.160–161.
23. Gy. Kókay, 'Patrióta vagy emberbarát? Hajnóczy József és Conrad Dominik Bartsch, a *Wiener Zeitung* szerkesztoje' and 'Hajnóczy József, a Széchényi könyvtár első könyvtárosa', in Gy. Kókay, *Könyv, sajtó és irodalom a felvilágosodás korában*, (Budapest: Akadémiai, 1983), pp.82–97, 179–89.
24. With regard to eighteenth-century Poland I have relied heavily on the studies of I. M. Sokol: 'Eighteenth-Century Polish Views on American Republican Government', in Király and Bárány, eds, *East-Central-European Perceptions of Early America*, pp. 89–96; and Daniel Stone, 'Poland and the Lessons of the American Revolution', in B. K. Király, ed., *East-Central-European Society and War in the Era of Revolutions, 1775–1856* (New York: Brooklyn College Press, 1984), pp.3–10.
25. On Kosciuszko and Pulaski, see E. Halicz, 'Kosciuszko and the Historical Vicissitudes of the Kosciuszko Tradition', in Király, ed., *East-Central-European Society*, pp. 55–74. On Mihály Kováts see Závodzsky, *American Effects*, pp.16–19.
26. On the insurrection of 1794, see A. Zahorski, 'The Attitudes of the Polish Estates toward the Kosciuszko Insurrection', in Király, ed., *East-Central-European Society*, pp.75–84.
27. Sokol, 'Eighteenth-Century Polish Views', pp. 90–2.
28. *Ibid.*, pp.93–5.
29. *Ibid.*, p.95.
30. Kontler, *Millennium*, pp.222–4.
31. On Bölöni, see Závodszky, *American Effects*, pp.103–25; A. A. Reisch, 'Sándor Bölöni Farkas's Reflections on American Political and Social Instututions' in Király and Bárány, eds, *East-Central-European Perceptions of Early America*, pp.59–71; Sándor Bölöni Farkas, *Napnyugati utazás. Napló*, (Budapest: Helikon, 1984); Sándor Bölöni Farkas, *Journey in North America, 1831* (Santa Barbara, CA: ABC-CLIO, Inc., 1978); A. Tocqueville, *Democracy in America*, (London: David Campbell, 1994)
32. Bölöni, *Journey*, pp.107–10, 112–13. Bölöni, *Napnyugati utazás*, p.73.
33. Bölöni, *Journey*, p.159.
34. *Ibid.*, pp.203, 97.
35. Bölöni, *Napnyugati utazás*, p.80.
36. G. Bárány, *Stephen Széchenyi and the Awakening of Hungarian Nationalism, 1791–1841* (Princeton, NJ: Princeton University Press, 1968), pp.85–6. Závodszky, *American Effects*, pp.74–8, 92–3, 96–8, 101–5.
37. On the influence of Washington and Franklin on Széchenyi, see Barany, *Stephen Szécheny*, pp.62–3, 85–6, 98, 133, 173, 221, 330–1. On Széchenyi and Jefferson see: Závodszky, *American Effects*, p.77. On Széchenyi and John Adams, see Bárány, *Stephen Szécheny*, p.127.
38. Závodszky, *American Effects*, p. 150.
39. I. Deák, *The Lawful Revolution: Louis Kossuth and the Hungarians in 1848–1849* (New York: Columbia University Press, 1979); A. Urbán, 'A Lesson for the Old

Continent: The Image of America in the Hungarian Revolution of 1848/49', *The New Hungarian Quarterly*, XVII (1976) 85–96.

40. On the birth of the 'American Scripture' see, for example, P. Maier, *American Scripture: Making the Declaration of Independence* (New York: Random House, 1998). The session of the Hungarian Parliament was held in one of the largest church buildings of the country in Debrecen where a huge mob was also present. Under such circumstances, the delegates who opposed the resolution were not brave enough to vote against it. Kontler, *Millennium*, p.257.

41. The members of the American committee were Thomas Jefferson, John Adams, Benjamin Franklin, Roger Sherman and Robert R. Livingstone, and the members of the Hungarian committee were Lajos Kossuth, István Gorove, Mihály Horváth, Imre Szacsvay and Antal Hunkár.

42. Maier, *American Scripture*, p.236. 'A magyar nemzet függetlenségi nyilatkozata' in K. Ballai, ed., *A magyar függetlenségi nyilatkozatok története*, (Budapest: Merkantil nyomda), p.99.

43. Ballai, *A magyar függetlenségi nyilatkozatok*, p.113.

44. M.J. Fraenkel, ed., *Az Amerikai Egyesült Státusoknak Függetlenségi Nyilatkozata és Alkotmánya* (Eger: 1848); Tocqueville Elek, *A demokrácia Amerikában*, (Buda: Magyar Királyi Egyetem, 1841–1843).

45. For nineteenth- and twentieth-century Poland I relied to a great extent on E. Kusielewicz, 'Poland's Changing Attitudes Toward the American Revolution' in Király and Bárány, eds, *East-Central-European Perceptions of Early America*, pp. 97–106. On the Polish Insurrection of 1830–31, see Király, ed., *East-Central-European Society*, pp.133–215.

46. Kusielewicz, 'Poland's Changing Attitudes', p.99.

47. *Ibid.*

48. *Ibid.*, p.100. Tocqueville, who visited the United States during the era of the defeat of the Polish insurrection, also gave an account of a mass demonstration supporting the Poles, at which the speaker identified the cause of the Polish insurrection with the cause of the American Revolution. A. Tocqueville, *Democracy in America*, (London: David Campbell, 1994) pp.302. On Kossuth's visit to the United States, see S. B. Várdy, 'Hungarians in the New World. An Unorthodox History of Hungarian Americans', in B. Várdy, *Magyarok az Újvilágban*, (Budapest: A Magyar Nyelv és Kultúra Nemzetközi Társasága, 2000), pp.44–55, 737.

49. Kontler, *Millennium*, pp.264–79. K. Vörös, 'The Image of America in Hungarian Mass Culture in the Nineteenth Century', *Etudes Historiques Hongroises*, Yearbook of the Institute of History of the Hungarian Academy of Sciences, (1985) 647–61.

50. J. Puskás, 'Emigrant Hungarians in the United States, 1880–1940', in J. Puskás, ed., *Kivándorló magyarok az Egyesült Államokban 1880–1940*, (Budapest: Akadémiai, 1982), pp.629–639.

51. Kusielewicz, 'Poland's Changing Attitudes', p.102.

52. *Ibid.*

53. *Ibid.*, pp.103–4.

54. Kontler, *Millennium*, pp.325–44. On Wilson and Hungary, see T. Glant, *Through the Prism of the Habsburg Monarchy: Hungary in American Diplomacy and Public Opinion during World War I* (Boulder, CO: Social Science Monographs, 1998), pp.41–60.

122   *Csaba Lévai*

33

55. Kontler, *Millennium*, pp.364–86.
56. *Ibid.*, pp.387–468.
57. *Az Egyesült Államok története I-II*, (Budapest: Gondolat, 1964); L. Solti, *1787: Az amerikai történetírás évszázados vitájának újabb állomásai*, (Budapest: Akadémiai, 1985); C.A. Beard, *Az Egyesült Államok alkotmányának gazdasági értelmezése*, (Budapest: Európa, 1988).
58. E. Szuhay-Havas, *Tizenhárom csillag: Az amerikai forradalom rövid története*, (Budapest: Kossuth, 1976); A. Urbán, ed., *Dokumentumok az Egyesült Államok történetéhez 1774–1918*, (Budapest: Tankönyvkiadó, 1981).
59. Kusielewicz, 'Poland's Changing Attitudes', 105–6.
60. A. Hamilton, J. Madison, and J. Jay, *A föderalista: Értekezések az amerikai alkotmányról*, (Budapest: Európa, 1998); C. Lévai, ed., *Új rend egy új világban: Dokumentumok az amerikai politikai gondolkodás korai történetéhez*, (Debrecen: Debrecen University Press, 1997); D.J. Boorstin, *Az amerikaiak: A gyarmatosítás kora*, (Budapest: Gondolat, 1991); C.N. Degler, *Az élőmúlt. Milyen erők formálták Amerika mai képét*, (Budapest: Európa, 1993); C. Sellers, H. May and N.R. McMillen, *Az Egyesült Államok története*, (Budapest: Maecenas, 1995); A. Urbán, *Köztársaság az Újvilágban: Az Egyesült Államok születése*, (Budapest: Tankönyvkiadó, 1984); P. Hahner, *Thomas Jefferson és a francia forradalom*, (Budapest: Osiris, 1998); C. Lévai, *A republikanizmus-vita: Vita az amerikai forradalom eszmetörténeti hátteréről*, (Budapest: L'Harmattan, 2003).

6
We, the Volk: Modern and Radical Constitutionalism from the American Revolution to the German Direct-Democracy Debate

Thomas Clark

Introduction

This chapter will explore radical constitutional thought during the American Revolution and assess whether or not it has influenced German debates on the subject. Its origin is anecdotal: reading a newspaper editorial on the risks of introducing direct democratic mechanisms on a national level in Germany sparked something of a transatlantic *déjà vu*. The arguments bore an uncanny resemblance to those in pamphlets, articles, and letters surrounding state and Federal constitutional debates of the founding era. The author warned of the limited intellectual and experiential horizons, the irrational passions, and the manipulability of the people, as well as the principal danger to minority rights without massive checks on the popular will. My curiosity awakened, I conducted a LexisNexis search for major mentions of the term 'American Revolution' in the German press, with predictably meager results: a report on a new Harley Davidson model, some reviews of Mel Gibson's 2000 movie *The Patriot*, and a comment on Joseph Ellis, but only two detailed references to American Revolutionary politics. Interestingly, both hits stemmed from conservative newspapers (*Frankfurter Allgemeine Zeitung* and *Die Welt*) and both were comments on the conservative nature of American Revolutionary thought. The Founding Fathers were credited with having displayed an intelligent distrust of equipping the people with too much unmediated power, creating an indirect democracy that limited participation primarily to the election of representatives and established electoral filters, as in voters choosing members of the Electoral College rather than directly electing the President.[1] Besides indicating that German public interest in the American Revolution is marginal at best, this result suggested that more conservative Germans made some use of American constitutionalism as a positive model as well as an arsenal of arguments against more plebiscitary mechanisms of government. In fact, one of the ways American constitutionalism has served in German discourse since the French Revolution is as the successful counter-example of ordered liberty to the anarchy and violence of French Jacobinism.[2] Are then, the American debates of 1776 and 1787 still alive in Germany today? Alexis de Tocqueville provided a different explanation:

> When the War of Independence was terminated and the foundations of the new government were to be laid down, the nation was divided between two opinions – two opinions which are as old as the world and which are perpetually to be met with, under different forms and various names, in all free communities, the one tending to limit, the other to extend indefinitely, the power of the people.[3]

Tocqueville tells us that when looking at the conflicts of the Revolution, we are dealing with a universal phenomenon, an inevitable structural component in the political discourse of liberty. My *déjà vu*, then, might not be the consequence of the diffusion of American Revolutionary thought, but rather result from similar political constellations causing analogous, but unrelated discursory formations. Since ideas never function independently of social contexts, this view in particular raises the question of whether socio-historical parallels in the two societies explain similarities in political discourse. There is a third factor to consider: old American and contemporary German ideas may share similarities, because they have common roots reaching from the enlightenment all the way back to antiquity. Indeed, if Periklean Athens, for all its exclusionary aspects, represents the Western paradigm of a highly plebiscitary democracy, then Plato's *Protagoras* contains one of its earliest and lasting critiques: that in all areas of life, people value the expertise of professionals, whereas 'when some matter of state policy comes up for consideration, anyone can get up and give his opinion, be he carpenter, smith or cobbler, merchant or ship-owner, rich or poor, noble or low-born, and no one objects to them'.[4] In defining politics as an art and devising a model republic governed by an elite specifically trained to excel at that particular art, Plato's *Republic* laid the foundation for a fundamental political discourse on the limits of popular sovereignty, which would ultimately leave its mark on the entirety of European and Anglo-American thought.

But even if we do assume that the American Revolution has influenced present-day German political discourse, it need not have been direct. The French used American models, including radical ideas from Pennsylvania during their Revolution, and these had a much greater practical impact on Germany than anything that occurred in America. Tom Paine's German reputation as an American, for one, was founded on his activities in France.[5] When considering the diffusion of American political ideas, a multi- rather than a bi-national approach may be warranted. Last but not least, direct democracy continued to be discussed in the United States, and the current debate there is still strongly informed by its Revolutionary roots, which is quite similar to that in Germany.[6] One could assume a transatlantic influence in the present to be more likely than a historical one, though again, we might just be dealing with structural analogies.

The fact that these five possibilities of historical, mediated or contemporaneous influence, functional analogy and shared ideological origins are by no means mutually exclusive makes for an extremely complicated picture, which scholars have agreed to disagree on. I will suggest the following here, as an invitation to further research rather than a solid conclusion: even the dominant forms of American constitutionalism had at best a tenuous impact on German thinkers, who, on the whole, tended to be far more conservative, lacked a deeper understanding of core American principles, and used them not so much as road maps, but rather as quarries for quite dissimilar constructions, or simply for rhetorical ammunition.[7] Thus a direct influence of American revolutionary radicalism is highly unlikely, especially since what radicalism there was in Germany was traditionally informed by historically and spatially contiguous French precedents.[8] Not until the Weimar constitution did even the basic notion of popular sovereignty constitute the unquestioned starting point of constitutional deliberation.[9] The plebiscitary features of that constitution were not influenced by American precedents, but were peculiarly German/French. They were – probably falsely – so thoroughly discredited by the failure of the Weimar Republic that the authors of the Federal Republic's Basic Law adopted a conservative model of constitutionalism, limiting and mediating popular sovereignty to ensure political stability. It was structurally and ideologically similar to that of the American Federalists of 1787 *and* roughly compatible with the demands of the American occupiers.[10] This explains why the

German movement for more direct democracy argues from similar positions as the radical Revolutionaries did. Both challenge the paradigm of modern constitutionalism with a radical constitutional alternative. In this essay I will briefly sketch the direct democracy agenda and outline my model of competing conceptions of modern and radical constitutionalism. I will then give a brief account of key moments when American political ideas played – or did not play – a part in German discourse: the late eighteenth century, the context of 1848, the Weimar Republic, and the aftermath of World War II.

Direct democracy in Germany

Direct democracy has become a relevant issue in Germany in the wake of increasing grass roots activism in the 1980s and even more so since reunification in 1990.[11] A dead letter in the 'old' Federal Republic, it is now emerging as a means to counter political apathy and reinvest the political order with the legitimacy the party system no longer seems to be able to convey. Direct democratic mechanisms, particularly in the form of 'Volksbegehren' and 'Volksentscheid', that is, popular initiative and referendum, have meanwhile been established for most municipalities and in all of the *Länder*, but there is still resistance to the concept, particularly among practitioners of *Staatsrecht* (constitutional law)[12] and conservatives,[13] and a great reluctance to introduce it on the federal level. Skeptics claim that ordinary citizens cannot be trusted with directly deciding political issues, because they lack the necessary information and expertise, or even interest, and are likely to be manipulated by special interests creating media spin in their favour.[14] Incompatible with the concept of representation, direct democracy will undermine the parliamentary system, federalism, and the separation of powers while furthering simplistic populist agendas and a yes/no approach to complex issues.[15] At the bottom of this one commentator sees a 'primal fear of the demos' particularly pronounced in Germany.[16] On the other hand, the popularity of the concept among the general population is apparently rooted in an increasing dissatisfaction with, distrust of and alienation from political elites in the form of parties who are viewed as serving their own or special interests instead of the public good.[17] Enshrined in the Basic Law as instruments to 'participate in the formation of the political will of the people', parties and the institutionalized 'party state' (Parteienstaat) are viewed by critics as encrusted obstacles to realizing genuine political participation that alienate government from the citizenry instead of functioning as mediators.[18] Respected justices, academics and even former President von Weizsäcker have attacked party oligarchy and ossification.[19] In the words of one scholar, 'a political class has emerged, which is neutralizing to the largest extent the control mechanisms of our constitution.'[20] The classical images that emerge in popular debate are 'on the one hand the corrupt politicians only thinking of their advantage versus the good people. On the other hand the knowledgeable, intelligent leaders versus a people that only follows its lowest instincts, ignorant and capricious.'[21]

The pros and cons raised in this debate bear a remarkable similarity to the political discourse of the American Revolution. One is reminded of the debates between Pennsylvania radicals and conservatives over the highly democratic and participatory 1776 constitution, conflicts over the instruction of representatives (actual versus virtual representation), the struggle between the Massachusetts assembly and citizens in the western counties closing down courts, and of course the Federalist howls of 'mob legislation' in state legislatures. Basic statements of political principle by John Adams, James Madison and other conservative or moderate Patriots expressed the very same views on the limited political capacity of ordinary citizens and their potential manipulation by 'demagogues' that one encounters in the German context.[22] Joshua Miller believes that '[c]ontemporary prejudices and arguments against direct democracy are, to a large extent, inheritances from the eighteenth century battles' against democrats who 'sought to preserve the principles of participation, local autonomy, and political community'.[23] Revolutionary radicals who were unwilling to accept traditional elites placed more trust in citizens than in representatives, and consequently fought for greater popular participation and mechanisms of control by the people.

Radical democracy in the American Revolution: the example of Pennsylvania

Two clearly direct-democratic traditions are often referred to concerning the American Revolution.[24] The first was not an innovation, but an ancient tradition: the New England town meeting. In this basic form of direct democracy, citizens could meet face-to-face to address and decide local issues, creating an Aristotelian identity of ruler and ruled, if only for circumscribed purposes. In 1778 this tradition of local autonomy resulted in a second principle in Massachusetts: popular ratification of the constitution, i.e. a referendum on the fundamental law, by the townships. While not duplicated for most Revolutionary state constitutions, the ratification process of the Federal Constitution (though indirectly, by representatives) set a precedent, which slowly became a fixture of American constitutionalism.

The radical democratic paradigm is not restricted to these practices, however. Americans Whigs had rejected the concept of virtual representation for the American-British relationship. Yet when it came to the question of 'who should rule at home' they followed Burke's stipulation that a representative must be concerned with the public good, not the particular interests of his constituents. Diverse citizens however, insisted on the right of instruction, which clearly defined representatives, in a recourse to the medieval roots of the practice, as mere delegates of a local constituency acting on its behalf.[25] While conservatives such as John Adams appeared democratic when insisting that an assembly be a mirror of its electors, acting as they would if fully assembled, this was only permissible if such an assembly was under the strict supervision of a vigorous executive equipped with veto powers and a council of wiser and more experienced 'Senators' clearly not mirroring popular prejudices and short-sightedness, and providing a further powerful check on the activities of the people's direct representatives.[26]

By far the most coherent expression of radical democratic constitutionalism was the body of ideas that brought forth and inscribed itself in Pennsylvania's 1776 constitution, which, despite its replacement with a 'modern constitution' in 1790, had a major impact on political discourse and prefigured many developments associated with Jacksonian democracy. Most importantly it featured the constitution as an instrument of the people to control their representatives (a popular convention created the document and a popularly elected council of censors was to assemble every seven years to investigate whether the constitution had been preserved inviolate or required amendment); and a form of government in which power was concentrated in a unicameral assembly controlling the executive and judiciary, while heavily dependent upon and truly representative of the people, since elections were annual, rotation enforced, sessions public, journals and bills published, and property qualifications for voters abolished.[27] Radical philosophy was succinctly expressed when James Cannon, perhaps the major architect of the Constitution, said about prospective members of the Constitutional convention:

> great and overgrown rich Men will be improper to be trusted ... Gentlemen of the learned Professions are generally filled with the Quirks and Quibbles of the Schools ... we would think it prudent not to have too great a Proportion of such in the Convention – Honesty, common Sense, and a plain Understanding, when unbiased by sinister Motives, are fully equal to the Task.[28]

Rhetoric in Pennsylvania was saturated with class antagonism as radicals chastised the opposition as self-serving aristocrats, tyrants, Tories, and traitors, while being attacked as incompetent demagogue upstarts satisfying their burning ambition on the backs of easily misled citizens. Pennsylvania radicalism emerged from the desire of various groups – western Farmers, urban artisans, the lower sort as embodied by the militia – to assert their interests against established elites, and they found a common vocabulary in concepts of popular sovereignty that stressed the virtue and political competence of commoners, and the civic dimension of labour and military service, rather than that of property.[29] Yet among the harshest critics of the Constitution were dedicated republicans such as Benjamin Rush (who had encouraged Paine to write *Common Sense*), whose doubts, in the end, resulted from their belief that even Americans were simply not ready for this much democracy. Commenting to David Ramsay on the 'present moral character of the people of the United States', he fumed that 'the people are as much disposed to vice as their rulers, and that nothing but a vigorous and efficient government can prevent their degenerating into savages or devouring each other like beasts of prey.'[30] Expressing a central notion of modern constitutionalism, he established distance between the people and their original sovereignty:

> It is often said 'the sovereign and all other power is seated *in* the people.' This idea is unhappily expressed. It should be – 'all power is derived *from* the people.' They possess it only on the days of their elections. After this, it is the property of their rulers, nor can they exercise or resume it, unless it is abused. It is important to circulate this idea, as it leads to order and good government.[31]

Modern versus radical democratic constitutionalism

When Tocqueville argued that the conflict over the scope of popular sovereignty during the Revolution was 'as old as the world', he was not entirely correct. It acquired a radically new form in 1776 as Americans, groping to legitimize their independence, came to develop a radically new understanding of constitutionalism and popular sovereignty. Horst Dippel has pointed out that the Virginia Declaration of Rights contained a set of ten principles which, taken together, represent a decalogue of modern constitutionalism that by the middle of the twentieth century had become essential, on a global scale, to any claim of political legitimacy. Tracing the complex and distinct paths of how various national political cultures have arrived from diverse origins at this basic consensus, he offers a new way of thinking about constitutional history comparatively. Modern constitutionalism encompasses (1) sovereignty of the people and (2) human rights, defined as (3) universally valid principles. Government must rest upon (4) a constitution embodying paramount law and consist of (5) representative, (6) limited, (7) responsible and accountable government characterized by (8) separation of powers, (9) judicial independence and impartiality. It must be (10) subject to reform or amendment by the people.[32]

Notwithstanding its impressive success, the liberal paradigm has been consistently challenged both by anti-democratic and radically democratic constitutionalism. Thus, German rulers in the post-Napoleonic era adopted the concept of the written constitution, but connected it to the monarchical principle, which remained central even to German liberalism.[33] Direct democracy movements and revolutionary era radicalism represent plebiscitary challenges to modern constitutionalism. If the ten principles from the Virginia Declaration represent the catechism of the latter, the Pennsylvania Constitution of 1776 is perhaps the most coherent expression of what has ever since formed the argumentative basis of direct democracy advocates challenging democratic liberalism, regardless of the particular institutional changes being demanded. Significantly, it does not reject either constitutions or representation as key mechanisms of governance (it is, in other words not a utopian reversion to some form of unadulterated *Ur*-Democracy). Rather, it introduces a strong democratic, i.e. popular participatory component into constitutional government by modifying some of modern constitutionalism's precepts. Thus, popular sovereignty is understood as not delegated to, but remaining in the people, who consequently must be included in political processes beyond the mere act of electing representatives. Representative government is maintained, but made more dependent on popular influence through short terms, direct elections, right of instruction or recall. Representatives are closer to being delegates than independent actors. The constitution, while it may enjoy a status beyond positive law, is on par with or even subordinate to the popular will. It is understood as a check on legislators more than a check on majority tyranny. Government by representatives is limited through popular checks as well as through constitutional barriers. Separation of powers is considered less important than the dependency of all government branches upon the people. The judiciary is less independent – judges may be popularly elected for limited terms instead of appointed by representatives for long or life terms. Finally, governmental accountability and the popular right to alter government are more strongly emphasized by providing according mechanisms.

Modern and radical constitutionalism, labelled liberalism and democracy by Joshua Miller, are embodiments of competing political philosophies, which he associates with the 'crucial' aspects of the classical polis, 'citizens sharing power and a common way of life'.[34] Benjamin Barber spoke of thin versus strong democracy.[35] Other designations that have been used are liberalism and populism (William Riker), majoritarian and consensus systems (Arendt Lijphart), or monism and pluralism (Ernst Fraenkel). Jack Balkin has juxtaposed these positions within a leftist context as Progressivism and Populism, democracy by virtue of elite guidance versus accepting the input of all citizens without establishing qualifications. According to populist understanding,

> political participation is not something to be forced on the citizenry, nor are popular attitudes some sort of impure ore that must be carefully filtered, purified, and managed by a wise and knowing state. From a populist standpoint, such attempts at managerial purification are paternalistic. They typify elite disparagement and disrespect for popular attitudes and popular culture. Government should provide opportunities for popular participation when people seek it, and when they seek it, government should not attempt to divert or debilitate popular will.[36]

Both modern and radical constitutionalism provide an answer to the fundamental republican question of how to manage power in order to most effectively maintain liberty. They are informed by divergent conceptions of politics as well as humankind. Modern constitutionalism is marked by the Platonic conviction that the 'people at large' are less qualified to master politics, because they are not members of a caste of social leaders, or experts equipped with political skill and socialized so as to think and act rationally. Politics is thus understood as an art or a science that requires special intellectual and moral abilities. Qualification and its limitation are expressed in the terminology noted above. The virtue, wisdom, disinterestedness, experience or professionalism of the elite is contrasted with the selfishness, limited horizon, disinterest, impulsiveness and irrationality of ordinary citizens. While modern constitutionalism concedes that elites cannot be fully trusted, because all people are principally self-interested and power corrupts (thus in fact contradicting the frequent 'virtue and wisdom' argument), there is no point in having them checked by even less reliable citizens. Rather, control is achieved by the mechanics of government, by checks and balances that ingeniously cancel out competing interests.[37]

Radical democracy's approach, on the other hand, is marked by a certain optimism in human nature and the better results of majority decisions. 'Everyman' (and starting in the late nineteenth century, 'Everywoman') is equally able to determine good and bad in politics as a matter of common sense, to use Paine's phrase. An occasional misjudgement is preferable to exposing liberty to the machinations of elites disconnected from the rest of society, holed up in institutions of governance that degenerate into self-preserving systems of power no longer primarily geared towards serving the public. Where scepticism enters the picture, the people rather than their leaders always enjoy the benefit of the doubt. And if the people, as one Revolutionary put it, are 'the only safe repository of power',[38] government must necessarily rely less on institutional mechanisms removed from the citizens-at-large and more on actively, deeply, and frequently involving them in political processes. A more direct democracy is the necessary consequence.

It should be noted that radical democracy can also be consciously exclusionary, by transferring power from leaders or institutions to the people, but defining those people narrowly. Thus, the Progressives of Balkin's nomenclature, who instituted many plebiscitary elements in state constitutions in the early twentieth century, advocated participatory democracy, but linked it to a political competence denied to immigrant and working class populations who were expected not to, and did in fact not turn out in significant numbers for initiatives or referendums.[39] Pennsylvania's Revolutionary radicals' inclusive conception of the people in terms of property highlighted their disfranchisement of African Americans.[40]

America, democracy, and Germany: of fears and fantasies

As with all perceptions of the other, German views of the American Revolution are in many ways expressions of Germans conditions.[41] Robert Palmer's dictum still holds that the French (before 1789) and Germans were fascinated with the Revolution, while the condition of their societies precluded political action, leading to 'an incredible outburst of discussion, speculation, rhapsody, and argument, a veritable intoxication with the *rêve américain*'.[42] As Horst Dippel has conclusively shown, the eighteenth-century 'German bourgeoisie combined excessive enthusiasm and sympathy for America and its revolution with a very low level of factual knowledge.'[43]

Even before the Revolution, the German press conveyed an image of the pre-revolutionary colonies remarkably close to Crevecoeur's depiction – a land of liberty and economic opportunity free from stultifying European hierarchies.[44] Shaped by enlightenment ideas, contemporary German intellectuals took an active interest in the Revolution, both defending and criticizing the American struggle for independence. Yet while scholars compiled impressive collections of data on North America, an in-depth knowledge of political discourse did not evolve.[45] America was perceived as the Enlightenment in action, a utopian foil onto which the desires of German liberals for liberty and equal rights could be projected, which they knew could not be realized at home. Ironically, while *Sturm und Drang* poets celebrated American liberty in a rather abstract fashion, more knowledgeable contemporaries by no means viewed events in the new United States as conducive to the German progress of liberty. One of the most influential liberals of the time, August Wilhelm Schlötzel, harshly criticized the Revolution. Viewing Britain as the ideal model for reforms achievable in Germany, he argued that the Revolution would convince German rulers that even moderate liberalization would ultimately lead to unabashed republicanism. From a Tory position, Schlötzel invoked the classical image of popular incompetence: 'I shudder at the prospect of an asiatic despotism ... but still more ferocious, in my opinion, is the democratic despot, the majority of the people. Against their rage all good men must declare a state of emergency, but who can tame them?'[46]

The limits of German thought become evident, if we consider the most radical and the best-informed German contemporaries of the American Revolution, Johann Christian Schmohl and Christoph Daniel Ebeling. Schmohl's exceptional text, radical and well-informed, explicitly celebrated the United States for realizing democracy by achieving equal political rights and popular sovereignty, issues that remained far more elusive to other authors. Yet while America was his ideal, even Schmohl asserted that England, from where he probably wrote his letter, was the European nation 'where alone the despotic government of one or the few not yet transforms the original sovereignty of the people into bondage'.[47] Compare this to Tom Paine's description of the English constitution as 'the base remains of two ancient tyrannies', except for the 'new Republican materials, in the Persons of the Commons' from which he developed his contrasting conception of a new American constitutionalism.[48] That Schmohl drowned on the way to America, is, perhaps, symbolic.

Christoph Daniel Ebeling, a scholar from Hamburg, whose never completed *Erdbeschreibung* represents the most ambitious and well-researched study of America of its time, was thoroughly acquainted with American events, corresponded with numerous Americans, and was a personal friend of Joel Barlow. He strongly identified with America, the 'Mother of liberty', and took great pride in his own Republic of Hamburg. In view of the chaos of the French Revolution, the United States served for him as a consoling model of a peaceful transition to liberty, and he hoped Germany could 'get rid of' nobility, courts, and Princes 'without great convulsions'.[49] Ebeling was aware of radical American thought, but he did not find it useful. He provided the best and most complete translation of *Common Sense* as well as summaries of the *Crisis* papers, and he commented on the radical constitution of Pennsylvania, showing more detachment in evaluating it than many American scholars up until the 1980s.[50] A friend of ordered liberty, Ebeling concluded that experience had shown the wisdom of the American attacks on radicalism that he summarized: unicameralism and the weak plural executive tipped the balance too much towards unmitigated popular power, laying bills before the people contributed to internal disorder, a Council of Censors reviewing the Constitution increased factionalism and governmental instability. Yet Ebeling was fair enough to point out that the fear of an aristocracy that had prompted unicameralism was not entirely unfounded, and that conditions in Pennsylvania mandated such a radical constitution to 'awaken, strengthen, and spread the republican spirit'.[51] His perspective on Germany was infinitely more modest. In 1817 he cast the German Confederation, an instrument of anti-democratic reaction,[52] in terms of constitutional progress: greater uniformity would replace provincial particularism, a future Prussian estate-parliament would be like a 'House of representatives', certain import duties were being removed, there was greater freedom of movement, and 'Censorship is much limited and mostly confined to newspapers.'[53] As for Paine, Ebeling lauded his love of liberty, but found his arguments unconvincing. Arnold considers Ebeling to be representative of many Germans: his initial enthusiasm for Paine cooled considerably as he became identified with the French Revolution and the *Age of Reason*.[54]

It was the French Revolution that initiated democratic activism and constitution-writing in Germany in the late-eighteenth century, an episode long ignored in a German historiography focused on the 'Vormärz' and 1848, but which laid the foundations for reformist and revolutionary sentiment in the nineteenth century.[55] And if any of the radical ideas of the American Revolution did arrive in Germany, it was through France, where certain fundamentals of modern constitutionalism would be challenged. The circle around Turgot, Condorcet, and La Rochefoucauld, chiding their friend Jefferson as the embodiment of the 'devil of aristocracy' for his moderate views,[56] celebrated the Pennsylvania Constitution (falsely attributed to Franklin) and its unicameral chamber as the only truly revolutionary American achievement. Turgot and the *américaniste* group, set against the *anglomanes* supporting balanced government, envisioned a unitary people identical to the national interest as against the counterproductive power of the privileged elites of the *ancien regime*.[57] Yet Pennsylvania's constitution, protecting fundamental rights, could not be abolished by the people, who had thus protected themselves from their representatives *and* themselves, while radical French conceptions, in the tradition of Rousseau, set the sovereign will of the nation above any constitution. Even if Germans had been aware of or (even less likely) sympathetic to Pennsylvania radicalism, it would have been dwarfed by the French Constitution of 24 June 1793, which explicitly located all sovereignty in a unified people, not the constitution, guaranteed citizens the right to participate in the legislative process and whose legislature had to have its bills confirmed by the people at large, to name the most important radical constitutionalist principles.[58]

In Germany, the American Revolution receded from public view as the Enlightenment faded into romanticism, nationalism, reaction and restoration.[59] It was not just a symbolic loss when Ebeling's huge collection of Americana was purchased by Harvard University.[60] Conservatives cited America as a moderate, traditional counter-example to the French radicalism and dogmatism they despised and feared, while assuring Germans that it was not a model adaptable to old world conditions. Liberals vaguely referred to America's 'people's democracy' without developing a clear conception of its possible meanings and implications.[61] America remained a foil for ambivalent European projections and a quarry for ideas.[62] A free spirit such as Heinrich Heine could rhapsodize in the abstract about America, 'the New World/Not Today's, which already/ Europeanized decays', but view the mass democracy celebrated by Jacksonians such as George Bancroft as a 'monstrous prison of liberty, where the invisible chains would press me more painfully than the visible ones at home and where the most despicable of all tyrants, the mob, exercises his raw dominion!'[63] Political thinkers, in a similar vein, viewed the United States as an asylum of liberty unachievable in the Old World, or considered its individualistic liberty undesirable and the treatment of African-Americans and Indians as a sign of hypocrisy.[64] Michael Dreyer has most emphatically argued that for all the many positive references to the American Constitution in the Paulskirche Assembly, even modern constitutionalism was simply too radical for Germans to accept or utilize. Self-government and popular sovereignty stood against the ruling monarchical principle, pluralism against the king as the wellspring of the nation, the constitution-based against the blood-based nation, denominationalism against the state religion, pragmatism against idealism and so forth.[65] The monarchical principle, which 'governed the German constitutional systems of the 19th century in text, theory, and practice', attempted to contain the development of constitutionalism and representation by positing the king, not the people, as constitutive power granting a constitution limiting himself.[66] As grants, and lacking higher legitimacy through special ratification procedures, constitutions were not securely established as higher law. Separation of powers was also rejected, leaving no foundation for effective judicial review.[67]

There are ironic parallels between Pennsylvania radicalism, which concentrated power in the single legislature bound to the people in order to protect them against government, and German principles keeping power close to the monarch, in order to protect the state from the people. While all political factions in the Paulskirche assembly necessarily referred to the American Constitution as the only established model of a federal state, thereby confirming not so much its model function as their attachment to the project of a German Federal state, conservatives, liberals and democrats alike were conditioned to think in a state-centred tradition, rather than in terms of popular power and the free agency of a society's constituent parts.[68] A democratic enemy of constitutional monarchy such as Julius Fröbel viewed the American system as a model to be perfected, a stepping stone on the way to a German 'social republic' where every person's 'happiness, freedom and dignity is recognized as the common purpose of all'. Fröbel considered the mechanism of Madisonian constitutionalism, born out of the realization of the heterogeneity of competing interests in an extended republic, as a means of combining the plurality of German states into a republic that would somehow be able to 'realize higher moral demands' that Americans were ignorant of.[69] He was apparently not aware that Antifederalist radicals had argued that it was precisely this sort of system that would destroy virtue by removing power from the people to a distant national elite in pursuit of its own interests. The parameters of the German struggle for unity, law and liberty were entirely different than those of 1776/1787. The Constitution finally created by the Paulskirche Assembly in 1849, never even to be enacted, was a product of a conservative modern constitutionalism that aimed at reconciling hereditary monarchy with popular representation, while clearly demarcating the latter's limits. It thus bore a certain similarity to the Federal constitution (in a Hamiltonian vein), but this was not due to a direct influence. The few delegates who had a decent knowledge of American government, such as Robert von Mohl, were focused on the issue of federalism, but continued in the belief that the United States Constitution was the product of unique American circumstances and thus not applicable to Germany.[70] After the failure of 1849 the study of American constitutionalism fell into no less neglect than the ideas of modern, not to speak of radical constitutionalism.[71]

America, democracy, and Germany: of failure and federalists

It required the cataclysm of a lost World War to bring democracy to Germany, both in 1919 and then again in 1949. While the Weimar constitution represented a Germanized version of radical constitutionalism, akin to Pennsylvania, but clearly inspired by the broad diffusion of Rousseauian ideas, the Basic Law of the Federal Republic was marked by an anthropological pessimism reminiscent of the American Federalists, but also reflecting the German liberal tradition of distrusting the people. In both cases, immediate American influence was particularly relevant in that Wilsonian foreign policy and post-1945 American interests set the frame work for reconstructing German government. Yet even under Allied occupation that frame work was broad (democratization, a federal system, and a capitalist economy were key American demands) and the interests of the United States and the diverse German groups were sufficiently compatible to avoid fundamental clashes.[72]

Rejecting the possibility of a 'Räterepublik', a republic of worker's councils, liberals and Social Democrats opted for a representative system, which however would contain strong plebiscitary elements. Hugo Preuss, the principal architect of the Weimar Constitution, 'conceived of democracy more as an organic unity of the people than as a system for the orderly resolution of conflict' in the tradition of the Jacobin constitution of 1793, rather than the American Federalists.[73] However, it was primarily the Socialists who pushed for including a national referenda as well as a legislative initiative and recall, while Preuss thought direct democracy better suited to small states.[74] The Reichstag was to represent a proportional replica of the popular will by including splinter parties. On the other hand, a directly elected President with far-reaching powers stood as the unitary representative of the popular will. He was viewed as an 'Ersatzkaiser', modeled on the strong US executive, rather than French or British parliamentary supremacy.[75] However, his right to dissolve the Parliament and initiate plebiscites indicated little enthusiasm for the American ideal of checks and balances, as did the absence of judicial review or individual redress to secure fundamental rights. Together with the easy amendability of the constitution, which, in the German tradition of legal positivism could be interpreted as an expression of sovereignty – now of the people rather than the monarch – and not as fundamental law,[76] the Weimar document represented a thorough rejection of modern constitutionalism in the attempt to realize popular sovereignty in Germany.[77]

Contemporary comments from America, reflecting Progressive-era dissatisfaction with the American constitution, considered this constitution, which in the words of Charles Beard 'vibrates with the tramp of the proletariat', as being quite advanced in stressing national consolidation over federal division of power, including social rights and stressing democracy.[78] But its utter failure in succumbing to National Socialism, unavoidable as it may have been under the circumstances of its rejection by key elements of German society and the volatility of postwar society and economy, was seen by post-Second World German leaders as proof of its absolute failure. This resulted in the peculiar situation that while they complained of and resisted, quite successfully, American attempts at influencing the political reconstruction of Germany (e.g. in retaining greater competencies for the Federal government), these German leaders generally adhered steadfastly to the fundamentally American principles of modern constitutionalism, even while arguing that specific American institutions, e.g. the Senate, could not function under German conditions.[79] The German-American political scientist Carl J. Friedrich, who was an important observer and liaison between General Lucius Clay and the Germans, observed that the Basic Law consisted of 'constitutional ideas partly German, partly French, partly English, and partly American', but that 'German concepts of democracy and government ... played a predominant role'.[80] Heinrich Wilms' recent exhaustive study comes to the conclusion that the Basic Law was an autonomous German achievement and yet deeply embedded in the Western constitutional tradition Germany had abandoned after 1849.[81]

The anti-plebiscitary bent of postwar German constitutionalism began with the fact that the members of the constitutional convention, strangely called the 'Parlamentarischer Rat', were not popularly elected, but appointed by the parliaments of the *Länder*, and the constitution was merely ratified by majorities in those assemblies, not the people at large. Fundamental rights were enshrined in the constitution, which would now be understood to constitute higher law. A powerful Supreme Court was instituted to practice judicial review. The strong President as well as the splinter parties of Weimar disappeared, leaving a parliamentary system geared towards stable majorities.

Plebiscitary elements were rejected from the Weimar experience, general ideological conviction, as well as the immediate concerns that communist agitation would lead to undesirable results.[82] The major argument, however, was the Weimar experience, where referenda had allegedly been abused by radical parties for ruthless agitation, thereby helping to destabilize the political order. While the desire to create an 'Anti-Weimar' is understandable, the argument was actually not empirically founded.[83] Employing the classical *topos* of popular manipulability, Theodor Heuss of the liberal-right Free Democratic Party, later President of the Federal Republic, called the referendum a 'premium for demagogues'. While considering it useful in the context of a small nation with established civic traditions, such as Switzerland, he viewed it as highly dangerous in times of 'massification and deracination'.[84] The German Founding Fathers and Mothers, most of whom had been victims of Nazism, understandably had limited faith in the people, believing, as Benjamin Rush had, that a democratic foundation had yet to be built in Germany in order to teach its citizens democracy. Carl Hodge speaks of a ' "marked generation" … motivated not by idealism but by a resignation to human fallibility that resembled nothing so much as the sober skepticism of Madison and Hamilton'.[85] Direct democracy was never a major issue during the debates. At the same time, while plebiscitary mechanisms had been installed in many *Länder*-Constitutions, the barriers (in terms of required votes and quorums) were set so high as to make them blunt instruments. Bavaria constituted the major exception, the model however having been Switzerland, not the progressive state constitutions in the United States, which themselves had looked to the Swiss example. What Balkin calls the 'progressive' conception of democracy by paternal guidance remained the core ideology of German leadership elites – judges, parliamentarians, party functionaries and scholars – well into the 1980s, as we saw at the beginning of this paper, despite the fact that the German people could arguably claim to have proven themselves reliable and competent democrats. Yet, as Haltern observes, 'it is amazing how the anti-plebiscitarian affect has persisted until today, and how strongly it still resonates in the dominant strand of German constitutional law'.[86] Meanwhile, however, the

German Federalists are being challenged with increasing success by distant cousins of Tom Paine and James Cannon. While there is no reason to believe that the American Revolution has influenced the current German debate in any direct way, this chapter has perhaps suggested why Germans might nonetheless find the study of the American Revolution to be of more than antiquarian value. It provides a complex discourse, addressing many of the fundamental questions of democratic practice that they are currently confronted with as they remeasure the scope and nature of political participation, rather than representing an inapplicable otherness or merely the modern constitutionalist half of the debate. The relative ignorance about and disinterest of Germans in American history might give way to a constructive exploration of the relation between modern and radical constitutionalism at its intellectual birthplace.[87]

Notes

1. R.D. Kaplan, 'Ein Lob dem Wahlmänner-System. Die indirekte Demokratie, geboren aus der Angst vor einem Cromwell, hält Amerika zusammen', *Die Welt*, 14 December 2000, 'Kein Hirt und eine Herde [No Shepherd and a Flock]', *Frankfurter Allgemeine Zeitung*, 11 September 1995.
2. G.-L. Fink, 'Die Amerikanische und die Französische Revolution: Analogien und Unterschiede im Spiegel der deutschen Publizistik [1789–1798]', *Modern Language Notes* (German Issue) CIII (1988) 564.
3. A. de Tocqueville, *Democracy in America*, ed., P. Bradley (New York: Knopf, 1945), I, pp.182–3.
4. Plato, *Protagoras*, trans. C.C.W. Taylor (New York: Oxford University Press, 1996), pp.15–16.
5. H. Arnold, 'Die Aufnahme von Thomas Paines Schriften in Deutschland', *Publications of the Modern Language Association of America*, LXXIV (1959), 365–86.
6. See T. Goebel, *A Government by the People: Direct Democracy in America, 1890–1940* (Chapel Hill, NC: University of North Carolina Press, 2002), pp.185–99; J.I. Miller, *The Rise and Fall of Democracy in Early America, 1630–1789. The Legacy for Contemporary Politics* (University Park, PA: The Pennsylvania State Univ. Press, 1991), p.7; J.C. Samples, ed., *James Madison and the Future of Limited Government* (Washington, DC: Cato Institute, 2002).
7. This follows M. Dreyer, 'Die Verfassung der USA. Ein Modell für deutsche Verfassungsentwürfe des 19. Jahrhunderts?', in J. Elvert and M. Salewski, eds, *Deutschland und der Westen im 19. und 20. Jahrhundert, Teil 1: Transatlantische Beziehungen*. Historische Mitteilungen (Stuttgart: Ranke Gesellschaft, 1993), pp.225–46.
8. This is evident from H. Dippel, *Die Anfänge des Konstitutionalismus in Deutschland: Texte deutscher Verfassungsentwürfe am Ende des 18. Jahrhunderts* (Frankfurt am Main: Keip, 1991), and J. Riethmüller, *Die Anfänge der Demokratie in Deutschland* (Erfurt: Sutton, 2002).

9. A.J. Jacobson and B. Schlink, 'Constitutional Crisis. The German and the American Experience', in A.J. Jacobson and B. Schlink, eds, *Weimar: A Jurisprudence of Crisis* (Berkeley, CA: University of California Press, 2000), p.2.

10. C.C. Hodge, 'Active at the Creation: the United States and the Founding of Adenauer's Republic', in C.C. Hodge and C.J. Nolan, eds, *Shepherd of Democracy? America and Germany in the Twentieth Century* (Westport, CT: Greenwood Press, 1992), p.95.

11. M.W. Richter, 'Exiting the GDR: Political Movements and Parties between Democratization and Westernization', in M.D. Hancock and H.A. Welsh, eds, *German Unification: Process and Outcomes* (Boulder, CO: Westview Press, 1994), p.109. East Germans showed much greater enthusiasm for direct democracy, while "Wesssies" tended to defend liberal democracy. See R. Rohrschneider, *Learning Democracy: Democratic and Economic Values in Unified Germany* (Oxford: Oxford University Press, 1999), pp.63–106.

12. In dominant forms of German constitutional thought even the concept of 'popular sovereignty' is considered meaningless or obsolete in view of constitutional supremacy. See H. Abromeit,'Volkssouveränität in komplexen Gesellschaften', in H. Brunkhorst and P. Niesen, eds, *Das Recht der Republik* (Frankfurt am Main: Suhrkamp, 1999), p.17.

13. Resistance is strongest among the Christian Democratic Union (CDU), while the Green Party and more recently the German Social Democratic Party (SPD) have taken a supportive stance. See G. Braunthal, *Parties and Politics in Modern Germany* (Boulder, CO: Westview Press, 1996), p.188. On the other hand, the CDU's Bavarian sister-party, the Christian Social Union (CSU) rules over the land with the most advanced and utilized system of direct democracy, while SPD- governed Bremen battled the introduction of initiative and referendum with all legally available means. See K. Hahnzog, 'Bayern als Motor für unmittelbare Demokratie', in H.K. Heußner and O. Jung, eds, *Mehr direkte Demokratie wagen: Volksbegehren und Volksentscheid: Geschichte – Praxis – Vorschläge* (München: Olzog, 1999), pp.159–76, R. Kampwirth, 'Bremen: Die Angst der Parteien vor dem "entfesselten Volk" ', in Heußner and Jung, eds, *Mehr direkte Demokratie wagen*, pp.177–88.

14. R. Leicht, 'Einspruch', *Die Zeit*, 24 April 1998.

15. See M. Efler, *Bundesweite Volksentscheide? Antworten auf die Einwände der CDU/CSU* (Mehr Demokratie e.V., n.d. [cited 18 Feb. 2004]), http://www.mehr-demokratie.de/fileadmin/bund/pdf_positionen/pos04.pdf; D. Schaal and G. Habermann, '22 Argumente für skeptische Zeitgenossen', in Heußner and Jung, eds, *Mehr direkte Demokratie wagen*, pp.333–50.

16. H.-G. Wehling, *Mehr direkte Demokratie als Antwort auf die Krise des Parteienstaats?* http://www.lpb.bwue.de/aktuell/skandal.htm

17. V. Kaina, 'Direkte Demokratie als Ausweg? Repräsentativverfassung und Reformforderungen im Meinungsbild von Politikeliten und Bevölkerung', *Zeitschrift für Politikwissenschaft* 12 (2002) 1045–72.

18. *Basic Law for the Federal Republic of Germany* (Deutscher Bundestag, 2000 http://www.bundestag.de/htdocs_e/info/030gg.pdf

19. D.P. Kommers, *The Constitutional Jurisprudence of the Federal Republic of Germany*, 2nd edn. (Durham, NC: Duke University Press, 1997), p.181.

20. H.H. von Arnim, *Strukturprobleme des Parteienstaates* (Bundeszentrale für politische Bildung, 2000), http://www.bpb.de/publikationen/MREFUM,6,0, Strukturprobleme_des_Parteienstaates.html#art6

21. Wehling, *Mehr direkte Demokratie?*
22. J.C. Samples, 'Madison and the Revival of Pure Democracy', in Samples, ed, *James Madison and the Future of Limited Government*, pp.165–89.
23. Miller, *Rise and Fall*, p.7.
24. See for example C.R. Kesler, 'Direct Democracy and Representation', in E. Abrams, ed., *Democracy How Direct? Views from the Founding Era and the Polling Era* (Lanham, MD: Rowman & Littlefield, 2002), pp.1–18; C. Stelzenmüller, *Direkte Demokratie in den Vereinigten Staaten von Amerika.* Beiträge zum ausländischen und vergleichenden öffentlichen Recht, 5 (Baden-Baden: Nomos-Verl.-Ges., 1994), pp.53–68.
25. G.S. Wood, *The Creation of the American Republic: 1776–1787* (New York: Norton, 1972), pp.162–96.
26. J. Adams, *Thoughts on Government Applicable to the Present State of the American Colonies: In a Letter from a Gentleman to His Friend* (Philadelphia: John Dunlap, 1776).
27. For an extensive discussion of Pennsylvania's radical constitutionalism see T.W. Clark, 'Virtuous Democrats, Liberal Aristocrats: Political Discourse and the Pennsylvania Constitution, 1776–1790' (PhD diss., J.W. Goethe University, 2001).
28. J. Cannon, *To the Several Battalions of Military Associators in the Province of Pennsylvania* (Philadelphia: broadside, 1776). Cannon was a schoolteacher and mathematician who had come to Philadelphia from Edinburgh in 1765. He was a gifted speaker and a skillful publicist. See W. Egle, 'The Constitutional Convention of 1776. Biographical Sketches of its Members', *Pennsylvania Magazine of History and Biography*, III (1879) 198–9.
29. Clark, 'Virtuous Democrats', pp.218–39; R. Schultz, *The Republic of Labor: Philadelphia Artisans and the Politics of Class, 1720–1830* (New York: Oxford University Press, 1993), pp.1–37.
30. B. Rush to D. Ramsay, *Letters of Benjamin Rush*, ed., L.H. Butterfield (Princeton, NJ: Published for the American Philosophical Society by Princeton University Press, 1951) p.453.
31. B. Rush, 'On the Defects of the Confederation', (1787) in D. Runes, ed., *The Selected Writings of Benjamin Rush* (Philadelphia, PA: Philosophical Library, 1947), p.28.
32. H. Dippel, 'Modern Constitutionalism: An Introduction to a History in the Need of Writing', *Tijdschrift voor Rechtsgeschiedenis*, 73 (2005) 153–69.
33. H. Wellenreuther, 'Die USA. Ein politisches Vorbild der bürgerlich-liberalen Kräfte des Vormärz?', in J. Elvert and M. Salewski, eds, *Deutschland und der Westen im 19. und 20. Jahrhundert, Teil 1: Transatlantische Beziehungen.* Historische Mitteilungen (Stuttgart: Ranke Gesellschaft, 1993), p.34.
34. Miller, *Rise and Fall*, p.11.
35. B.R. Barber, *Strong Democracy: Participatory Politics for a New Age* (Berkeley, CA: University of California Press, 1984), pp.3–25, 117–38.
36. J.M. Balkin, 'Populism and Progressivism as Constitutional Categories', *Yale Law Journal*, CIV (1995) 1945.
37. For the argument that Americans arrived early at the model of the mechanical polity, see M.W. Kruman, *Between Authority & Liberty: State Constitution Making in Revolutionary America* (Chapel Hill, NC: University of North

Carolina Press, 1997). For a detailed discussion see Clark, 'Virtuous Democrats', pp.152–76.
38. Demophilus, 'The Genuine Principles of the Ancient Saxon, or English Constitution (Philadelphia, 1776)', in C.S. Hyneman and D.S. Lutz, eds., *American Political Writing During the Founding Era, 1760–1805* (Indianapolis, IN: Liberty Press, 1983), p.363.
39. Goebel, *A Government by the People*, p.59.
40. Clark, 'Virtuous Democrats', p.215.
41. For an overview of German perceptions of America in general, see M. Nolan, 'America in the German Imagination', in H. Fehrenbach and U.G. Poiger, eds, *Transactions, Transgressions, Transformations: American Culture in Western Europe and Japan* (New York: Berghahn Books, 2000), pp.3–25.
42. R.R. Palmer, *The Age of the Democratic Revolution* (Princeton, NJ: Princeton University Press, 1959), p.242.
43. H. Dippel, *Germany and the American Revolution, 1770–1800: A Sociohistorical Investigation of Late Eighteenth-Century Political Thinking* (Chapel Hill, NC: University of North Carolina Press, 1977), p.346.
44. See V. Depkat, 'Zwischen Wildnis und Kultur: Nordamerika als "Land des Fortschritts" in deutschen Zeitschriften, 1750–1789', in A. Blome and V. Depkat, *Von der "Civilisirung" Rußlands und dem "Aufblühen" Nordamerikas im 18. Jahrhundert: Leitmotive der Aufklärung am Beispiel deutscher Rußland- und Amerikabilder* (Bremen: Edition Lumière, 2002), pp.73–114.
45. Dippel, *Germany and the American Revolution*, p.346; E.E. Doll, 'American History as Interpreted by German Historians from 1770 to 1815', *Transactions of the American Philosophical Society*, XXXVIII (1949) 510.
46. Quoted in E. Douglass, 'German Intellectuals and the American Revolution', *The William and Mary Quarterly, 3rd ser*. XVII (1960) 209.
47. J.C. Schmohl, *Über Nordamerika und Demokratie: ein Brief aus England*, ed., Reiner Wild. (St. Ingbert: Röhrig, 1992), p.7.
48. T. Paine, *Common Sense* (Philadelphia: William Bradford, 1776), p.10.
49. Ebeling to M. Carey, 25 September 1792; Ebeling to the American Philosophical Society, 14 October 1793; and Ebeling to Carey, 20 September 1794, quoted in Doll, 'American History as Interpreted by German Historians', 477–83.
50. See Clark, 'Virtuous Democrats', pp.21–7.
51. C.D. Ebeling, *Die Vereinten Staaten von Nordamerika: Sechster Band, Christoph Daniel Ebelings Erdbeschreibung und Geschichte von Amerika* (Hamburg: Bohn, 1803), p.317; and Ebeling, *Die Vereinten Staaten von Nordamerika: Vierter Band, Christoph Daniel Ebelings Erdbeschreibung und Geschichte von Amerika* (Hamburg: Bohn, 1797), p.268.
52. J.L. Snell and H.A. Schmitt, *The Democratic Movement in Germany, 1789–1914* (Chapel Hill, NC: University of North Carolina Press, 1976), p.23.
53. C.D. Ebeling and W.C. Lane, 'Glimpses of European Conditions from the Ebeling Letters', *Proceedings of the Massachusetts Historical Society*, LIX (1926) 375–76.
54. Arnold, 'Die Aufnahme von Thomas Paines Schriften in Deutschland', 367–8.
55. See H. Dippel, *Die amerikanische Verfassung in Deutschland im 19. Jahrhundert: das Dilemma von Politik und Staatsrecht* (Goldbach: Keip, 1994), p.15; Dippel,

Die Anfänge des Konstitutionalismus in Deutschland, pp.11–31; Riethmüller, *Die Anfänge der Demokratie in Deutschland*, pp.195–8.

56. Palmer, *The Age of the Democratic Revolution*, p.470.
57. J. Appleby, 'America as a Model for the Radical French Reformers of 1789', *The William and Mary Quarterly, 3rd ser.*, XXVIII (1971) 269, 273–4. Pennsylvanians had defended unicameralism in terms of a singularized public good, but also as a forum for building consensus among competing interest groups. See Clark, 'Virtuous Democrats', pp.286–91. Appleby argues however, that British and American ideas were being selectively adapted to fit competing French theories and thus they were empirical complements more than genuine influences.
58. See 'Constitution of 1793', in S.F. Scott and B. Rothaus, eds, *Historical Dictionary of the French Revolution, 1789–1799*, 2 vols (Westport, CT: Greenwood Press, 1985), I, pp.238–42.
59. Riethmüller, *Die Anfänge der Demokratie in Deutschland*, p.197. This is the classical interpretation of the origins of Germany's anti-democratic "Sonderweg". See H. Kohn, *German History: Some New German Views* (London: George Allen & Unwin, 1954), p.46.
60. See Dreyer, 'Die Verfassung der USA. Ein Modell für deutsche Verfassungsentwürfe des 19. Jahrhunderts?', p.227.
61. J. Heideking, 'Das "Modell Amerika" in der deutschen Verfassungsgeschichte vom Vormärz bis zur Weimarer Republik', paper delivered at the conference *Amerikanische Einflüsse auf Verfassungsdenken und Verfassungspraxis in Deutschland*, Atlantische Akademie Rheinland-Pfalz, 1997 (electronic manuscript in possession of the author).
62. Wellenreuther, 'Die USA. Ein politisches Vorbild der bürgerlich-liberalen Kräfte des Vormärz?', p.41.
63. H. Heine, 'Vitzliputzli', in H. Heine, *Werke and Briefe in zehn Bänden*, ed., H. Kautfmann (Berlin: Aufban-Verl., 1961), II, p.57; H. Heine, *Ludwig Börne: Eine Denkschrift*, in H. Heine, *Historisch-Kritische ECSAMtansgabe der wenke*, ed., M. Windfurn (Hamburg: Hoffmann & Compe Veslag, 1978), XI, p. 37.
64. Wellenreuther, 'Die USA. Ein politisches Vorbild der bürgerlich-liberalen Kräfte des Vormärz?', p.37.
65. Dreyer, 'Die Verfassung der USA. Ein Modell für deutsche Verfassungsentwürfe des 19. Jahrhunderts?', pp.244–6.
66. W. Heun, 'Das monarchische Prinzip und der deutsche Konstitutionalismus des 19. Jahrhunderts', *Fundamentos. Cuadernos monográficos de Teoría del Estado*, II (2002). http://www.uniovi.es/constitucional/fundamentos/segundo/index.html.
67. W. Heun, 'Supremacy of the Constitution, Separation of Powers, and Judicial Review in Nineteenth-Century German Constitutionalism', *Ratio Juris,* XVI (2003) 195–205.
68. Dreyer, 'Die Verfassung der USA. Ein Modell für deutsche Verfassungsentwürfe des 19. Jahrhunderts?', p.246.
69. J. Fröbel, *Monarchie oder Republik* (Mannheim: Heinrich Hoff, 1848), p.6.
70. Dippel, *Die amerikanische Verfassung in Deutschland*, pp. 27–31.
71. For a good summary of the view that sees a definite influence of American constitutional ideas in 1848 see G. Moltmann, 'The American Constitutional Model and German Constitutional Politics', in R.C. Simmons, ed., *The United*

States Constitution: The First Two-Hundred Years (Manchester: Manchester University Press, 1990), pp.90–103. But, of course, the popularity of the United States Constitution as the acme of modern constitutionalism would also be an argument against the presence of American-inspired radicalism.

72. J. Heideking, 'Im zweiten Anlauf zum demokratischen Verfassungsstaat: amerikanische Einflüsse auf die Weimarer Reichsverfassung und das Grundgesetz der Bundesrepublik Deutschland', in H. Bungert, M. Frey and C. Mauch, eds, *Verfassung – Demokratie – Politische Kultur. U.S.-amerikanische Geschichte in transatlantischer Perspektive* (Trier: WVT, 2002), pp.183–5.

73. R. Brunet, *The New German Constitution*, transl. Joseph Gollomb (New York: A.A. Knopf, 1928), p.521; Heideking, 'Im zweiten Anlauf zum demokratischen Verfassungsstaat', pp.191–2; C. Schoenberger, 'Hugo Preuss. Introduction', in A.J. Jacobson and B. Schlink, eds, *Weimar: A Jurisprudence of Crisis* (Berkeley, CA: University of California Press, 2000), p.114.

74. Brunet, *The New German Constitution*, pp.521–4. The constitution provided for the following forms of immediate popular participation: direct election of representatives and the President, referenda on laws enacted by the parliament on Presidential order, referenda on laws deferred by at least a third of the Reichstag on petition of at least 5 per cent of voting population, popular vote on legislative initiative of the people if this is rejected or amended by the Reichstag, on petition by at least 10 per cent of voting population, referendum on demand of President over bills not agreed upon by Reichstag and Reichsrat, referenda on constitutional amendments by the Reichstag not endorsed by the Reichsrat, a vote on recall of the President, after a 2/3 vote by the Reichstag. See Brunet, *The New German Constitution*, p.540.

75. Quoted in Heideking, 'Im zweiten Anlauf zum demokratischen Verfassungsstaat', p.186, n.14.

76. For this complex debate during the Weimar period see P.C. Caldwell, *Popular Sovereignty and the Crisis of German Constitutional Law: The Theory & Practice of Weimar Constitutionalism* (Durham, NC: Duke University Press, 1997).

77. See C.J. Friedrich, 'Rebuilding the German Constitution, I', *The American Political Science Review*, XLIII (1949) 463–64.

78. C. Beard, 'Foreword', in *The New German Constitution* (New York: A.A. Knopf, 1928), p.vii; E. Freund, 'The New German Constitution', *Political Science Quarterly*, XXXV (1920) 181, 184, 203.

79. *Der Parlamentarische Rat:1948–1949. Akten und Protokolle*, vol. 9 (Munich: Oldenbourg, 1996), pp.62, 65. For extensive discussions on American and other foreign influences on the creation of the Basic Law see E. Spevack, *Allied Control and German Freedom. American Political and Ideological Influences on the Framing of the West German Basic Law (Grundgesetz)* (Münster: LIT, 2001); H. Wilms, *Ausländische Einwirkungen auf die Entstehung des Grundgesetzes* (Stuttgart: Kohlhammer, 1999).

80. Friedrich, 'Rebuilding the German Constitution, I', 462.

81. Wilms, *Ausländische Einwirkungen auf die Entstehung des Grundgesetzes*, p.315. Previous scholars have argued all positions, from the Basic Law being an indigeneous achievement, to the belief that it was the result of Allied German negotiation with either side dominant, to it being a creation of the Allies. See Spevack, *Allied Control and German Freedom*, pp.13–33.

82. For a detailed study see O. Jung, *Grundgesetz und Volksentscheid. Gründe und Reichweite der Entscheidungen des Parlamentarischen Rates gegen Formen direkter Demokratie* (Opladen: Westdeutscher Verlag, 1994).

83. J. Rux, 'Direkte Demokratie in der Weimarer Republik', *Kritische Vierteljahresschrift für Gesetzgebung und Rechtswissenschaft*, LXXXV (2002) 273–98.

84. *Der Parlamentarische Rat: 1948–49. Akten und Protokolle*, IX, p.111.

85. Hodge, 'Active at the Creation', p.95. See also R. Pommerin, 'Konrad Adenauer and the United States', in R. Pommerin, ed., *The American Impact on Postwar Germany* (Providence, RI: Berghahn Books, 1995), p.2.

86. U. Haltern, 'Progressivism, Populism, and Constitutional Review in Germany', Harvard Jean Mannet Working Paper No. 5/96, http://www. jeanmonnetprogram.org/papers/96/9605ind.html.

87. R.R. Doerries, 'The Unknown Republic: American History at German Universities', *Amerikastudien/American Studies*, L. (2005) 99–125.

7
John Taylor of Caroline's *Construction Construed, and Constitutions Vindicated* and *New Views of the Constitution of the United States* – with Some Reflections on European Union

Joseph Eugene Mullin

The American Revolutionary period, from 1763 to 1789, may be seen as a series both of conflicts about local autonomy and of experiments in confederation and federation building. Thereafter, as the federal government gradually grew stronger, its strengthening caused a deepening controversy in the South and North, surfacing into crises with the Alien and Sedition Laws, the Louisiana Purchase, the Hartford Convention, and the Missouri Compromise. The extension of slavery eventually became the paramount issue, of course, but the protective tariff, the national bank, and internal improvements all provoked intense debate about the relative powers of the states and of the federal government. During the first American decades states feared consolidation, thought challenges to political rights would proceed from the centre, and fought Washington over issues that now appear to have been settled, not least by the Northern victory in 1865. Slavery and Southern rebellion seemed to verify that danger could easily proceed from the periphery, and the ratification of the Fourteenth Amendment subsequently protected constitutionally guaranteed rights from state abuse. The twentieth century, especially through the long Democratic dominance of the federal government during the New Deal and its aftermath (from 1933 to roughly 1980), confirmed federal primacy.

However, since the Reagan administration the Republican Party has succeeded in downsizing the federal government by starving the federal

budget, reasserting state predominance in matters like welfare administration, and proclaiming a vague 'new federalism'. Conservative
intellectual circles, citing strict construction of the Constitution,
'judicial restraint', and 'original intent', argue a stronger position for the
states relative to the national government than we have imagined in
the last one hundred years. The Tenth Amendment, which reserves to
the states or the people all powers not granted to the federal
government, is effectively reviving. Simultaneously, the Fourteenth
Amendment's guarantee to citizens of equal rights, due process and
equal protection suddenly is used to undermine affirmative action. My
point is that the tensions between a regionalism or a states' rights position and a federal or a national loyalty are not entirely resolved, even *in
American terms*. As old American controversies stir and redefine themselves, old American voices, made apparently irrelevant by events, speak
with renewed vigour and relevance. And all of this is happening while
Europe contemplates regional and state primacy, and debates sovereignty for a transnational confederation or federation – or a yet stronger
Union. I am suggesting, therefore, that the historical American debate
about regional and central power has indeed a contemporary interest
for Europe, reexamining discarded alternatives and, indeed, unheeded
warnings.

One of these old American voices belongs to John Taylor of Caroline
(1753–1824), a soldier, a planter, an occasional pamphleteer, and a some-
time legislator. (He introduced, for example, the Virginia Resolutions
into the Virginia legislature in 1798, and he served three short terms as
his state's interim appointee to the United States Senate.) In the years of
the Federalist presidencies he wrote opposing Hamilton's banking
schemes: the funding of the debt, the assumption of the state debts, and
the national bank. He wrote the popular *Arator* (1813), a collection of
newspaper pieces on his farming experience and methods, which was a
sort of handbook of Virginia agrarian practice.[1] However, his last years
constituted the most productive period of his life, for it was during that
decade that he composed and published his lifetime of speculation on
the American constitution-making experience.

*An Inquiry into the Principles and Policies of the Government of the United
States* (1814) constituted a delayed response to John Adams' *Defence of the
Constitutions* (1787). But for a long time John Taylor of Caroline, though
acknowledged to be the most articulate of the Virginia Republicans, the
person who best gave voice to Jeffersonian political values – a voice clearer,
more organized, and more sustained than Jefferson's own – enjoyed
only diffident respect. Henry Adams acknowledged Taylor's brilliance as

a relentless voice for local or regional power, but felt he had had no influence whatsoever, writing as he had a decade or two after practical events had resolved most of Taylor's constitutional preoccupations. Adams doubted Taylor had been read 'north of Baltimore by any but curious and somewhat deep students'.[2] Adams thought Taylor was at best a brilliant anachronism. Vernon Parrington recognized Taylor as the 'intellectual leader of the Jeffersonian Republicans' and appreciated Taylor as a significant figure of '*American letters*'.[3] In a skillful analysis of *An Inquiry*, Arthur Schlesinger, Jr. remarked on its literary distinction in the seventeenth-century baroque manner, 'a kind rare in America and ignored by literary historians'.[4] Charles A. Beard considered Taylor's *Inquiry* 'among the two or three really historic contributions to political science which have been produced in the United States'.[5] Such accolades arouse our curiosity. In sum, Taylor's *Inquiry* argued that persons and parties greedy for dominance were consciously undermining the various balances in the American system. Taylor saw a dangerous conspiracy of wealth and station, centered in the presidency and the federal courts. He wished to limit the President to a single term and to remove his executive privilege, powers of patronage, and dominance in foreign affairs. He wished to make the federal bench elective and to remove the Supreme Court power to review Congressional legislation. Nowadays, interest in a number of these reforms is again stirring, though others yet remain dormant.

Construction Construed, and Constitutions Vindicated (1820) replied to central decisions of the Marshall Court that strengthened judicial powers. *Tyranny Unmasked* (1822) countered growing congressional support for a protective tariff, which was supportive of minority capital and inimical to majority agricultural interests. Finally, *New Views of the Constitution of the United States* (1823), which followed the publication of the journal of the federal convention (1818) and of Robert Yates's *Secret Proceedings and Debates of the Convention* (1821), reflected upon what Taylor 'discovered were distortions of original meaning and a nationalistic bias permeating *The Federalist*'.[6] In *New Views* Taylor took an anticipatory, opposing, but now forgotten view to Judge Joseph Story's three-volume *Commentaries on the Constitution* (1833), which became the classic of early constitutional construction. Joseph Story makes no mention of Taylor in those *Commentaries*, though he must have been aware of him. James McClellan reports that on a later occasion Story snorted his disbelief that there could be 'new views' of the Constitution, with the sublime confidence that the Marshall Court's reading of the Constitution was a 'canonical' interpretation, something very close to 'original intent'.[7] So, despite his prescience, John Taylor had found no audience. As recently as thirty-five years ago Taylor's long-out-of-print works could be located only in research libraries. Today, nearly two centuries after their first publication, all of his major writings are back in print, edited by regionalist scholars of reputation like M. E. Bradford, and discussed approvingly by Robert E. Shalhope and such major American historians as Forrest McDonald. It is possible today to buy Taylor's works in new editions, read them, and contemplate their arguments, even 'north of Baltimore'.

In the first new edition of *New Views of the Constitution of the United States* since its publication in 1823, McClellan remarks that John Taylor of Caroline is 'the only Republican to present a systematic exposition of states' rights doctrines'.[8] Jefferson himself, writing to Spencer Roane in 1821, said *Construction Construed, and Constitutions Vindicated* 'is the most logical retraction of our government to the original and true principles of the Constitution. ... It contains the true political faith, to which every catholic republican should steadfastly hold'.[9] McClellan finds that *New Views of the Constitution of the United States* offers 'one of the most insightful and closely reasoned analyses of the *original intent* [italics mine] of the Constitution from a states' rights perspective ever written'.[10]

I intend to focus on *Construction Construed, and Constitutions Vindicated* and on *New Views of the Constitution of the United States* and consider topics raised by John Taylor of Caroline that address the relationship of state sovereignties to a larger political union. These relationships are the central preoccupation of Taylor's writing. The nature of a federal constitution, the means of its ratification, and the consideration of just whom that union represents; the general problem of explicit and implied federal powers; the matter of a federal judicial review of national legislation; the power of a federal legislature to tax directly; concerns about currency and banking (with ramifications for state/federal political and economic relations, together with the danger of manipulation of the currency or budget to the advantage of classes or regions); and treaty and war-making powers for a federal entity. All of these are subjects on which the members of the European Union are and will continue to be ruminating for the next few decades, and upon which John Taylor's observations and reflections nearly two centuries ago have continuing relevance.

'We the people of the United States'

Who made the Constitution? Or, in whose name was the Constitution made? John Taylor's argument goes like this: the American Constitution, even though it commences with the apparently unambiguous phrase 'We the people of the United States', is a pact among the people of the several states and not among the people of America. Times may have changed, amendments and Supreme Court decisions may have altered the Constitution or its received meaning, but it is important to remember that the delegates to the Constitutional Convention were chosen by the states and that the Constitution was ratified, not by a national referendum or plebiscite, but by the states through conventions that represented the people of each state. 'The Constitution was thus a compact among the states, resting on the sovereignty of the people as expressed through their state conventions', observes James McClellan.[11] Moreover, amendment of the constitution does not require a national vote, but rather requires the approval of three-quarters of the states, each state making its decision discretely, whether by vote of its state legislature or of a state convention called for the specific purpose of determining its decision about the proposed amendment. (This means that the nearly thirty five million residents of California cannot overwhelm the six New England states, whose combined population number only half that of California.) Taylor is explicit about the process of amending the constitution:

> Had this constitution originated from, or been made by the people inhabiting the territories of the whole union, its amendment would have remained to them, as the amendment of state constitutions belongs to the people of a state. But as such a body of associated people, did not exist, the amendment of the union is left in the hands of the existing bodies politick, to which, as its authors, it obviously belonged. No majority in congress can either call a convention, or amend the constitution; but the legislatures of two-thirds of the states may compel congress to call one, and those of three-fourths, may amend it. Thus a supremacy of the states, not only over congress, but over the whole constitution, is twice acknowledged; first, by their power over the legislative and executive departments instituted for executing the union; and secondly, by their power over the union itself.[12]

The fallacy, that is, the 'new doctrine', with which Taylor takes issue – and this fallacy has become the standard modern interpretation, or 'construction' of the Constitution – is 'that the government of the union is responsible to the sovereignty of the people residing throughout the union, and not to the sovereignty of the people residing in each state'.[13]

Let us hear Taylor in another exposition of the same fundamental point:

> The journal of the convention states 'that the constitution was transmitted to Congress, and by it to the state legislatures; that these legislatures, by separate laws, appointed state conventions for the consideration of the constitution; and that it was ratified by the delegates of the people of each state.' Every step in its progress, from beginning to end, defines it to be a federal and not a national act. The deputies who framed it were federal and not national deputies. They transmitted it to Congress, because the assent of that body was required by the federal union of 1777. It was transmitted by Congress to the state legislatures, because the federal principle required it. And it was ratified by each state, because each state was sovereign and independent.[14]

The process was not as smooth or uncontroversial as Taylor suggested here, but such was the process nonetheless.[15] Considering all these facts therefore, 'We the people of the United States' needs to be understood, not as 'we the citizens of a united nation', but rather as 'we the citizens of the several states, federated as we already have been by *The Articles of Confederation* and here gathered once again to reaffirm and strengthen our political arrangement'. Or, more simply put, not 'We the people of the *United* states', but 'We the people of the united *States*'.

Note, as evidence, the central position the states play in every department of the new government. First, in the Senate the states are represented as such, and with equal weight. In Taylor's time, of course, the state legislatures elected their states' representatives in the United States Senate. Since the ratification of the Seventeenth Amendment in 1913, the voters of each state have taken this elective responsibility upon themselves, but any 'reform' of representation, if that is what was envisioned in 1913, remained unrealized: the states still have equal representation in the Senate.[16] Today, regardless of population, each state still elects only two senators, a confirmation that the Senate continues to represent the several states as such. It is also worth remembering that Article V of the Constitution, in detailing the amendment process, explicitly excludes any proposed amendment that denies any state its equal representation in the Senate without that state's specific consent. Any such amendment would be entirely outside the bounds of the present constitution.

Second, the House members are elected directly by the people, representing *state* districts. Each state has at least one representative of its own. As the Constitution puts it, 'The House of Representatives shall be composed of Members chosen ... by the *People of the several States* [italics mine], and the Electors shall have the Qualifications requisite for Electors of the most numerous Branch of the State Legislatures' (I: 2: 1); and, as Taylor pointedly observed (of the situation before the 1820s), 'the right of suffrage is placed upon different grounds in different states'.[17] There is this further consideration: House legislative districts are subject to reformation by the *state* legislatures every ten years, following the result of the decennial census. Each member of the House represents a single district of a single state. John Taylor makes a revealing observation: 'The representatives of no states feel any responsibility to the people of other states, nor have the people of one state any influence over the representatives of another. The influence over this house [of representatives] is therefore state or federal, and its responsibility to a consolidated nation quite chimerical.'[18] It is true that James Madison (*Federalist, Number XXXIX*) is of a different opinion about the House being a national rather than a federal institution. His point of argument is essentially that the House is *composed* in the same manner as a state House of Representatives, but this point is misleading. Consider again, in riposte, the words of the Constitution itself, 'The House of Representatives shall be composed of Members chosen every second Year by the People of the several States' (I: 2: 1).

Third, John Taylor is at pains to note that the President is chosen by electors from the several states, whose sole responsibility is to vote the presidential choice of each state. (It is accurate, if unorthodox, to observe that on a presidential election day not one national election but many state elections are held, and the results of those separate elections are tallied later in the electoral college.) Even more telling, if the electoral college is unable to deliver a majority of its vote to any one candidate, then the incoming House of Representatives makes the decision, in which each state delegation, regardless of its size, has a single vote for President (II: 1: 3; significantly, a procedure unaltered by the Twelfth Amendment). It is clear upon reflection that the President is not chosen and was not intended to be chosen by the people of America, but by the people of the several states in an indirect manner. Speaking of the President, Taylor says that 'The mode of his election is federal, and not national, because the constitution intended to establish a federal and not a national government. If the states should ever part with this federal feature of the constitution [i.e., the electoral college], it will be a great and probably a conclusive stride towards a consolidated, and perhaps a monarchical government.'[19] Where Taylor stands in defense of a federal arrangement is clear. Moreover, his reasoning is also clear – and surprisingly persuasive – even if time has altered our understanding of the American government and we have developed or evolved into another kind of United States.

So, to repeat Taylor's observations: the people of each state elect their senators, their representative, and the electors who vote for President. The Constitution is amended by *state citizens*, and while it is possible to imagine a new constitutional convention revising or even dissolving the American union, it is more difficult to imagine a dissolution of the states themselves, simply because they are the more fundamental American political units. Grasping this, one can understand John Taylor's point that the federal government possesses no more than those few powers granted to it. Energetic readings of the 'necessary and proper' clause (I: 8: 18) or of the 'supremacy clause' (VI: 1: 2) abuse the intention and spirit of the Constitution. 'Implied powers' – whatever the judicial determinations of the John Marshall's Supreme Court – may hardly be said to exist, for so-called 'implied' powers were likely *retained* simply because they were not granted, not granted that is, by state citizens who had another more basic political society to which they belonged.

Taylor argues that no superiority of federal over state power, or vice versa, exists. In citing the eminent David Ramsay, Taylor insists that 'The sovereignty was in the people', and 'the characteristic of that sovereignty was displayed by their authority in written constitutions'.[20] This result was clear to Taylor, a position he finds perfectly consistent with Alexander Hamilton, whose 'plain arguments' in *Federalist, Number XXXVI*,

> supply us with a conclusive construction of the constitution, namely, that federal and state legislatures are co-ordinate, co-equal, and independent neither being controllable by the other; that only legal supremacy appertains to both; that their mutual independence was intended to inspire them with mutual moderation; and that if collisions occur which they cannot amicably settle, the control of the people over both, and not a dictatorial supremacy of one, or some portion of one, is an umpire.[21]

To Taylor, early American constitutional history was the story of a struggle with centralizing political forces that refused to face the people directly with their interpretations of supremacy. Instead, these nationalistic forces relied on constitutional interpretation, or in other words, 'construction', which they contested in courts, and between state and federal court systems. Which is to say that John Taylor was combating the Marshall court while that court was sitting.

The 'necessary and proper' clause (I: 8:18) and broad construction

The complex history of the 'necessary and proper' clause and the considerable commentary upon that history are matters too vast for our appreciation here. Suffice it to say that in the landmark opinion of the Marshall court in the case of *McCulloch v. Maryland* the power granted to Congress by the Constitution, 'To make all laws which shall be necessary and proper for carrying into Execution the foregoing Powers [i.e., I: 8: 1–17], and all other Powers vested by this Constitution in the Government of the United States or in any Department or Officer thereof' was given a generous interpretation by the Chief Justice, known for his nationalist judicial tendencies. The *McCulloch* case involved a judgment about the constitutionality of the establishment of a national bank. Bernard Schwartz explains that Marshall followed the reasoning of Alexander Hamilton in his own *Bank Opinion*, that 'if the establishment of a national bank would aid the government in the exercise of its granted powers, the authority to set one up would be implied'.[22] It has to be admitted that Hamilton's reasoning speaks neither to 'necessary' (i.e., 'logically inevitable') nor 'proper' (i.e., 'consistent') powers: his argument is purely pragmatic. And pragmatism is the drift of John Marshall's famous argument in his case decision: 'Let the end be legitimate, let it be within the scope of the constitution; and all means which are appropriate, which are plainly adapted to that end, which are not prohibited, but consist with the letter and spirit of the constitution, are constitutional.'[23] Here Marshall appears to have seized on 'proper' exclusively.

John Taylor himself quotes Marshall's opinion, but he sees the entire question of implied powers in the larger context of state and federal powers. He affirms 'the principle of dividing, limiting, balancing and restraining political powers, to which all our constitutions [state constitutions and The Articles of Confederation] have unequivocally resorted, as the only resource for the preservation of a free government.'[24] Taylor feared that 'If the means to which the government of the union may resort for executing the powers confided to it, are unlimited, it may easily select such as will impair or destroy the powers confided to the state governments.'[25] Taylor argues that one of the surest ways to know the limitations on federal means is to study the powers granted directly to the states: 'the unspecified means which congress may use to effect the ends committed to the care of the government of the union, are also limited by the powers delegated and reserved to the states.'[26] This is an extraordinary observation, and an argument no one advances today. In Taylor's mind, nothing could be 'more manifestly unconstitutional' than federal legislation justified by the 'necessary and proper' clause with 'capacity to subvert the distinct division of powers between the general and state governments'.[27]

John Marshall's famous formula – 'Let the end be legitimate' – therefore makes no argument for the 'necessity' of an apparent implied power, and he finds such a power to be 'proper' when judged merely in terms of the federal Constitution itself. Taylor insists, on the contrary, that the Constitution exists within a fabric of fundamental law, with explicitly defined powers, in each American state. It is as if Taylor were accusing Marshall simply of begging the question about implied powers: that is, of assuming the priority of the federal constitution when that is the matter under consideration. Taylor tries once again to order this subject properly:

> The declaration of independence declares the colonies to be free and independent states; the constitutions of many states assert the sovereignty of the people; and the sovereignty has hitherto been considered as the highest political degree. In that sense it has been claimed, held and exercised by the people of every state in the union from the revolution to this day.[28]

The people of the states formed a federal union, granted some explicit powers to that federal government, and retained others. The Tenth Amendment, after all, records as a *fact* that powers *are* retained by the people or by the states (and the states possess those powers because they were granted to them by the citizens in constitutions pre-dating the Constitution of 1787). The Tenth Amendment is not, therefore, an appeal for generosity from a 'superior' federal entity, anymore than the First Amendment is, say, merely an *appeal* for legislative restraint in matters of religious and political practice. Taylor is simply arguing that powers *held* by the states cannot be read as implied federal powers under the 'necessary and proper' clause for some Hamiltonian convenience. Taylor understands the meaning of 'proper' in terms of an entire constitutional process of balancing equal and equally restrained governments in which true 'supremacy' lies only in the sovereignty of the people of the states themselves.

The Supremacy Clause

The Supremacy Clause affirms,

> This Constitution, and the Laws of the United States which shall be made in Pursuance thereof; and all Treaties made, or which shall be made, under the Authority of the United States, shall be the supreme Law of the Land; and the Judges in every State shall be bound thereby, any Thing in the Constitution or Laws of any State to the Contrary notwithstanding.

This clause seems definitive. Ostensibly, it claims that federal law is superior to state law where the two may collide: indeed, that federal law is 'supreme'. However, John Taylor doubts that the Supremacy Clause is so simple. He observes that state sovereignties made and can amend or revoke the Constitution itself; thus, to take just this one example, the 'supremacy' referred to in VI: 1: 2 is in some sense subordinate to these state sovereignties. Taylor's solution to this riddle is clear: first, 'the laws and treaties to be supreme must ... be made in conformity with the powers bestowed, limited and reserved by the constitution'.[29] Taylor argues that matters reduce themselves, as they must, to a strict understanding of granted and implied powers. Furthermore, he explicitly observes that by those 'powers bestowed, limited, and reserved ... we must determine whether a law or treaty has been constitutionally made, before the question of its supremacy can occur'.[30] This calls for reflection. Conflicts cannot be dismissed simply with a vague reference to federal legal supremacy. Taylor sharply notes that 'The supremacy is not bestowed upon the federal government', or upon a department of that government.[31] So, supremacy 'is not extended to [federal] judicial decisions' either.[32] Supremacy extends only to the Constitution in its bestowed powers, and to laws and treaties constitutionally in accord with them. Again, as ever, Taylor understands the federal Constitution as part of a web of fundamental, that is constitutional, constructions in both the states and in the federal union. Elsewhere, Taylor summarizes his view of judicial supremacy:

> Whenever the constitution operates upon collisions between individuals, it is to be construed by the [supreme] court, but when it operates upon collisions between political departments [at state or federal level], it is not to be construed by the court, because the court has a power to settle the collisions of individuals, but no power to settle those of political departments.[33]

It has been an old argument against judicial review that a creature of the Constitution – the Supreme Court – could not interpret the meaning of the Constitution. That point is made here by Taylor in regard to federal supremacy: the Supreme Court would have no jurisdiction in matters pertaining to other constitutions, namely the several state constitutions made in separate acts by the people of each state. Forrest McDonald identifies this same point in his examination of *Tyranny Unmasked*,

> To allow a *branch* of the confederal government to be the arbiter of either that government's own powers or the *powers of the parties to the compact that gave it existence* would be to pervert the very idea of compact, the inviolability of compact or contract being one of the cardinal features of the God-given natural constitution.[34]

The Supremacy Clause, therefore, may be said to apply explicitly to delegated powers in the Constitution, but not to reserved powers or those imaginary 'implied' powers dear to the constitutional theory of Hamilton and Marshall. Taylor is combating a claim for 'the convenience or necessity of uniformity' in constitutional means, which he understands to be merely a cover for a consolidation of political power. Let us not pretend that a power for internal improvements or the creation of a national bank are 'implied' in powers granted to 'regulate Commerce', 'coin Money', or establish 'post Roads' (I: 8: 3, 5 and 7). Let us, instead, discuss amending the constitution to establish a national bank, or to provide internal improvements. The forces for consolidation want a bank and internal improvements, to be sure. Even more, they want a general permission to legislate far and wide for convenience. Thus, the Marshall decision in *McCulloch v. Maryland* produced a far greater change in the Constitution than appropriate amendments would have permitted. Loose construction of the Constitution, Taylor acknowledged, would more likely produce a surer revolution than frequent amendments to the federal and state constitutions. He saw it as being politically intolerant to deny the several states the power to take their own paths in most fundamental legal matters, where the sovereignty of the people can be most effectively and safely exercised. To consolidate power in a federal government, to insist that its laws and courts have political supremacy, was to step back into the time of the Hanoverian kings.

One certain abuse to flow from a consolidation of federal, legal and judicial supremacy is the transference of wealth from one class or district, to another. Taylor worried about the creation of a permanent, commercial-paper-holding class, and he feared the transfer of the profits of labour from one portion of the union to another. Taylor was referring to debt, interest on debt, and various legislative bounties, and more specifically on contemplating tariffs on imported manufactured products. He observes: 'To define the nature of a government truly, I would say, that a power of distributing property, able to gratify avarice and monopoly, designated a bad one; and that the absence of every such power, designated a good one'.[35] The concept of federal supremacy through judicial construction made all this political mischief convenient, without any reformation of constitutional principles. Again, false construction made for stealthy subversion and easy corruption.

John Taylor summarizes the question of supremacy by posing this question:

> If the constitutional rights and powers, established by the people between legislative, executive and judicial departments, and between state and federal departments, do in the language of the court *retard, impede, burden or controul* each other, where does the authority lie for removing the inconvenience, admitting it to be one; in the people, or in an implied supremacy of one of these departments, intended by the people to be controuled?[36]

He begins his reply rhetorically: 'If in the latter, the constitution is exposed to be altered by laws or adjudications without restraint.'[37] And, so, the 'inconvenience' is to be removed by the people, through altering fundamental law, i.e., constitutions, and, if necessary, by using erected balances to frustrate a call for 'convenience or harmony' at the expense of rights retained by the states or the people. That is to say, there are times when actions such as the Virginia and Kentucky Resolutions, written in opposition to the Alien and Sedition Laws, would be an appropriate though temporary response that was entirely in keeping with the Ninth and Tenth Articles of the Bill of Rights.

Judicial review

There are several arguments supporting the theory that the Supreme Court possesses the power of judicial review of the Constitution and its laws. The case has been made that the American Revolution itself was a kind of judicial review, that the existence of a Bill of Rights certainly implies a necessity to construe the Constitution, that the Supremacy Clause (as generally understood since Marshall's time) requires the power of judicial review, that *Federalist* understood judges must give preference to constitutional formulas rather than legislative acts when these should conflict (*Number LXXVIII*),[38] and that the Judiciary Act of 1789 fully expected the Supreme Court to exercise judicial review as part of its appellate responsibilities.[39] Still, it is fair to observe that Chief Justice Marshall selected with caution those cases (e.g., *Marbury v. Madison*) that became the foundation for the concept of judicial review: Marshall was alert to judicial and political objections to his position, and he was prudent in his political circumspection in the face of the Virginia and Kentucky Resolutions.

John Taylor takes a different view from Hamilton and Madison. He understands that Hamilton, in arguing for a national government, intends to resolve disputes through the superiority of the national legislature 'with a power to *pass all laws whatsoever*', subject only to the control of the electorate.[40] Taylor also understands that Madison prefers a federal judiciary with power to settle controversies between the state and federal spheres. Madison claims neither sphere 'is subject to the other, and both ... are independent and supreme'; yet, as Taylor retorts, 'although the whole of each is independent of the whole of the other, yet the whole of one is subjected to and dependent upon a part of the other'.[41] Both Madison and Hamilton miss that 'mutual check or control between independent state and federal spheres' for which both had argued during other phases of the ratification process.[42] Now Taylor finds the concept of judicial review contrary to the spirit of the entire constitutional process, which began with the Declaration of Independence, continued through the ratification of The Articles of Confederation and the state constitutions, and culminated in the acceptance of the Constitution of 1787. These various constitutional acts 'unite in establishing the principle, that the guardianship of each belonged to the people as organized into states, and they have never surrendered a power, essential for the preservation of their liberty, to a chamber of men inducted, like bishops, for life, by executive selection'.[43] To try it once more:

> There are some principles necessary for the existence of the political system of the United States. One of these is, the supremacy, both of the state and federal constitutions, over the repositories of power created by their articles. Another, that this is a limited supremacy in both cases, subject in one, to the supremacy of the people in each state, and in the other, to the supremacy of three-fourths of the states. And a third, that no power created by these constitutions, can

violate their articles, or evade the supremacies to which the
constitutions are themselves subject.[44]

Powers granted to state and federal departments will conflict, circumstances do change, and principles will need reformulation and renewal.
Neither a Supreme Court nor a national government possesses the explicitly granted powers, sophistication, tradition, and capacity to resolve conflicts in a political union without reference to the people and deference to
their sovereignty. Democratic life requires reflection and active political
engagement. Conflicts are resolved by sovereign citizens using their intelligence and experience. Deferring to political entities that claim political
supremacy for 'the convenience or necessity of uniformity' (a constant
danger in federated governments) undermines democratic practice and
confidence. This is certainly John Taylor of Caroline's lesson in construing
political constitutions, and his most impressive political legacy.

Ratification

The Seventh Article of the Constitution provides that 'The Ratification
of the Conventions of nine States shall be sufficient for the Establishment
of this Constitution between the States so ratifying the Same.' The
Constitution calls for ratification by conventions and not by the state legislatures. This preference is an act of returning to the source of state as well
as federal sovereignty, that is, to the people of the states themselves. Now,
sovereignty is a complex and thorny problem: here let us note only what
Madison, Hamilton, and Taylor have to say on the matter. Madison avers
that 'The express authority of the people alone could give due validity to
the Constitution.'[45] Hamilton agrees, making a more detailed observation:

> It has not a little contributed to the infirmities of the existing political
> system that it [*The Articles of Confederation*] never had a ratification by
> the PEOPLE. Resting on no better foundation than the consent of the
> several legislatures, it had been exposed to frequent and intricate ques-
> tions concerning the validity of its powers, and has in some instances
> given birth to the enormous doctrine of a right of legislative appeal.

Hamilton is prophetically looking down the long road toward nullification.
He continues,

> The possibility of a question of this nature proves the necessity of
> laying the foundation of our national government deeper than in the

mere sanction of delegated authority. The fabric of American empire ought to rest on the solid basis of THE CONSENT OF THE PEOPLE. The streams of national power ought to flow immediately from that pure, original fountain of all legitimate authority.[46]

Hamilton confirms that sovereignty lies with the people, but his discussion betrays his intention that the national government would assume superiority over the states in the future. Madison is also aware of the needs of a national legislature in its relations with the states. He wrote to Washington in early 1787 that ratification by convention, going beyond 'the ordinary authority of the Legislature ... will be the more essential as inroads on the *existing Constitutions* of the states will be unavoidable'.[47] Both loose and strict constructionists wished ratification to be based on the consent of the governed as directly as possible, though they might very much disagree as to the effects this sanction had on the *Constitution* and its governmental branches. Joseph Story calls to his aid this very passage in developing the same argument for ratification by convention.[48]

   John Taylor is more suspicious of power than either Hamilton or Madison, and has the benefit of a hindsight that included his observation of how Hamilton and Madison performed when they assumed positions of influence. The long English struggle for political dominance in the seventeenth and eighteenth centuries confirmed that 'No English sovereignty regal, parliamentary or republican, recognized sovereignty or a right to self-government in the people'.[49] So, in the colonies

> before the American revolution, the natural right of self-government was never plainly asserted, nor practically enforced; nor was it previously discovered, that a sovereign power in any government, whether regal or republican, was inconsistent with this right, and destructive of its value. Then the divine sovereignty claimed by governments of every form, was completely exploded or reclaimed by the natural or divine right of self-government, not to be again surrendered, but to be retained and employed in creating and controlling governments, considered as trustees invested with limited functions [note, again, the clarifying Ninth and Tenth Amendments to the *Constitution*], and not as sovereigns possessing powers derived from that source of despotism.[50]

Conventions called for specific and fundamental purposes, like ratifying a constitutional, express sovereignty definitively. But for Taylor the question of convention or legislative approval, though important, was not as vital as the recognition that the approval be in the name of the people *of the states*, since they were the only source of any political arrangement for union.

In the Founding era there was no talk of referenda or plebiscites. Local gatherings of citizens could make essential local decisions and, of course, might also petition the legislature in other matters. The town meeting was a tradition in most of New England, for example. But a little arithmetic illustrates that conventions for single purposes called in individual states, while not referenda, were nothing like the conventions of political parties in our own time. One might well wonder who are those delegates at the national conventions in the United States, how did they get there, who chose them, and whom do they nominally represent? Most passive viewers have few answers to these questions. At the Connecticut ratifying convention in 1788, 168 men represented the approximately 230,000 people who lived in the state. That is roughly one delegate for every 1370 inhabitants. However, discounting women and children, and considering the question of property or other qualifications for male suffrage, the ratio of delegate to potential voter was more like one to three hundred. In Massachusetts there were 355 delegates for a general population of 360,000, or a ratio closer to one to two hundred. I believe Connecticut and Massachusetts have the most favourable ratios (the numbers are particularly troublesome in states with slave populations), but they are not drastically different from the other states. These ratifying conventions may not be referenda, but they are nothing like our expectation nowadays of what a 'convention' denotes. Conventions constituted a remarkable way for citizens to *discuss* as well as express their considered decision about a single central political question, especially in comparison with modern referendums that provide for no discussion and depend upon the seriousness of the press and the candour of the government in power to lay the foundation for an informed vote. So, when Hamilton or Madison, or even their critic John Taylor, insists that ratifying *conventions* in the states should approve a new constitution, each is asking for *direct* participation and vote by those who are the source of sovereignty – for while the people 'bestow' limited powers upon governments, they do not receive limited rights or prerogatives from them.[51] In Taylor's judgment, I believe, something as fundamental as a European constitution ought to flow from an expression of popular sovereignty *within each European state*, and that sovereignty might express itself best in a referendum or a ratifying convention. Only by such a means would authority for a European constitution go beyond the authority for a mere piece of legislation, which could, after all, be overturned by subsequent legislation of a later national parliament.

The American colonies, for all their differences, were products of the same political history, sharing a similar consciousness of sovereignty and a common-law tradition. They understood themselves as defending 'the rights of Englishmen' in their very acts of resistance to the Crown. Their independence came at the same legal moment, with the same declaratory act. Rebellion threw upon them a need for further interdependence. The people of the nations of modern Europe, on the contrary, have their own distinct histories and ways of conceiving of their political identities. European nations have more matters of history and identity to sort through than the Americans ever had.

John Taylor would be interested in the notion of sovereignty in the various member states of the European Union, wherein it resides, and how sovereignty finds the means to delegate powers to a continental political system. To put it in somewhat more contemporary terms, Taylor would be interested in narratives that European countries have about the relation of the people to their governments. Something as fundamental as a European constitution ought to flow from an expression of popular sovereignty within each European state. (I am aware of no public discussion addressing the source of sovereignty that is being conducted in tandem with public debate about the adoption of the proposed constitution for the European Union. One would expect in the new republics of Eastern Europe especially that sovereignty would be an increasingly controversial, indeed a pressing, inquiry.) That European countries are all versions of parliamentary democracy hides the fact that they have their own ways of explaining sovereignty to themselves. Constitutional monarchies are not republics, for example. What does it mean that a British person is a 'subject' and a French person a 'citizen'? What kind of authority have the various peoples of these European nations given to their governments to negotiate on their behalf for any European association?

Let us consider regional development funds as an example. They are a transfer of wealth, as John Taylor would be quick to point out. Where does development money come from? The practical question is stark: who gave the authority for whose taxes to be appropriated and transferred? If I were Dutch or German I would like to know whether *my* taxes built the splendid new Vasco da Gama Bridge across the Tagus in Lisbon, and if so, why? I would also like to know when and how I gave authority for it. I would be concerned with a political precedent for funding other faraway projects – wars, potentially – without specific authority voted in my own legislature, by my immediate representatives. Speaking in these ostensibly hostile terms is merely voicing the large and essential problem of sovereignty – if not calling for national referenda, at least insisting upon more clearly understood and credited sources of sovereignty and its representations.

Could or should a European Parliament or the Council of Ministers alter basic European arrangements without national referenda or conventions? Can the act of national parliaments grant sufficient sanction to continental political arrangements? The absence of national *referenda* to ratify decisions taken in Brussels raises a concern that powerful national or international minorities have agendas of their own. In John Taylor's mind this consideration would be at least as important as the nature of that continental association itself, because a continental union built on disregard for the sovereignty of the people of the several nations is certain to produce a union dangerous to the liberties, which that union professes to encourage and protect. John Taylor of Caroline does give witness, from long observation, to such an unhappy eventuality unfolding in his own time.

Notes

1. See J.E. Mullin, 'The American Georgic', *Diacrítica*, IX (1994), 291–307.
2. H. Adams, *The History of the United States of America during the Administrations of Thomas Jefferson and James Madison* (New York: Library of America, 1986), II, p.1314.
3. V.L. Parrington, *Main Currents in American Thought, 1800–1860* (New York: Harcourt Brace, 1927), II, p.14.
4. A. Schlesinger, Jr., *The Age of Jackson* (Boston: Little, Brown, 1953), p.22.
5. C.A. Beard, *Economic Origins of Jeffersonian Democracy* (New York: Macmillan 1943), p.323.
6. John Taylor of Caroline, *New Views of the Constitution of the United States*, (1923), ed., J. McClellan (Washington, DC: Regnery Publishing, 2000), p.liii.
7. *Ibid.*, p. xi.
8. *Ibid.*, p. xiv.
9. F. McDonald, *States' Rights and the Union: Imperium in Imperio, 1776–1876* (Lawrence: University Press of Kansas, 2000), p.252, n.14.
10. Taylor, *New Views*, p.xi.
11. *Ibid.*, p.xxvi.
12. J. Taylor, *Construction Construed, and Constitutions Vindicated* (1820), (New York: DaCapo Press, 1970), p.45.
13. *Ibid.*, p.45.
14. Taylor, *New Views*, p.38.
15. See J.N. Rakove, *Original Meanings: Politics and Ideas in the Making of the Constitution* (New York: Knopf, 1996), pp.94–130.

16. See D. Lazere's harsh criticism of the institution of the Senate in this respect: 'America the Undemocratic', *New Left Review*, CCXXXII (November–December 1998) 3–40.
17. Taylor, *Construction Construed*, p.44.
18. Taylor, *New Views*, p.237.
19. *Ibid.*
20. Taylor, *Construction Construed*, pp.63, 64; quoting David Ramsay, *History of the United States* [1789], II, pp.172, 174.
21. Taylor, *New Views*, p.97.
22. B. Schwartz, *A History of the Supreme Court* (New York: Oxford University Press, 1993), p.46; see also S. Cornell, *The Other Founders: Anti-Federalism & the Dissenting Tradition in America, 1788–1828* (Chapel Hill, NC: University of North Carolina Press, 1999), p.187.
23. Cited in Schwartz, *Supreme Court*, p.46.
24. Taylor, *Construction Construed*, p.83.
25. *Ibid.*
26. *Ibid.*, p.86.
27. *Ibid.*, p.93.
28. *Ibid.*, pp.120–21.
29. *Ibid.*, p.124.
30. *Ibid.*
31. *Ibid.*, p.123.
32. *Ibid.*, p.129.
33. J. Taylor, *Tyranny Unmasked* (1822), ed., F.T. Miller (Indianapolis, IN: Liberty Fund, 1992), p.204.
34. *States' Rights and the Union: Imperium in Imperio, 1776–1876*, pp.78–9; italics mine.
35. Taylor, *Construction Construed*, p.15.
36. *Ibid.*, p.174.
37. *Ibid.*
38. See Schwartz, *Supreme Court*, pp.41ff.
39. C.L. Black, Jr, *A New Birth of Freedom: Human Rights Named and Unnamed* (New Haven, CT: Yale University Press, 1999), p.121.
40. Taylor, *New Views*, p.127.
41. *Ibid.*, p.126.
42. *Ibid.*, p.128.
43. *Ibid.*, p.152.
44. *Ibid.*, pp.198–9.
45. J. Madison, A. Hamilton and J. Jay, *The Federalist Papers*, ed., I. Kramnick (Harmondsworth: Penguin, 1987), *Number XLIII*, p.285.
46. *The Federalist Papers, Number XXII*, pp.183–4.
47. J. Madison, *Writings* (New York: Library of America, 1999), p.83.
48. J. Story, *Commentaries on the Constitution of the United States*, 3rd edn [1858] (Union, NJ: The Lawbook Exchange, 2001), II, pp.652–3. [§1855].
49. Taylor, *Construction Construed*, p.34.
50. *Ibid.*, p.37.
51. *Ibid.*

8
Revisioning the American Revolution in the Era of the Hollywood 'Blockbuster'

Andrew Pepper

It is a curious anomaly that an event which occupies such a sanctified position in the meta-narrative of American history – what Simon Newman refers to in his introduction as 'a beacon for others around the world committed to a republican form of government' – should have been so resolutely overlooked by the majority of Hollywood filmmakers.[1] Indeed, while Americans and Europeans alike have learned about the United States from films about the conquest of the West, the Civil War, the Second World War and Vietnam, the American Revolution has been routinely ignored by Hollywood. Since the United States celebrated its bicentennial in 1976, only two major films have been made, or at least partly financed by Hollywood, which feature the events of the Revolution in a meaningful way: Hugh Hudson's ill-fated *Revolution* (1985), a film whose abject box office performance effectively bankrupted its British production company Goldcrest, and Roland Emmerich's *The Patriot* (2000), a star-driven 'blockbuster' film made by the production team also responsible for *Independence Day* (1996) and *Godzilla* (1998). This chapter provides a comparative reading of both films and, in doing so, makes two central claims: first, the issue that should concern us when considering how history is represented in films is not one of 'accuracy' – whether films are faithful to, or falsify, the so-called historical record – but rather how a film's engagement with historical events has been shaped by the material conditions under which filmmakers construct and disseminate their narratives and audiences watch and make sense of them; second, and consequently, any comparative study of two films made about the American Revolution will reveal less about the intricacies of the course of revolution itself and more about the changing historiographic status of the revolution in the contemporary era, and indeed about changing practices of filmmaking, distribution and consumption in what has become an increasingly globalized marketplace.

Accordingly the chapter argues that both films constitute important interventions in debates not only about the meaning and relevance of the American Revolution for our own cultural and political moment – both in the United States and Britain – but also in the different way in which national histories are appropriated to service the needs of particular kinds of filmmaking. At stake here is the question of whether both films were received in different ways by American and European audiences and, indeed, whether the American Revolution has come to mean or signify something different for Americans and Europeans in our own historical moment. My comments here will be confined to British, rather than European filmgoers and critics, not least because in the light of the films' subject matter and the fact that *Revolution* was produced by a largely British production team and *The Patriot*, by a largely American team, a comparison between American and British responses to the films seems most apposite. In very broad brush terms, it would certainly be fair to argue that there are, and have been, very significant political and cultural differences between America and Britain over the past quarter-century; differences which have, in turn, produced contrasting attitudes towards imperialism, conflict and history/culture. Since the early 1980s successive American administrations have actively sought to combat the so-called 'Vietnam syndrome' and, in doing so, tap into a discourse of patriotic self-belief that has, to some extent or another, been a feature of American civic culture since the early nineteenth-century. Meanwhile Hollywood, with obvious exceptions, has generally reflected this larger political ethos of American self-belief and self-confidence projected by successive administrations from Reagan through to the current George Bush. Hence, in the case of American history, the tendency has been to produce essentially affirmative films, such as *Saving Private Ryan* (1998) and *Pearl Harbor* (2001), which celebrate the heroism of American combatants in the face of hostile external threats. In contrast, attempts by the Thatcher government in the 1980s to construct a culture of affirmation and patriotism, found limited success with regards to events like the Falklands War, but was generally countered by a more fractious, antagonistic social and political culture. Generally, too, films made about Britain in the 1980s and 1990s (or about British history) were less patriotic and affirmative than their American counterparts.

However, as I point out in this chapter, there is no compelling evidence in the particular cases of *Revolution* and *The Patriot* to suggest that audiences and critics in Britain and America responded to the films in radically different ways. That's to say, American audiences were predisposed to make and enjoy 'affirmative' films like *The Patriot* and reject 'critical' films like *Revolution*, and Britons were predisposed to accept *Revolution* and reject *The Patriot*. What I argue, instead, is that a comparative analysis of both films ends up revealing much more about changes in the cultural and political landscape, and practices filmmaking in America *and* Europe between the mid-1980s and the turn of the new century. As such, this chapter argues that *Revolution*, in part a throwback to a type of 'new wave' cinema that emerged in Hollywood in the late sixties and seventies (and influenced by European auteurs like Goddard and Truffaut),[2] constitutes a compelling and at times uncomfortable (for the viewer at least) attempt to challenge some of the foundational myths upon which traditional understandings of the American Revolution and American exceptionalism are based. It proposes that the film's failure at the American box office, to some extent, reflects its attempts to unsettle some of the more commonly held, patriotic beliefs and assumptions about the revolution – and while it falls some way short of claiming that Hudson's film was, in relative terms, well-received in Europe for precisely these reasons, it argues that the film did attract a small but enthusiastic following, both in the United States and Britain, among left-minded critics and viewers precisely because of its willingness to contest certain conventional 'truths'. Conversely, the chapter argues that *The Patriot* constitutes a new type of formally conventional and politically conservative 'blockbuster' or 'high concept' cinema now predominating in the global realm. As such, the events of the 1770s and 1780s are utilized to serve two related purposes: first, to celebrate, in traditional ways, the American Revolution as a heroic landmark for human progress and a progressive assault against the forces of colonial tyranny, and second, to make the point that the values supposedly earned or guaranteed by the revolution (such as freedom, individual rights, and equality) are, in the contemporary context, not simply American, but universal. The chapter compares this 'preferred' reading of the film, whereby the freedom and equality fought for and won by the Patriot armies are constructed as America's gift to a 'grateful' world, with a series of 'oppositional' readings;[3] these include objections by British critics to the film's problematic inclusion of highly embellished and exaggerated atrocities committed by Crown forces; African-American criticisms of the film's unwillingness to confront the issue of slavery; and those readings which interpret the film's apparently well-intentioned postulations as part of a contemporary shift in the way in which order is exercised and maintained *across* boundaries of race, class and even nation. Indeed, the extent to which a film like *The Patriot*, no longer made only with American finance or exclusively for American audiences, ends up express- ing the concerns and preoccupations, not of an imaginary 'America', but rather of multinational conglomerates such as Sony – in short, the political and economic logic of free-market neo-liberalism currently in the global ascendancy – will be addressed in the chapter's conclusion.[4]

While explanations for Hollywood's apparent lack of interest in the American Revolution remain speculative – Michael Ventura most daringly argues that Hollywood has tended to shy away from the revo- lution for the same reason that American television networks refused to air a dramatized reading of the Declaration of Independence during the 1976 Bicentennial: because to do so would be to remind people of the document's incendiary, subversive claims and hence how far 'America' had fallen from its original promise – filmmakers tackling it as a subject inevitably find themselves caught between a rock and a hard place.[5] Those who depict it as far-reaching and genuinely revolutionary, run the risk of exposing the ever-growing gap between the rhetorical claims of, say, the Declaration of Independence and what Gregory Jay calls 'the stubborn realities of particularity and exclusion', associated with the United States from its inception.[6] However, those who suggest that the break with colonial Britain was somehow limited in scope, and that the revolution itself was essentially a conservative one, maintaining property claims and existing social hierarchies, implicitly undermine a strongly-held belief in America's 'exceptional' status that has percolated through American cinema from the early twentieth century onwards.

Still, in spite of these dilemmas and in the light of the rhetorical claims of American exceptionalism, one could very well argue that the story of the founding of the American nation – virtuous, heroic rebels overcoming a tyrannical oppressor – has played an influential role, both in the development of American cinema in general, and in the ways in which subsequent episodes and events from American history have been represented by Hollywood filmmakers. In so far as Hollywood has typically sought to contain and resolve contradictions between competing values and mythologies through a strategy of displacement (displacing contra- dictions arising from the 'real' into melodrama as a means of resolving them), then this mythologized account of the revolutionary has found its way into films as diverse as *My Darling Clementine* (1946) and *Star Wars* (1977). Furthermore, if cultural myths, as Hellmann contends, 'enable a nation to cohere by reconciling, in the ambiguous relations of narrative, conflicts that its people cannot solve in the sharply delineated realm of analytical thought', then we should perhaps see their assimilation into Hollywood films as a form of ideology as much as an expression of national preoccupations.[7] Slotkin, for example, argues that myth does not 'argue its ideology' but rather 'exemplifies' it. 'It projects models of good and bad behaviour that reinforce the values of ideology, and affirm as good the distribution of authority and power that ideology rationalizes.'[8] As such, the displacement of the historically 'real' into myth is part of a wider process whereby cultural forms avail themselves to the task of re-inscribing the status quo. The question that lies at the heart of this chapter is how or whether the displacement of the historically 'real' into narrative forms, which themselves borrow heavily from myth, impacts upon their contradictory status as vehicles of ideology and pedagogically instructive texts. Audiences in the United States and Europe may well be aware of perceived bias in films such as *The Patriot* or, for that matter, *Saving Private Ryan*, but that does not preclude the fact that such films have provided these audiences with much of their understanding of American history in general and specific events like the American Revolution and the Second World War in particular. And while it has always been the case that history which purports to be the 'ultimate reality and source of truth' in fact 'manifests itself in narrative constructs' or 'stories designed to yield meaning through narrative ordering',[9] the question that most concerns me is how this process is affected or intensified by its translation into a type of narrative – the Hollywood movie – typically known for its affirmative vision of American life. Of course, one needs to be careful about conceiving of the 'Hollywood movie' as a standardized product, just as one also needs to be aware that the practices and processes of making films – and financing and distributing them – have changed, especially in the last twenty years. Still, if the term Hollywood now more than ever is shorthand for a type of spectacular, ideologically conservative, star-driven filmmaking, then the question of how such larger systemic changes might have affected Hollywood's role as American historian, and scribe of the American Revolution in particular, does require our attention.

Revolution: history, myth and subversion

If it is unfair to berate Hollywood filmmakers for the fact that they re-write history – for history itself is by no means a pure, unmediated account of the past – then one should perhaps ask how films like *Revolution* or *The Patriot* can help us to better understand the complexities and contingencies of particular historical episodes or events. Here,

Revolution, a film which focuses on the struggle between the colonial armies and the forces of the British Crown initially in New York and ultimately at Yorktown, constitutes both a success and a failure. Certainly there is little in the film to explain what might have motivated the rebellion against Britain, aside from the rambling sentiments of Pacino's Tom Dobb who talks wistfully to his injured son about 'making a place for ourselves' where 'there ain't no kings or queens' to 'tell us what to do'. Nonetheless the film skillfully elucidates the ambivalence of those who, like Tom Dobb, found themselves thrust into battle on the side of the Continental Army without explicitly believing in what they were fighting for, and highlights albeit heavy-handedly, via a schism between archetypal patriot Daisy McConnahay (Natassja Kinski) and her loyalist family, the way in which the wider conflict split families and communities. Furthermore, just as John Shy claims that the war itself was revolutionary in so far as the act of mobilizing against the British had a transforming effect on the colonial population, it is only once Dobb has suffered at the hands of the enemy that, evoking the spirit of Paine's *Common Sense*, he talks of wanting 'to make a place for ourselves' where 'there ain't no one to bow down to' and 'where there ain't no lord or lady better than you'.[10] Even more significantly, the film, like Ray Raphael's study of the American Revolution, starts to explore, or at least open up the class divisions created by the conflict.[11] Though the men who enlist for the newly formed Continental Army are promised 150 acres of land and Dobb, whose fishing boat is requisitioned for the cause, is promised 200 dollars in addition, at the end of the film the same people are told that land and money owing to them has been sold by Congress to pay for the war debt. The resulting disturbances may be muted, but the point is well made; the poor go to the wall while McConnahay, a speculator who initially supported the Crown, but who subsequently changed sides, benefits financially and politically in this new America. As a powerless Dobb is jostled from the centre of the frame by an unruly mob, the visual imagery evokes disarray rather than consensus and unity of purpose. Behind the thin veneer of a newly created national 'sameness' lie a myriad of competing, potentially explosive class claims and differences.

Nonetheless, in spite of the film's perceived pedagogical ambitions, what is of more relevance for the purposes of this chapter is not how 'accurately' *Revolution* recreates particular episodes and events from the American Revolution, but rather how, or how far, this process is shaped by a desire to offer a particular reading or interpretation of the past, by the narrative conventions of Hollywood cinema, or indeed by the cultural and political imperatives informing the film's moment of production. Traditionally, the western has tended to set the limits of Hollywood's engagement with history or, to put this another way, Hollywood has sought to narrate the growing pains of nation through the mythologized exploits of a single, heroic figure borrowed from the western. As Slotkin notes, 'When history is translated into myth, the complexities of social and historical experiences are simplified and compressed into the actions of representative individuals or "heroes." '[12] So what of Tom Dobb and *Revolution* in general? Does he slide comfortably into the outlaw hero's cowboy boots and does the film reduce and simplify the complexities of 'real' history? Certainly it would be fair to argue that the film's attempts at historical revisionism take place through the lens of generic revisionism; that is to say, its means of telling the 'truth' about history is to summon up the slower, darker, more contemplative mood of westerns such as *McCabe and Mrs Miller* (1971) rather than the bombast of earlier Second World War films, such as *The Sands of Iwa Jima* (1949). Indeed, like the European 'new wave' films upon which they drew their inspiration, revisionist movies like *McCabe and Mrs Miller*, *M*A*S*H* (1970) and *Little Big Man* (1970) were not necessarily any more 'realistic' than their earlier counterparts, but rather self-consciously sought to challenge myths about the viability of individual heroism or the ability of such figures to shape and order the chaotic 'mess' of public history.

From the beginning, Dobb struggles to assert himself. In fact, he is dwarfed by his surroundings, by the sheer physicality of a New York City in turmoil. The film's mis-en-scene here is revealing. As the moving camera attempts to follow him through the teeming streets, Dobb is jostled from the centre of the frame, disorientating both him and the viewer. A little later, as the conscripts leave the city by boat, the camera pulls back slowly to reveal Dobb in a sea of equally blank-looking faces. Visually, as with the earlier street scenes, the effect is to situate him in a context where the collective is privileged over the individual, in a situation over which he has no control. Of course the classic western often began this way, with the outlaw hero reluctant to sacrifice his independence in order to help the wider community achieve some kind of desirable collective goal.[13] In *Revolution*, Dobb reluctantly agrees to join the war effort in order to protect his son and eventually to 'make a place for ourselves', but his efforts make little or no difference to the collective cause. Underlining this point, in a scene that self-consciously evokes the climax of John Ford's *Stagecoach* (1939), British dragoons – stand-ins for Ford's Apaches – pursue and attack a coach driven by Daisy

McConnahay, the woman that Dobb loves. Rapid editing between close-ups of the pursuers, the galloping horses and the stagecoach itself intensify the connection. But whereas Ford's hero, the Ringo Kid (John Wayne), is instrumental in repelling the Apaches, Dobb can only watch from a distance as the British attack and upend the stagecoach. His decision to chase after it on foot strikes one not as heroic but as the desperate response of a man who is all too aware of his own limitations.

Many of Ford's films strive to integrate the outlaw into an enabling community. Though the dictates of the outlaw code precludes permanent engagement, the solidarity that is fostered through some kind of encounter with a hostile, external force is genuinely uplifting, and even where the outlaw's anti-social tendencies threatens to undermine this solidarity – as in *The Searchers* (1956) – the communal goal of settling the land cannot be achieved without his help. *Revolution* works to an altogether different end, namely the isolation and entrapment of individuals who, as Kolker puts it, 'though part of a large organization, are forced to be alone'.[14] Alienated both from the Patriot army which he grudgingly serves and his son who interprets his self-interest as cowardice, Dobb veers between action and passivity. Occasional successes, such as his rescue of his son from a heavily fortified British army camp, are punctuated by long periods of introspection and melancholy. Failure, or rather ambivalence, is Dobb's leitmotif. As the film lurches towards its climax – the last stand of the British at Yorktown – it flirts with conventionality in so far as the wider conflict is displaced into a stand-off between Dobb and Peasy (Donald Sutherland), a British soldier who has previously captured and beaten Dobb's son. Still, even here, the film's willingness to flout convention is evidenced. Dobb wounds Peasy and has the opportunity to kill him but, at the behest of his son, decides not to, allowing Peasy to make his escape.

There are a number of ways to read this palpable sense of ambivalence. The first is to frame it in terms of artistic failure; that is, to interpret the film's contemplative pace, its willed incoherence, and its dramatic confusion as a failure on the part of its makers. The film's abject performance, particularly at the American box office, and its mauling at the hands of many American film critics, lends a certain amount of credibility to this argument. *Time's* Richard Corliss, for example, described it as a 'chaotic two hour and four minute mess' and claimed that preview audiences had 'giggled derisively through it'.[15] Pauline Kael, in *The New Yorker*, believed the film was so bad 'it puts you in a state of shock', and said of the disjointed introductory sequence: 'this is the American Revolution as you might expect to see it on MTV'.[16] I am not suggesting that these criticisms are somehow invalid, or that their negative treatment of the film stems, first and foremost, from uneasiness about its critical, not necessarily celebratory agenda. In the same way, I would not want to suggest that audiences and critics in Britain, for example, warmed to the film for precisely these reasons. What I would like to argue, however, is the film's apparent disjointedness can be read in alternative ways. Certainly, the film cannot work out what to do with Pacino's character, or how to make sense of his twin role as conscientious objector and standard bearer for the emerging nation. To some extent, attempts to wrap him up in the Stars and Stripes, as the film's trailer sets out to do, reflect a traditional preoccupation with celebrating an uncomplicated 'American-ness'. His ambivalence, meanwhile, speaks to, and about, a more critical impulse to unsettle the assumed link between the film's protagonist and archetypal heroic patriot.

More particularly, this incoherence or tension must be situated quite explicitly in the context of 1980s America; that is to say, one might think about how the contradictory ideologies informing the production of the film shape the way in which the film represents history. For a start, there is something unconvincing about the film's flirtation with a celebratory vision of America and American national identity – a vision that was central to Ronald Reagan's presidency.[17] To be sure, in the climate of a Reagan-inspired attempt to resuscitate a positive sense of American national identity from the trauma of defeat in Vietnam and the so-called 'crisis of confidence' that paralyzed Carter's administration, the decision to wrap Pacino in the American flag in the film's trailer made perfect box office sense. At the same time, however, the film is ultimately uninterested in occupying the patriotic territory claimed by movies like *Rambo: First Blood Part II* (1985). Rather, *Revolution* is curious in that it wants to explore the legacy of America's 'crisis of confidence'. To put it another way, if the critical cinema of the 1970s – inspired by both Vietnam and Watergate – was essentially one of anxiety and ambiguity, then *Revolution* is intrigued by this legacy without ever fully committing itself to continuing it. As such, the film both embraces and recoils from patriotic sentiment, knowing full well that a film about failure and vulnerability might not play well to audiences in the thrall of Reagan's can-do boosterism, but perhaps suicidally, wanting to privilege failure over jingoistic populism nonetheless. As Adrian Turner notes, 'Al Pacino is not John Wayne as David Crockett defending democracy and dying at the Alamo; nor is he John Rambo, a one-man task force regaining for America a whimsical self-respect and national pride after the humiliations of Vietnam and Iran ... *Revolution* subverts this image of heroism.'[18]

The film's engagement with the legacy of the 1970s manifests itself most obviously in its willed incoherence and formal disjointedness, as though part of Hudson's desire is not to make a 'bad' film, but rather a difficult film, one that requires audiences to work at eliciting meaning from it. Building upon this starting point, I want to argue that what is being evoked here is not the confused ideological undercurrents of the mid-1980s but an alternative, possibly even subversive way of 'seeing' history. If American cinema has tended to treat history as popular myth – that is to say, to displace the complexities, discontinuities and contingencies of the 'real' into a simplified form where such contradictions can be resolved – then what we see in *Revolution* represents a different approach to history, one in which the sweep of public events takes precedence over the private exploits of individuals, and where neatly packaged answers and clear visual and narrative signposts are absent. For all its flaws, therefore, the film's determination to unsettle our expectations, to withhold clues about how to read character and motivation, to disempower its protagonist and show war to be dirty, brutal and shorn of heroic aura, serves to throw into relief the more general relationship between cinema and history. Accordingly, *Revolution* may not be 'true' in the sense that it sets out to dispassionately and objectively record what really happened, but as Robert Rosenstone argues, the idea that 'truth' and 'accuracy' are necessarily synonymous is itself problematic. As he explains, 'The historical film will always include images that are, at once, invented and, at best, true ... true in the sense they symbolize, condense, or summarize larger amounts of data; or true in that they impart an overall meaning of the past.'[19] What we see in *Revolution*, then, is a fictional recreation of the 'real' as seen through the eyes of an invented figure, Tom Dobb, but one that is 'true' in so far as it imparts 'an overall meaning of the past', or at least one that shows what it might have been like to have lived in or through the events of the revolution. When we see Tom Dobb being caught up in circumstances over which he has no control, what we are actually witnessing is the surrender of the private individual to the collective. As Michael Ventura points out:

> Hudson's subject is the emotional context of a rebellion. How it swings in wild extremes, both brutal and lyrical. Here everyone and everything is dirty and confused and bold and contradictory and desperate and sweet and unkempt ... [The film's characters] only have a story in so far as they're swept up into the flow of the rebellion, and to be swept up is, by definition, not to have a story of one's

own. To be part of such movements is to surrender one's private story to the collective story.[20]

The film's failure at the box office can be explained by its willed ambivalence and its refusal to jump onboard a populist patriotic bandwagon, and perhaps too by its narrative incoherence and its weak characterization, theatrical dialogue and wooden acting. But I would like to propose an additional reason for its failure; one that relates to the political project of revolution and the attendant anxieties produced when social and political hierarchies are questioned by mainstream cinema. If Ventura's point that American filmmakers 'haven't dared to portray the American Revolution' because 'there's no way to do it without being at least incendiary if not downright subversive' is true, then it perhaps explains the small number of films made about the event. Certainly, as he concludes, however the 'revolutionaries' are represented, 'you've still got the most articulate principles of rebellion ever spoken; the invention ... of modern guerrilla war; and the application of political terrorism'.[21] *Revolution* may not be entirely successful in articulating these principles and imperatives, but in so far as it exposes the chaos and upheaval associated with radical change, the class divisions opened up, and the gap between utopian rhetoric and lived reality, then it makes for viewing that is by no means comfortable and reassuring. In the light of the film's revisionist ambitions which are, in turn, the product of its preoccupation with a 1970s culture of despondency and vulnerability, the film challenges a patriotic, benign reading of the American Revolution, which posits it as a landmark in human progress and suggests that the revolution, *in spite* of its incendiary rhetoric, was essentially a conservative one, or at least a struggle which ended up securing the interests of the landed class. Certainly when Dobb arrives back in New York at the end of the film, little or nothing has changed: land and money promised to him has gone to pay off the war debt, speculators and businessmen have assumed control of the city and the streets throng with the injured and dispossessed. The lasting images of the film, meanwhile, are the grim, impressively staged battle scenes which impress, in the final analysis, not simply because they reveal war to be brutal, dirty and shorn of any heroic aura, but also because they allow audiences the time and space to reflect on the damage wrought on individuals and groups. As the British film critic Dilys Powell concludes, 'I can think of no film which with such amplitude of vision offers a more powerful impression of an old, simple war and the heartless annihilators of warfare.'[22]

The Patriot: history and the
politics of authenticity

If Hudson's *Revolution* constitutes a type of critically-minded film that seeks to contest the myth of the individualist hero, underline the brutalizing, dispiriting elements of warfare in general and portray the American Revolution in particular as a conflict fought between elites in order to secure their own interests, then Emmerich's *The Patriot* provides an alternative and, in many ways, deeply conservative approach to the historical retrospective film, conflict in general and the American Revolution in particular. For one thing, the film's makers come across as so beholden to the task of making the sets and costumes look as 'real' as possible – to the point that advisors from the Smithsonian were employed to advise on matters as diverse as military regalia and the type of cooking utensils used by escaped slaves – that discussions about the authenticity or otherwise of the film's artefacts end up standing in for more interesting debates about the politics of historical representation; how the past is represented and what this reveals both about the event itself and the cultural and political circumstances informing the film's own historical moment. In fact, therefore, dubious claims about the film's historical 'accuracy' obscure the much more significant issue of the extent to which the film's attempts to re-imagine the events of the American Revolution are shaped, first and foremost, by the demands of a particular kind of popular narrative cinema. To put this another way, rather than marking a new departure in the way in which Hollywood filmmakers engage with American history *per se, The Patriot* conforms to a very familiar narrative formula: what Ray describes as the 'reluctant hero' template most readily identified with the western whereby an 'exceptional' figure is persuaded by the needs of his community to temporarily sacrifice his hard-earned independence in order to further some kind of socially or politically significant collective cause, only to regain his independent status in the final frames of the film.[23]

In the case of *The Patriot*, this requires Benjamin Martin (Mel Gibson), a widowed homesteader who, like the western's gunslinger, has a reputation for and a history of violence, to come out of self-imposed retirement and commit himself to the collective cause of fighting against the forces of the Crown and those colonists loyal to the British monarch. In the light of this latter distinction, it would perhaps be unfair to suggest that the film tells us nothing at all about the tensions within North American colonial communities in the early years of the conflict. Indeed, a scene depicting a debate in the Charleston Assembly indicates that its representatives in 1776 were by no means agreed upon which course of action to follow, whether to fight for independence or remain loyal to the Crown. That said, what could have potentially turned into a sophisticated argument about competing interests or, as Richard B. Morris explores, how or whether the social, political and economic disruption caused by the war generated fundamental changes in the institutional structures of government, quickly becomes an issue that is addressed and resolved in the context of Martin's private affairs.[24] Though, as we find out, he is opposed to 'taxation without representation' and believes in 'self-government', he is unwilling to commit himself to the cause, because he feels he can better protect his family by remaining at home; especially, as he remarks, because 'the war will be fought not on some distant battlefield but amongst us'. In other words, the question of whether it is appropriate for the colonists to take up arms against the Crown ultimately boils down to the issue of Martin's desire to protect his family. Whereas *Revolution* demanded the surrender of the individual to the collective, *The Patriot's* view of history is dependent on the opposite, on the surrender of the collective to the individual. The result is predictable – Martin eventually joins the cause only because his home is attacked by British soldiers and one of his sons is killed. This scene is indicative of the film's process of simplification. From the moment when Colonel Tavington (Jason Isaacs) arrives at Martin's home on horseback and rejects Martin's pleas for clemency, choosing to demonstrate 'something of the rules of war' by shooting dead one of Martin's sons, a highly complex, multi-faceted conflict between the British and Americans, loyalists and patriots, and colonizer and colonized, boils down to a personal feud between two men. As such, the film's claims to accuracy are rendered moot. This much is made clear by its climactic battle scene; the final encounter between the Crown and Continental armies in the Carolinas. Notwithstanding the unlikely scenario of Martin riding into battle carrying the Stars and Stripes – the Continental Army had not yet adopted the flag – the scene's melodramatic excess and individualized view of history is firmly underlined when Martin retrieves the fallen standard and drives the sharp end of the pole into Tavington's horse, before defeating his archenemy in a hand-to-hand duel involving knives and tomahawks. In other words, the moment that Martin triumphs over Tavington, independence from the Crown is effectively realized.

If there is something eminently typical about the way in which *The Patriot*, to paraphrase Slotkin, simplifies or compresses 'the complexities of social and historical experiences' into 'the action of representative heroes', then we perhaps should not be too surprised that the view of historical events we are given in the film is, to say the least, a skewed one.[25] Of more significance is the historiographic status of the American Revolution for our own cultural and political moment. Here the film would appear to support a quite conventional account of the events of the 1770s and early 1780s whereby those supporting the Patriot cause were fighting simply for an amorphous notion of 'freedom' and that, as a result, the American Revolution constitutes an heroic landmark for humankind and a shot across the bow of tyranny and oppression in all of its guises. One hardly needs to add that this 'preferred' reading of the film would have been well-received by a patriotic and nationalistic constituency in the contemporary United States. Indeed, the film's supporters claim that while its makers inevitably employed some kind of dramatic licence, its basis in historical 'truth' is verifiable: the production notes claim that Martin's character is based on a number of 'real' figures who waged a guerrilla war against the Crown across the Carolinas. 'Martin's slippery elusiveness', we are told, 'is reminiscent of [Francis] Marion, who would attack the British and retreat into the swamps, earning him the sobriquet "The Swamp Fox" ', but at the same time Martin's 'independent spirit, his talent for recruiting men to join his militia, and his effective guerrilla campaign reflect [Thomas] Sumter' as well as Andrew Pickens and Daniel Morgan whose '1000-strong force of light infantry, riflemen, regular army and militia led the crucial colonial victory at the Battle of Cowpens which is represented in the film'.[26]

It goes without saying that, for its advocates, the film's apparent historical accuracy is evidenced by its 'correct' reading of the American Revolution and vice versa. It perhaps also goes without saying that the film's perceived inaccuracies are evidenced by its 'incorrect' reading of the Revolution and vice versa. Accordingly, African-American critics like Spike Lee were moved to anger by the film's careful elision of any references to slavery: African-Americans who work on Martin's farm do so under their own volition and for a fair wage. In an open letter to the *Hollywood Reporter*, he described the film as 'pure, blatant American propaganda', and pointed out that when 'talking about the history of this great country, one can never forget [it] was built upon the genocide of the Native Americans and the enslavement of African people', and that to imply otherwise was nothing short of 'criminal'.[27] In a different but related attack, many British film critics felt aggrieved by the film's attempts to caricature the Crown's military leaders, notably Tavington, who in one scene locks a cowering group of women and children in a church and burns it to the ground. As Andrew Pulver summarily remarked, 'If the occasional intrusion of smiling, happy black faces point to one blind spot in *The Patriot*'s historical vision, then the elaborate demonization of the British is another ... Historians – who, unlike film-makers or, indeed, critics, are sticklers for facts – are unanimous in asserting that such activities were entirely unknown: basically, this is a historical film that is *way* off-beam'.[28] However, as George Custen argues, '[t]o address history from the point of view of "accuracy" alone is to accept that such a condition exists and that it is disinterested, rather than ideologically motivated'.[29] In other words, the issue of whether 'facts' do, in fact, reveal a larger historical truth is open to question. My point is that an obsessive focus on the question of historical (in)accuracy ultimately manifests itself in banal list-making where a film's failings are held up and evaluated against an historical record which is itself, by no means secure and beyond challenge. As such, one can easily find examples from the film that both support and undermine particular historical claims. Just as John Shy's assertion that the British force under Banastre Tarleton 'acquired in the course of its operations a reputation for inhumanity that drove apathetic citizens towards the rebels for protection'[30] would seem to vindicate some part of the film's depiction of Tavington, his point that the rebel militia was 'poorly trained, badly led ... and seldom comprised of the deadly marksmen dear to American legend'[31] and functioned, first and foremost, not as a military force, but as catalyst for politicizing the rural population against the Crown, is directly contradicted by *The Patriot*, which suggests that the militia was instrumental in driving the British army not just from the Carolinas, but also out of America.

More particularly, this focus on questions of historical accuracy ends up obscuring some of the more insidious ways in which a film like *The Patriot* sets out to convince us of the 'rightness' of its message. Indeed, while the polemic intent of Spike Lee's criticisms of *The Patriot* are useful for political mobilization against racism, his analysis fails to notice that the film's racial politics are beholden less to *Gone With the Wind*-style plantation movies, with their emphasis on absolute racial differences, than to a more contemporary cultural and political logic that insists upon eradicating racial differences, or at least pretending that they have no profound social or political consequences. Thus while the filmmakers enthusiastically pointed to their faithful recreation of an 'authentic' Gullah village populated by runaway and freed slaves originating from Angola, Congo and the Ivory Coast – experts from the Smithsonian museum were consulted in order to get the details right – this kind of exclusive focus on, say, the authenticity of the film's wattle and daub huts, obscures the more important question of the village's function in the narrative as a whole. On the one hand, then, the Gullah villagers, with their own indigenous culture and language, are free, in the context of the film, to do whatever they choose, unbounded by the strictures of white authority. On the other hand, however, they are free only in so far as they are permitted to occupy certain carefully demarcated spaces and given particular unchallenging tasks to perform. In this sense, a shift away from racial politics in which difference is conceived of in absolutist terms does not herald the arrival of a race-less utopia in which all differences can be disregarded. As Hardt and Negri argue, referring to the mutation of older colonial patterns of rule into newer 'friendlier' forms, what they call Empire 'does not create divisions but rather recognizes existing or potential differences, celebrates them, and manages them within a general economy of command'.[32]

Accordingly the scene in which Martin's eldest son Gabriel (Heath Ledger) marries local sweetheart Anne (Lisa Brenner) in the 'safe' confines of the Gullah village is an instructive one. The question of security is an important one, since Gabriel and his father are, by this stage in the film, being actively pursued by the British. As the camera slowly zooms in on Gabriel and Anne, the onlookers from the village, who are literally outside of the tent, are erased from the frame. The villagers might be 'hosting' the wedding, but their role is a marginal one; as night falls, we are shown shots of a maracas and xylophone, and hear the unmistakable sounds of what is now referred to as World Music. In other words, despite the hybrid possibilities inherent in the way in which the scene insists upon incorporating and mixing of white colonial and 'maroon' cultures, the freed and escaped slaves are ultimately little more than a colorful backdrop to the wedding celebrations, or rather they are incorporated into a hierarchy or chain of command with Martin, and his family, at its helm. Indeed this applies not just to racial differences but also to class ones, for however much the film wants to pretend that the rhetoric of the Declaration of Independence is binding, once British rule is brought to an end, it is instructive that the first act performed by the militia who served under Martin is to rebuild his burnt out home. Explaining this, Hardwick, an ex-slave who has earned his freedom by fighting in the militia, says to Martin, '[Your son] said if we won the war we could build a whole new world. Just figured we'd get started right away with your home.' Hardwick is standing next to another militia-man, a white man, who admitted, earlier in the film, that he didn't 'like the idea of giving muskets to slaves'. The fact that he has changed his opinion speaks to, and about, this 'new world' where 'all men are created equal under God.' Or rather, the fact that some men, namely Martin, are more equal than others is conveniently overlooked.

While *Revolution* hinted at the possibility that the chaos of war might lead to radical social and political change, and hence presented the re-inscription of pre-existing class hierarchies at the end of the film as a crushing disappointment, *The Patriot* wants us to believe that the British constitute the only impediment to political liberty and social freedom, and that once removed, a new classless, racially harmonious society can magically take root. The fact that Emmerich's film ends not with the violent social upheavals seen in *Revolution*, but rather with a polite group of poor whites and freed slaves volunteering to rebuild Martin's homestead is indicative. That is to say, such a vision is so seductive because it appears to be inclusive and consensual, and therefore free of ideology, but is in fact politically loaded *precisely because* of this absence. As Slavoj Zizek argues, referring to a contemporary political phenomenon: 'In post-politics ... via the process of negotiation of interests, a compromise is reached in the guise of a more or less universal consensus. Post-politics thus emphasizes the need to leave old ideological divisions behind and confront new issues, armed with the necessary expert knowledge and free deliberation that takes people's concrete needs and demands into account.'[33] As early as the mid-nineteenth century, Alexis de Tocqueville worried that a reductive view of freedom might take precedence over a more far-reaching interpretation of liberty and popular sovereignty in the fledgling Republic, and argued that the greatest threat posed to this freedom came from the 'tyranny of the majority'.[34] In Emmerich's film, Martin's status as 'reluctant hero' might mean that he is able to masquerade as a figure for whom independence and personal autonomy are of paramount importance but, in the final analysis, his personal vision is eerily reminiscent of Zizek's account of post-politics. Indeed, one might ask how or to what extent Martin and the film's preference for tolerance and inclusionism speaks about, and to, a 'neo-liberal' political and cultural logic currently at work both in the United States and the global realm.

It is worthwhile, here, to note that the makers of *The Patriot* were also responsible for *Independence Day* (1996), the global blockbuster which features a poster-perfect alliance of multi-ethnic Americans battling aliens and making America and then the rest of the world safe. The most obvious reading of the film is that a form of old-fashioned American imperialism underpins the film's universal liberalism, a reading supported by the content and tone of President Whitmore's (Bill Pullman) climactic speech in which he declares: 'We are reminded not of our petty differences but of our common interests ... From this day forth, the Fourth of July will no longer be remembered as an American holiday but as the day that the world declared in one voice that we will not go quietly into the night.' In other words, *Independence Day's* appeal to an imaginary universal liberalism is at once conceived as an American celebration and as the manifestation of a triumphant America bestriding a world – and a new world order – apparently formed in its image. But, as Gregory Jay notes, the crucial point is that this new global and American order secures its power through the manufacturing of universal consent rather than through the reaffirmation of imperialist structures of power or through acts of military coercion:

> With the Americans in the lead, the whole earth prepares to be reborn on the Fourth of July. It is as if scapegoating the extraterrestrial will vanquish the legacy of imperialism and make the Third World grateful once more for the superior power of the West ... Any doubt about the racism of the film is resolved when, to illustrate victory, the camera pans an African savannah where traditionally dressed tribesmen wave spears in jubilation at the sight of the downed alien craft. The actuality of the postcolonial condition ... is erased by a visual narrative that returns the happy primitives to their place in the world.[35]

A similar point could be made about *The Patriot* in so far as everything here, too, is allocated to its proper place and the poor whites and freed slaves are happy to assume their subservient positions *vis-à-vis* Gibson's white landowner. One could add that the freedom being articulated by Gibson's Martin in eighteenth-century North America is identical to the freedom being demanded by Gibson's William Wallace in *Braveheart* (1995) or, for that matter, by Whitmore in *Independence Day*. In this context, values which are typically identified as American (choice, diversity and, particularly freedom) are reconstituted as universal values and, as such, a concept like freedom has more than one possible meaning. On the one hand, a sovereign America stands for, and indeed guarantees freedom not just from the tyranny of the eighteenth century British Crown, but against oppressive regimes across the world in our historical moment. On the other hand, these apparently 'American' values are subsumed into a larger universal category – that of, say, the global capitalist economy – and do not merely lose their particularity but rather become proxies for less appealing formulations. As such, the film's representation of the American Revolution serves to articulate a definition of freedom that is so undifferentiated that it means almost nothing. As Tocqueville feared, a reductive interpretation of freedom could simply invoke the right of individuals and corporations to pursue their own interests regardless of the consequences for others. The film's amorphous conception of freedom may, in a literal sense, be de-politicizing in so far as it is founded upon a false notion of consensus whereby everyone's view is apparently taken into account, but it is also de-politicizing in a profoundly political sense. To put this another way, the film's unacknowledged desire to clear the ground not simply for a mindless, unquestioned patriotism, but rather for an empty freedom (that, in turn, reinforces the concerns and ambitions of global corporations like Sony) makes it a very political film.

This is particularly so, because its visual style serves to encourage audience passivity and an uncritical acceptance of what is on the screen. Indeed, like other 'blockbuster' films, it is ultimately less concerned with articulating coherent political arguments and, at least superficially, maintaining the pretense of cinematic verisimilitude than it is with bombarding audiences with a numbing series of spectacular action sequences that serve to gratify and reassure rather than to provoke or challenge. To illustrate this point, it is instructive to consider a scene from the film in closer detail. The scene in question takes place after Gibson's Martin has witnessed the murder of one of his sons by Tavington and the capture of another. Taking his two youngest sons, he ambushes the platoon that is transporting Gabriel to their camp and proceeds to attack them. The scene takes place after the last Crown soldier drops his weapon and starts to runs away. Martin removes his tomahawk, steadies himself and plants it squarely in the man's back. The scene cuts to a shot of the youngest sons freeing Gabriel. Out of the frame, we hear Martin grunt. It cuts back to Martin who is kneeling over the dead soldier, disemboweling him with his tomahawk and then to a close-up of his bloody face. The scene cuts back to his three children who stare at him, ashen-faced. Finally it returns to Martin who turns to face them, his hair, face, and clothes covered in fresh blood.

Initially shocking, what is excessive about the scene and what threatens to unravel the film – the unsanctioned brutality, the cold-blooded slaying of a soldier who had dropped his weapon, and the sheer scale of the violence – is quickly mitigated by subsequent reaction. The attack is reported to the British high command, not as an horrific slaughter, but as a morale-boosting victory for the patriot cause, while any guilt that Martin might have felt is assuaged shortly afterwards by one of the sons who claims to be 'satisfied' with the deaths. Even the son who is most repulsed by the violence relents and offers Martin a reconciliatory hug. On reflection, what is most striking about the way in which the scene is constructed is that Martin's children witness the slaughter in order to replicate how the film asks that we, as viewers, watch it. Their gaze, as Anthonia Quirke argues about this particular scene, 'mitigates – sanctifies, even – their father's behavior by presenting the whole thing to us as a familial rites of passage'.[36] In other words, Martin's violence is justified, because it serves as implicit support of the white, middle class family. Moreover, precisely because of the gratifying scale of the 'spectacle' (which of course transcends all national and linguistic boundaries) and the solace we receive immediately following it, (where we are reassured the everything is alright) the scene ends up evoking *Braveheart*, or for that matter *Lethal Weapon* and *Independence Day*, more than *Revolution*. Even more so because its perpetrator is not Benjamin Martin, but Mel Gibson; that is to say, the potential for reading this scene in ambiguous ways is nullified, because its perpetrator is Gibson, and his 'star' image all but guarantees that our identification with him will never be broken. The result, as Miller says about much contemporary Hollywood film-making, ends up being 'a spectacle that has been meticulously engineered to "gratify" at every single moment ... [and whose] images are designed to keep us happy, thereby composing a heavy atmosphere of ... easy shocks along with constant solace, flattery and admiration'.[37]

Perspectives from America, Europe and the World

It would be far too easy, and for that matter quite misleading, to claim that *The Patriot* performed well at the US domestic box office, where audiences appreciated its unabashed patriotic sentiments, but poorly elsewhere; in the United Kingdom, for example, where audiences might not have warmed to the film's unapologetic portrayal of British soldiers as war criminals, or in France and Germany where antipathy about an overbearing American patriotism remains strong among certain sections of the population. In fact, *The Patriot* earned almost as much at the international box office as it did at the domestic American box office, taking $113 million at the latter and $112 million at the former. More particularly, the film took a respectable $6.9 million in the United Kingdom, $6 million in France and $14.4 million in Germany; a performance that compares unfavorably with more popular films like *Saving Private Ryan* or *Independence Day*, but very well in comparison with more recent Hollywood combat films such as *Black Hawk Down*

(2001), *U–571* (2000) and *We Were Soldiers* (2002).[38] Yet rather than undoing the logic of this chapter, this statistical data supports its two related lines of argument. First, I have been careful not to overlook the way in which the film operates within a traditional sovereign context; that is to say, how it ends up articulating an uncomplicated, patriotic conception both of the American Revolution (as a heroic struggle against tyranny and oppression) and of America in our own historical moment (as guarantor of an undefined freedom). Hence it is no surprise that the film played well both to its Fourth of July 'opening weekend' audiences in the United States in 2000, as well as to American troops stationed in Bosnia later that same year. Gibson himself is reported to have prepared the following message for soldiers about to view the film: 'I'm glad you're there. I hope you enjoy the film because I enjoyed making it. It deals with personal freedom, which is something people take for granted.'[39] Second, the fact that the film performed well at the box offices in the United Kingdom, France, Germany and throughout Europe underscores the extent to which it was produced and marketed not exclusively for American audiences, but rather for audiences throughout the world already well versed in a particular type of visually spectacular 'high concept' or 'blockbuster' cinema. This is not to suggest that particular sections of cinema-going audiences in France and Germany either necessarily liked the film or were unable to see through its naively patriotic message (clearly this is or was not the case), but rather that the international popularity of action films, the 'star' appeal of Mel Gibson and the relentless marketing campaign that necessarily accompanies summer blockbusters throughout the world all combined to ensure that the film found an enthusiastic audience within *and* outside the US. To put this another way, while there were many filmgoers and critics, in America *and* Europe, who strongly objected to *The Patriot* (on the grounds of its dubious history), the fact that the film found a very sizeable audience at the domestic American and international box office speaks about the 'success' of the film to market itself as a blockbuster and 'everyone's story'. As I have argued here, there is something deeply insidious about this process, but it says more about the globalisation of American values, or rather the transfiguration of so-called American values into universal ones, than about perceived differences between American and European audiences or different responses to the American Revolution. As J.C. Columbani declared in *Le Monde*, in a very different context, 'We're all American now.'[40]

What we find in *The Patriot*, then, is a digitally re-mastered version of the past whose 'high concept' style, to use Justin Wyatt's term, speaks to important structural changes in the film industry and 'can be described most productively … as one strain of contemporary American cinema whose style has a direct economic motive'.[41] To put this another way, if high concept films are founded upon the availability of an exploitable presence – something which 'can motivate moments which are excessive in the film'[42] – then Gibson himself is such a presence, and the function of the 'excessive' behaviour displayed in scenes such as the one in which he slaughters a British soldier is not to engage with the messiness of history or force audiences to question their own identification with the film's protagonist, but rather the opposite: that is, to thrill and titillate unthinking audiences reared on violent action films and expecting Gibson to do as he has done throughout his own movie career: kill 'bad' people in the name of an unquestioned 'good'. As such, *The Patriot's* version of the past, of an American past, is aimed at an audience that is no longer exclusively or even predominantly American. The point, here, is not whether non-American audiences are actually seduced by such images – indeed one can only imagine how some filmgoers in cities across the world, from Berlin to Baghdad, might find the notion of the United States as the ultimate defender and arbiter of 'freedom' a hard one to swallow – but rather that Hollywood filmmakers like *The Patriot's* Roland Emmerich are having to think about such questions as, 'how can I construct this film in order to maximize revenue, not just in America, but also in Europe, the Far East etc.?' As Frederick Wasser concludes, 'The trend line is not absolute but the economic circumstances of current production demands that fewer and fewer films will address a specific community or national audience in a profound way.'[43]

Notes

1. The author would like to acknowledge Edinburgh University Press for allowing the reproduction of parts of this chapter from T. McCrisken and A. Pepper's *American History and Contemporary American Film* (2005).
2. For a fuller account of the rise and fall of this type of revisionist, critically-minded Hollywood film, see the following: P. Biskind, *Easy Riders Raging Bulls: How the Sex-Drugs-and-Rock'n'Roll Generation Saved Hollywood* (New York: Simon & Schuster, 1998); R. Kolker, *A Cinema of Loneliness: Penn, Stone, Kubrick, Scorsese, Spielberg, Altman*, 3rd edn (New York and Oxford: Oxford University Press, 2000); M.C. Miller, ed., *Seeing Through Movies* (New York: Pantheon, 1990).
3. For a fuller definition and account of the way in which these terms can be utilized in the analysis of popular film, see S. Hall, 'Encoding, Decoding' in Simon During, ed., *The Cultural Studies Reader* (London: Routledge, 1993), pp.90–103.

4. The most comprehensive and indeed persuasive account of this newly emerging world order or structure of rule can be found in M. Hardt and A. Negri, *Empire* (Cambridge, MA: Harvard University Press, 2000).

5. M.Ventura, 'A Revolution Worth Having', *LA Weekly*, 27 December 1985, 21.

6. G. J. Jay, *American Literature and the Culture Wars* (Ithaca, NY: Cornell University Press, 1997), p.79.

7. J. Hellmann, *American Myth and the Legacy of Vietnam* (New York: Columbia University Press, 1986), p.218.

8. R. Slotkin, *The Fatal Environment: The Myth of the Frontier in the Age of Industrialization* (Norman, OK: University of Oklahoma Press, 1998), p.19.

9. See J. Culler quoted in T. Bennett, 'Outside literature: Texts in History' in K. Jeffries, ed., *The Postmodern History Reader* (London and New York: Routledge, 1997), p.219.

10. J. Shy, 'The Military Conflict as a Revolutionary War', in M. Penman, ed., *Perspectives on the American Past Vol. 1: To 1877* (Chicago: Heath, 1996), p.135.

11. R. Raphael, *A People's History of the American Revolution* (New York: Harper Perennial, 2002).

12. R. Slotkin, *Gunfighter Nation: The Frontier Myth in Twentieth Century America* (New York: Athenum, 1992), p.13.

13. R. Ray, *A Certain Tendency of Hollywood Cinema 1930–1980* (Princeton, NJ: Princeton University Press, 1985).

14. Kolker, *A Cinema of Loneliness*, p.109.

15. R. Corliss, 'Losing Battle', *Time*, 6 January 1986, 55.

16. P. Kael, 'Revolution', *The New Yorker*, 13 January 1986, 67.

17. See L. Cannon, *President Reagan: The Role of a Lifetime* (New York: Touchstone, 1991); R. Dallek, *Ronald Reagan: The Politics of Symbolism*, Revised Edition (Cambridge, MA: Harvard University Press, 1999).

18. A. Turner, 'Rambo's Revenge', *Guardian*, 6 February 1986, 13.

19. R. Rosenstone, 'Oliver Stone as Historian' in R.B. Toplin, ed., *Oliver Stone's USA* (Lawrence, KS: University Press of Kansas, 2000), p.7.

20. Ventura, *LA Weekly*, p.21.

21. *Ibid.*, p.21.

22. D. Powell, 'Yankee Doodles', *Punch*, 5 February 1986, 84.

23. Ray, *A Certain Tendency of Hollywood*, p.90.

24. R.B. Morris, 'A People's Revolution', in M. Penman, ed., *Perspectives on the American Past*, pp.118–27.

25. Slotkin, *Gunfighter Nation*, p.13.

26. S. Fritz and R. Aberly, *The Patriot: The Official Companion* (London: Carlton, 2000), p.25.

27. See D. Campbell, 'Film director Lee spikes Patriot guns,' *Guardian*, 8 July 2000, 16.

28. A. Pulver, 'Taking a liberty' *Guardian*, G2, 14 July 2000, 5.

29. G. Custen, *Bio/Pics: How Hollywood Constructed Public History* (New Brunswick, NJ: Rutgers University Press, 1992), p.11.

30. Shy, 'The Military Conflict', p.135.

31. *Ibid.*, p.138.

32. Hardt and Negri, *Empire*, pp.200–1.

33. S. Zizek, *The Ticklish Subject* (London: Verso, 1999), p.198.

34. See A. de Tocqueville, *Democracy in America*, transl. H. Mansfield and D. Winthrop (Chicago and London: University of Chicago Press, 2000), pp.235–248.
35. Jay, *American Literature and the Culture Wars*, p.63.
36. A. Quirke, 'Old leatherface gets blood on his hands,' *Independent on Sunday*, Culture, 16 July 2000, 3.
37. Miller, ed., 'Introduction', *Seeing Through Movies*, p.233.
38. At the international box office, Saving Private Ryan earned $268 million, but Black Hawk Down, just $50.5 million, U-571 $37.5 million and We Were Soldiers, $36.5 million; see http://www.boxofficeguru.com/intlarch6.htm. For a more detailed breakdown of The Patriot's performance at the United Kingdom, French and German box offices, see http://www.imdb.com/title/tt0187393/business
39. See A. Shales, 'Patriots and bleeding hearts', *World Jewish Review*, 5 July 2000, http://www.jewishworldreview.com/cols/shales07500.asp
40. Following the 11 September attacks on New York and Washington DC, J.M. Columbani wrote a lead article in *Le Monde* with the headline 'Nous sommes tous Américains' (13 September 2001).
41. J. Wyatt, *High Concept: Movies and Marketing in Hollywood* (Austin, TX: University of Texas Press, 1994), p.8.
42. *Ibid.*, p.31.
43. F. Wasser, 'Hollywood Goes Global: The Internationalization of American Cinema', in S.R. Ross, ed., *Movies and American Society* (New York and Oxford: Blackwell, 2002), p.358.

Bibliography

Ackerman, B. *We the People*, vol. 1, *Foundations* (Cambridge, MA: Harvard University Press, 1991).

Acton, J.E.E.D. *Essays on Freedom and Power* (Boston, MA: Beacon Press, 1949).

——. *Lectures on Modern History* (London: Macmillan, 1906).

Adams, H. *The History of the United States of America during the Administrations of Thomas Jefferson and James Madison*, 2 vols (New York: Library of America, 1986).

Anderson, B. *Imagined Communities: Reflections on the Origins and Spread of Nationalism* (London: Verso, 1983).

Appleby, J. 'America as a Model for the Radical French Reformers of 1789', *William and Mary Quarterly*, 3rd ser., XXVIII (1971), 267–86.

Armitage, D. 'Making the Empire British: Scotland in the Atlantic World, 1542–1707', *Past and Present*, CLV (1997), 34–63.

Arnold, H. 'Die Aufnahme von Thomas Paines Schriften in Deutschland', *Publications of the Modern Language Association*, LXXIV (1959), 365–86.

Bailyn, B., ed. *The Debate on the Constitution*, 2 vols (New York: Library of America, 1993).

Balkin, J.M. 'Populism and Progressivism as Constitutional Categories', *Yale Law Journal*, CIV (1995), 1935–90.

Barany, G. *Stephen Széchenyi and the Awakening of Hungarian Nationalism, 1791–1841* (Princeton, NJ: Princeton University Press, 1968).

——. 'Hoping Against Hope: The Enlightened Age in Hungary', *American Historical Review*, LXXXVI (1971), 319–57.

——. 'The Appeal and the Echo', in Király, B. K. and Bárány, G. eds, *East-Central-European Perceptions of Early America* (Dordrecht: The Peter De Ridder Press, 1977), 107–39.

Beard, C.A. *Economic Origins of Jeffersonian Democracy* (New York, Macmillan, 1915).

Bemis, S.F. *The Diplomacy of the American Revolution* (Bloomington and London: Indiana University Press, 1957).

Bergamasco, L. and Rossignol, M.J. eds, 'L'Amérique: des colonies aux républiques', *Cahiers Charles*, XXXIX (Paris: Université Paris 7-Denis Diderot, 2005).

Black, C.L., Jr. *A New Birth of Freedom: Human Rights Named and Unnamed* (New Haven, CT: Yale University Press, 1999).

Bölöni, S.F. *Journey in North America, 1831* (Santa Barbara, CA: ABC-CLIO, Inc., 1978).

Bradford, M.E. *A Better Guide Than Reason: Federalists and Anti-Federalists* (New Brunswick, NJ: Rutgers University Press, 1994).

Brewer, J. *Party Ideology and Popular Politics at the Accession of George the Third* (Cambridge: Cambridge University Press, 1976).

——. *The Sinews of Power* (London: Unwin Hyman Inc., 1989).

——. 'The Misfortunes of Lord Bute: A Case-Study in Eighteenth-Century Political Argument and Public Opinion', *The Historical Journal*, XVI (1973), 3–43.

Brock, W.R. *The Character of American History*, 2nd edn (London: Macmillan, 1965).

Brogan, D. *America in the Modern World* (New Brunswick, NJ: Rutgers University Press, 1960).

——. *The American Character* (1944) (New York: Knopf, 1950).

——. *The American Political System* (London: H. Hamilton, 1933).

——. *American Themes* (London: H. Hamilton, 1948).

——. *Politics and Law in the United States* (Cambridge: Cambridge University Press, 1942).

——. *U.S.A., An Outline of the Country, its People and Institutions* (London: Oxford University Press, 1941).

Burgoyne, R. *Film Nation: America Looks at US History* (Minneapolis, MN: University of Minnesota Press, 1997).

Clark, T.W. 'Virtuous Democrats, Liberal Aristocrats : Political Discourse and the Pennsylvania Constitution, 1776–1790', PhD diss., J.W. Goethe University, 2001.

Clavière, E. and Brissot de Warville, J.P. *De la France et des Etats-Unis ou de l'importance de la révolution d'Amérique pour le bonheur de la France; des rapports de ce royaume et des Etats-Unis, des avantages réciproques qu'ils peuvent retirer de leurs liaisons de commerce et enfin de la situation actuelle des Etats-Unis* (London: s.n., 1787).

Claydon, T. and McBride, I. eds, *Protestantism and National Identity: Britain and Ireland, c. 1650–c. 1850* (Cambridge: Cambridge University Press, 1998).

Colley, L. *Britons: Forging the Nation 1707–1837* (New Haven, CT: Yale University Press, 1992).

——. 'Britishness and Otherness: An Argument', *The Journal of British Studies*, XXXI (1992), 309–29.

Conway, S. ' "A Joy Unknown for Years Past": The American War, Britishness, and the Celebration of Rodney's Victory at the Saints', *History*, LXXXVI (2001), 180–99.

——. 'From Fellow-Nationals to Foreigners: British Perceptions of the Americans, circa 1739–1783', *The William and Mary Quarterly*, 3rd ser., LIX (2002), 65–100.

Cornell, S. *The Other Founders: Anti-Federalism & the Dissenting Tradition in America, 1788–1828* (Chapel Hill, NC: University of North Carolina Press, 1999).

Cummins, L. Townsend. *Spanish Observers and the American Revolution, 1775–1783* (Baton Rouge and London: Louisiana State University Press, 1991).

Custen, G.F. *Bio/Pics: How Hollywood Constructed Public History* (New Brunswick, NJ: Rutgers University Press, 1992).

Deák, I. *The Lawful Revolution: Louis Kossuth and the Hungarians in 1848–1849* (New York: Columbia University Press, 1979).

Deutscher Bundestag. *Der Parlamentarische Rat: 1948–1949. Akten und Protokolle*, vol. 9 (Munich: Oldenbourg, 1996).

Devine, T.M. *The Tobacco Lords: A Study of the Tobacco Merchants of Glasgow and their Trading Activities c. 1740–1790* (Edinburgh: Donald, 1975).

Dippel, H. *Germany and the American Revolution 1770–1800: A Sociohistorical Investigation of Late Eighteenth-Century Political Thinking* (Wiesbaden: Steiner, 1978).

——. *Die amerikanische Verfassung in Deutschland im 19. Jahrhundert: das Dilemma von Politik und Staatsrecht* (Goldbach: Keip, 1994).

——. 'Modern Constitutionalism: An Introduction to a History in the Need of Writing', *Tijdschrift voor Rechtsgeschiedenis*, LXXIII (2005), 153–69.

Donovan, R. K. *No Popery and Radicalism: Opposition to Roman Catholic Relief in Scotland, 1778–1782* (New York: Garland, 1987).

Dorigny, M. *Révoltes et révolutions en Europe et aux Amériques (1773–1802)* (Paris: Belin, 2004).

Dreyer, M. 'Die Verfassung der USA. Ein Modell für deutsche Verfassungsentwürfe des 19. Jahrhunderts?', in Elvert, J. and Salewski, M. eds, *Deutschland und der Westen im 19. und 20. Jahrhundert, Teil 1: Transatlantische Beziehungen* (Stuttgart: Ranke Gesellschaft, 1993) pp.225–46.

Dubois, L. *A Colony of Citizens: Revolution and Slave Emancipation in the French Caribbean, 1787–1804* (Chapel Hill, NC: University of North Carolina Press, 2004).

Ebeling, C.D. *Die Vereinten Staaten von Nordamerika : Vierter Band, Christoph Daniel Ebelings Erdbeschreibung und Geschichte von Amerika* (Hamburg: Bohn, 1797).

——. *Die Vereinten Staaten von Nordamerika : Sechster Band, Christoph Daniel Ebelings Erdbeschreibung und Geschichte von Amerika* (Hamburg: Bohn, 1803).

Ebeling, C.D., and Lane, W. C. 'Glimpses of European Conditions from the Ebeling Letters', *Proceedings of the Massachusetts Historical Society*, LIX (1926), 324–76.

Echeverria, D. *Mirage in the West. A History of the French Image of American Society to 1815* (Princeton, NJ: Princeton University Press, 1957).

Ellis, J.J. *Passionate Sage: The Character and Legacy of John Adams* (New York: Norton, 1994).

Fagerstrom, Dalphy I. 'Scottish Opinion and the American Revolution', *William and Mary Quarterly*, 3rd ser., XI (1954), 252–75.

Faÿ, B. *L'esprit révolutionnaire en France et aux Etats-Unis à la fin du XVIIIè siècle.* (Paris: Edouard Champion, 1924).

Fichtner, P.S. 'Viennese Perspectives on the American War of Independence', in Király, B.K. and Bárány, G. eds, *East-Central-European Perceptions of Early America* (Dordrecht: The Peter De Ridder Press, 1977), 19–29.

Fink, G.-L. 'Die Amerikanische und die Französische Revolution: Analogien und Unterschiede im Spiegel der Deutschen Publizistik [1789–1798]', *Modern Language Notes*, CIII (1988), 540–68.

Furet, F. *Penser la révolution française* (Paris: Gallimard, 1978).

Gaspar, D.B. and Geggus, D.P. eds, *A Turbulent Time. The French Revolution and the Greater Caribbean* (Bloomington and Indianapolis, IN: Indiana University Press, 1997).

Gauchet, M. *La Révolution des droits de l'homme* (Paris: Gallimard, 1989).

Glant, T. *Through the Prism of the Habsburg Monarchy: Hungary in American Diplomacy and Public Opinion during World War I* (Boulder, CO: Social Science Monographs, 1998).

Godechot, J. *France and the Atlantic Revolution of the Eighteenth Century, 1770–1799* (New York and London: Free Press, 1965).

——. *La grande nation. L'expansion révolutionnaire de la France dans le monde* de 1789 à 1799, 2nd edn (Paris: Aubier, 1983).

Gould, E.H. *The Persistence of Empire: British Political Culture in the Age of the American Revolution* (Chapel Hill, NC: University of North Carolina Press, 2000).

——. 'American Independence and Britain's Counter-Revolution', *Past and Present*, CLIV (1997), 107–41.

Greene, J.P. 'Empire and Identity from the Glorious Revolution to the American Revolution', in Marshall, P. J. ed., *The Eighteenth Century* (Oxford: Oxford University Press, 1998), 208–30.

Halácsy, K. 'Benjamin Franklin's Image in Hungary', *The New Hungarian Quarterly*, XVII (1976), 121–25.

Halicz, E. 'Kościuszko and the Historical Vicissitudes of the Kościuszko Tradition'; in Király, B. K. ed., *East-Central-European Society and War in the Era of Revolutions, 1775–1856* (New York: Brooklyn College Press, 1984), 55–74.

Heideking, J. 'Im zweiten Anlauf zum demokratischen Verfassungsstaat: amerikanische Einflüsse auf die Weimarer Reichsverfassung und das Grundgesetz der Bundesrepublik Deutschland', in Bungert, H., Frey, M. and Mauch, C. eds, *Verfassung – Demokratie – Politische Kultur. U.S.-Amerikanische Geschichte in Transatlantischer Perspektive* (Trier: WVT, 2002) pp.179–98.

Henretta, J. *Salutary Neglect: Colonial Administration Under the Duke of Newcastle* (Princeton, NJ: Princeton University Press, 1972).

Herr, R. *The Eighteenth Century Revolution in Spain* (Princeton, NJ: Princeton University Press, 1958).

Heußner, H. K. *Mehr Direkte Demokratie wagen: Volksbegehren und Volksentscheid: Geschichte – Praxis – Vorschläge* (München: Olzog, 1999).

Heun, W. 2005. 'Das monarchische Prinzip und der deutsche Konstitutionalismus des 19. Jahrhunderts' [Electronic Journal], *Fundamentos. Cuadernos monográficos de Teoría del Estado, Derecho Público e Historia Constituciona* (2000). Available from http://www.uniovi.es/constitucional/fundamentos/segundo/index.html

Higonnet, P. *Sister Republics : the Origin of French and American Republicanism* (Cambridge, MA: Harvard University Press, 1988).

Jacobson, A. J. and Schlink, B. eds, *Weimar: A Jurisprudence of Crisis* (Berkeley, CA: University of California Press, 2000).

Jay, G.J. *American Literature and the Culture Wars* (Ithaca, NY: Cornell University Press, 1997).

Kaina, V. 'Direkte Demokratie als Ausweg? Repräsentativverfassung und Refomforderungen im Meinungsbild von Politikeliten und Bevölkerung', *Zeitschrift für Politikwissenschaft*, XII (2002), 1045–72.

Karsky, B. and Marienstras, E. eds, *Autre temps, autre espace. Etudes sur l'Amérique pré-industrielle* (Nancy: Presses Universitaires de Nancy, 1986).

——. *Travail et loisir dans les sociétés pré-industrielles* (Nancy: Presses Universitaires de Nancy, 1991).

Kesler, C.R. 'Direct Democracy and Representation', in Abrams, E. ed., *Democracy How Direct? Views from the Founding Era and the Polling Era* (Lanham, MD: Rowman & Littlefield, 2002) pp.1–18.

Kidd, C. *British Identities before Nationalism: Ethnicity and Nationhood in the Atlantic World, 1600–1800* (Cambridge: Cambridge University Press, 1999).

——. *Subverting Scotland's Past: Scottish Whig Historians and the Creation of Anglo-British Identity, 1689– c. 1830* (Cambridge: Cambridge University Press, 1993).

——. 'North Britishness and the Nature of Eighteenth-Century British Patriotisms', *The Historical Journal*, XXXIX (1996), 361–82.

Kókay, G. *A magyar hírlap és folyóirat irodalom kezdetei 1780–1795* (Budapest: Akadémiai, 1970).

Kolker, R. *A Cinema of Loneliness: Penn, Stone, Kubrick, Scorsese, Spielberg, Altman*, 3rd edn (New York and Oxford: Oxford University Press, 2000).

Kontler, L. *Millennium in Central Europe: A History of Hungary* (Budapest: Atlantisz, 1999).

Kusielewicz, E. 'Poland's Changing Attitudes Toward the American Revolution', in Király, B.K. and Bárány, G. eds, *East-Central-European Perceptions of Early America* (Dordrecht: The Peter De Ridder Press, 1977) pp.97–106.

Kutnik, J. 'The Declaration of Independence in Poland', *Journal of American History*, LXXXV (1999), 1385–88.

Lacorne, D. *L'invention de la république. Le modèle américain* (Paris: Hachette, 1991).

Landsman, N.C. 'Nation, Migration, and the Province in the First British Empire: Scotland and the Americas, 1600–1800', *The American Historical Review*, CIV (1999), 463–75.

Langley, L. D. *The Americas in the Age of Revolution, 1750–1850* (New Haven, CT and London: Yale University Press, 1996).

Lazare, Daniel. 'America the Undemocratic', *New Left Review*, CCXXXII (1998), 3–40.

Lévai, C. 'The Tokay is Much More Superior To What You Sent me last Year Under That Name: Thomas Jefferson and His Hungarian Wines', *Hungarian Journal of English and American Studies*, VIII (2002), 85–94.

——. 'Early American History in Europe from an East-Central-European Perspective', in Béghain, V., Chéntier, M. and Gabilliet, J.-P. eds, *The Cultural Shuttle. The United States in/of Europe* (Amsterdam: VU University Press, 2004), 283–9.

Liss, P.K. *Atlantic Empires: The Network of Trade and Revolution, 1713–1826* (Baltimore, MD and London, Johns Hopkins University Press, 1983).

Luce, H. 'The American Century', *Life*, 17 February 1941, 61–5.

Lynch, J. *Bourbon Spain, 1700–1808* (Oxford: Blackwell, 1989).

Mably, G. Bonnot de. *Observations sur le gouvernement et les loix des Etats-Unis d'Amérique* (Amsterdam and Paris: Hardouin, 1787).

Madison, J. *Writings* (New York: Library of America, 1999).

Madison, J., Hamilton, A. and Jay, J. *The Federalist Papers*, ed. Isaac Kramnick (Harmondsworth: Penguin, 1987).

Marientras, E. *Les mythes fondateurs de la nation américaine: essai sur le discours idéologique aux Etats-Unis à l'époque de l'indépendance: 1763–1800* (Paris: Maspéro, 1976).

——. 'Nous, le peuple': les origines du nationalisme américain* (Paris: Gallimard, 1988).

Marienstras, E. and Vincent, B. eds, *Les Oubliés de la Révolution américaine: femmes, Indiens, Noirs, quakers, francs-maçons dans la guerre d'Indépendance* (Nancy: Presses Universitaires de Nancy, 1990).

Marienstras, E. and Wulf, N. 'The Declaration of Independence in France', *Journal of American History*, LXXXV (1999), 1299–324.

McCrisken, T. and Pepper, A. *American History and Contemporary Hollywood Film* (Edinburgh: Edinburgh University Press, 2005).

McDonald, F. *States' Rights and the Union: Imperium in Imperio, 1776–1876* Lawrence, KS: University Press of Kansas, 2000).

McFarlane, A. 'Rebellions in Late Colonial Spanish America: A Comparative Perspective', *Bulletin of Latin American Research*, XIV (1995), 313–39.

Miller, J.I. *The Rise and Fall of Democracy in Early America, 1630–1789. The Legacy for Contemporary Politics* (University Park, PA: The Pennsylvania State University Press, 1991).

Moltmann, G. 'The American Constitutional Model and German Constitutional Politics', in Simmons, R. C. ed., *The United States Constitution: The First Two-Hundred Years* (Manchester: Manchester University Press, 1990) pp.90–103.

Morris, R.B. *The American Revolution Reconsidered* (Westport, CT: Greenwood, 1979).

Mullin, J.E. 'The American Georgic', *Diacritica.*, IX (1994), 291–307.

——. 'Standing Armies, War Powers, and Selective Service—A Reflection', *O Lago de todos os Recursos: Homenagem a Hélio Osvaldo Alves*, (Lisbon: Centro de Estudos Anglísticos da Universidade de Lisboa, 2004), 145–57.

——. 'The United States Constitution and the American Transcendentalists', *Diacrítica*, XI (1996), 135–43.

Nelson, W.E. *Marbury v. Madison, WI: The Origins and Legacy of Judicial Review* (Lawrence, KS: University Press of Kansas, 2000).

Palmer, R.R. *The Age of the Democratic Revolution: A Political History of Europe and America, 1760–1800*, 2 vols (Princeton, NJ: Princeton University Press, 1959–64).

Parrington, V.L. *Main Currents in American Thought, 1800–1860* (New York: Harcourt Brace, 1927).

Phelan, J. Leddy. *The People and the King: The Comunero Revolution in Colombia, 1781* (Madison, WI: University of Wisconsin Press, 1978).

Potofsky, A. 'G.A Ducher and the Collapse of "Doux Commerce" during the American Revolution', in Bergamasco, L. and Rossignol, M. J. eds, 'L'Amérique: des colonies aux républiques', *Cahiers Charles* XXXIX (Paris: Université Paris 7-Denis Diderot, 2005).

Puskás, J. 'Emigrant Hungarians in the United States, 1880–1940', in J. Puskás, ed., *Kivándorló magyarok az Egyesült Államokban 1880–1940* (Budapest: Akadémiai, 1982) pp.629–39.

Racine, K. *Francisco de Miranda: A Transatlantic Life in the Age of Revolution* (Wilmington, DE: Scholarly Resources, 2003).

Rakove, J.N. *Original Meanings: Politics and Ideas in the Making of the Constitution* (New York: Knopf, 1996).

Raphael, R. *A People's History of the American Revolution* (New York: Harper Perennial, 2002).

Ray, R.B. *A Certain Tendency of Hollywood Cinema 1930–1980* (Princeton, NJ: Princeton University Press, 1985).

Raynal, G.T. *Révolution de l'Amérique* (London: L. Davis, 1781).

Reisch, A.A. 'Sándor Bölöni Farkas's Reflections on American Political and Social Instututions', in Király, B. K. and Bárány, G. eds, *East-Central-European Perceptions of Early America* (Dordrecht: The Peter De Ridder Press, 1977), 59–71.

Robertson, M.L. 'Scottish Commerce and the American War of Independence', *The Economic History Review*, IX (1956), 123–31.

Rodríguez, M. *La revolución americana de 1776 y el mundo hispanico: Ensayos y documentos* (Madrid: Techos, 1976).

Roider, K.A. 'William Lee: Our First Envoy to Vienna', *Virginia Magazine of History and Biography*, 80 (1978), 163–68.

Rosenstone, R.A., ed. *Revisioning History: Film and the Construction of a New Past* (Princeton, NJ: Princeton University Press, 1995).

——. *Visions of the Past: The Challenge of Film to Our Idea of History* (Cambridge, MA: Harvard University Press, 1995).

Rossignol, M.J. *The Nationalist Ferment. The Origins of U.S. Foreign Policy, 1789–1812* (Columbus, OH: The Ohio State University Press, 2003).

Rudé, G. 'The Gordon Riots: A Study of the Rioters and their Victims', *Transactions of the Royal Historical Society*, VII (1955), 429–37.

Ruigómez de Hernandez, M.P. *El gobierno español del despotismo ilustrado ante la independencia de los Estado Unidos de América* (Madrid: Ministerio de Asuntos Exteriores, 1978).

Rux, J. 'Direkte Demokratie in der Weimarer Republik', *Kritische Vierteljahresschrift für Gesetzgebung und Rechtswissenschaft*, LXXXV (2002), 273–98.

Samples, J.C. *James Madison and the Future of Limited Government* (Washington, DC: Cato Institute, 2002).

Sarrailh, J. *La España Ilustrada de la segunda mitad del siglo XVIII*, trans. A. Alatorre (Mexico and Buenos Aires: Fondo de Cultura Económica, 1957).

Schlesinger, A., Jr. *The Age of Jackson* (Boston, MA: Little, Brown, 1953).

Schwartz, B. *A History of the Supreme Court* (New York: Oxford University Press, 1993).

Shalhope, R.E. *The Social Philosophy of John Taylor of Caroline: A Study in Jeffersonian Democracy* (Columbia, SC: University of South Carolina Press, 1980).

Shy, J. *A People Numerous and Armed: Reflections on the Military Struggle for American Independence* (Ann Arbor, MI: University of Michigan Press, 1991).

Slotkin, R. *The Fatal Environment: The Myth of the Frontier in the Age of Industrialization* (Norman, OK: University of Oklahoma Press, 1998).

——. *Gunfighter Nation: The Frontier Myth in Twentieth Century America* (New York: Athenum, 1992).

Sokol, I.M. 'Eighteenth-Century Polish Views on American Republican Government', in Király, B.K. and Bárány, G. eds, *East-Central-European Perceptions of Early America* (Dordrecht: The Peter De Ridder Press, 1977) pp.89–96.

Spevack, E. *Allied Control and German Freedom. American Political and Ideological Influences on the Framing of the West German Basic Law (Grundgesetz)* (Münster: LIT, 2001).

Stavig, W. *The World of Túpac Amaru: Conflict, Community and Identity in Colonial Peru* (Lincoln, NE and London: University of Nebraska Press, 1999).

Stein, S.J. and Stein, B.H. *Apogee of Empire: Spain and New Spain in the Age of Charles III, 1759–80* (Baltimore, MD and London: The Johns Hopkins University Press, 2003).

Stone, D. 'Poland and the Lessons of the American Revolution', in Király, B. K. ed., *East-Central-European Society and War in the Era of Revolutions, 1775–1856* (New York: Brooklyn College Press, 1984) pp.3–10.

Story, J. *Commentaries on the Constitution of the United States*, 3rd edn [1858] (Union, NJ: The Lawbook Exchange, 2001).

Taylor, J. *Arator, Being a Series of Agricultural Essays, Practical and Political* (1813) ed. M.E. Bradford (Indianapolis, Liberty Fund, 1977).

——. *Construction Construed, and Constitutions Vindicated* (1820) (New York: DaCapo Press, 1970).

——. *An Inquiry into the Principles and Policy of the Government of the United States* (1814) (New Haven, CT: Yale University Press,1950).

——. *New Views of the Constitution of the United States* (1822) ed. James McClellan (Washington, DC: Regnery Publishing, 2000).

Taylor, J. *Tyranny Unmasked* (1822) ed. F. Thornton Miller (Indianapolis: Liberty Fund, 1992).

Toplin, R.B., ed. *Oliver Stone's USA: Film, History and Controversy* (Lawrence, KS: University of Kansas Press, 2000).

Urbán, A. 'Lesson for the Old Continent: The Image of America in the Hungarian Revolution of 1848/49', *The New Hungarian Quarterly*, XVII (1976), 85–96.

Utrilla, J.F. Yela. *España ante la independencia de los Estados Unidos*, 2 vols (Lérida: Gráficos Academia Mariana, 1925).

Várdy, B.S. 'Hungarians in the New World. An Unorthodox History of Hungarian Americans', in Várdy, B.S. ed., *Magyarok az Újvilágban* (Budapest: A Magyar Nyelv és Kultúra Nemzetközi Társasága, 2000) pp.737–65.

Venturi, F. *The End of the Old Regime in Europe, 1776–1789: I. The Great States of the West*, translated by R. Burr Litchfield (Princeton, NJ: Princeton University Press, 1991).

Vörös, K. 'The Image of America in Hungarian Mass Culture in the Nineteenth Century', *Etudes Historiques Hongroises* (1985), 647–61.

Vovelle, M., ed. *Révolution et république. L'exception française* (Paris: Kimé, 1994).

Walker, C.F. *Smouldering Ashes: Cuzco and the Creation of Republican Peru, 1780–1840* (Durham, NC and London: Duke University Press, 1999).

Wellenreuther, H. 'Die USA. Ein politisches Vorbild der bürgerlich-liberalen Kräfte des Vormärz?', in Elvert, J. and Salewski, M. eds, *Deutschland und der Westen im 19. und 20. Jahrhundert, Teil 1: Transatlantische Beziehungen* (Stuttgart: Ranke Gesellschaft, 1993) pp.23–41.

Wilms, H. *Ausländische Einwirkungen auf die Entstehung des Grundgesetzes* (Stuttgart: Kohlhammer, 1999).

Wood, G.S. *The Radicalism of the American Revolution* (New York: Knopf, 1992).

Zahorski, A. 'The Attitudes of the Polish Estates toward the Kościuszko Insurrection', in Király, B.K. ed., *East-Central-European Society and War in the Era of Revolutions, 1775–1856* (New York: Brooklyn College Press, 1984) pp.75–84.

Závodszky, G. *American Effects on Hungarian Imagination and Political Thought, 1559–1848* (Highland Lakes, NJ: Atlantic Research and Publications, Inc., 1995).

Index